T0269946

MOGULS

ALSO BY MICHAEL BENSON

Betrayal in Blood

Lethal Embrace (with Robert Mladinich)

Mommy Deadliest

A Killer's Touch

Knife in the Heart

Gangsters vs. Nazis

ALSO BY MICHAEL BENSON AND FRANK DIMATTEO

Carmine the Snake: Carmine Persico and His Murderous Mafia Family

Lord High Executioner: The Legendary Mafia Boss Albert Anastasia

Mafia Hit Man: Carmine DiBiase, the Wiseguy Who Really Killed Joey Gallo

The Cigar: Carmine Galante, Mafia Terror

Red Hook: Ground Zero of the Brooklyn Mafia

MOGULS

THE LIVES AND TIMES OF HOLLYWOOD FILM PIONEERS NICHOLAS AND JOSEPH SCHENCK

Michael Benson and Craig Singer

CITADEL PRESS
Kensington Publishing Corp.
www.kensingtonbooks.com

CITADEL PRESS BOOKS are published by

Kensington Publishing Corp.
900 Third Avenue
New York, NY 10022

All Kensington titles, imprints, and distributed lines are available at special quantity discounts for bulk purchases for sales promotions, premiums, fund-raising, educational, or institutional use. Special book excerpts or customized printings can also be created to fit specific needs. For details, write or phone the office of the Kensington sales manager: Kensington Publishing Corp., 900 Third Avenue, New York, NY 10022, attn Sales Department; phone 1-800-221-2647.

10 9 8 7 6 5 4 3 2 1

First Citadel hardcover printing: October 2024

Printed in the United States of America

ISBN: 978-0-8065-4308-6

ISBN: 978-0-8065-4310-9 (e-book)

Library of Congress Control Number: 2024936517

To all the filmmakers who've knocked on the door, who fought the doubt and rejection, the nepotism and agendas, to stay the course and damn the torpedoes, who with the help of a small army of like-minded artists and eccentrics executed their stories and saw their dreams come to life

AUTHORS' NOTE

This book is a work of nonfiction. It depicts actual events as truthfully as can be verified by research. Dialogue and actions consistent with these historical figures have been supplemented.

CONTENTS

FOREWORD

WITH THE POSSIBLE EXCEPTION OF THE WRIGHT BROTHERS—and *maybe* the Marx Brothers—there are perhaps no other male siblings who did more to bring the world closer together than Joseph and Nicholas Schenck, two of the men who created Hollywood as we know it. From the silent film era to this very day, movies spawned a cultural revolution felt not just here in America, but around the world. Movies have changed the way we think, act, dress, learn, and relate to one another. Movies have formed our collective perception of race and gender roles, then also challenged those perceptions. Movies have opened our eyes to discrimination, the horrors of war, environmental issues, poverty, injustice, and hunger. Movies have tickled, terrified, and thrilled us, showed us what love looks like and taken us to places we had once only been able to read about or see in photographs. At their best, movies have not only entertained us, but also inspired us to action.

For most of us, it seems movies were always there, fully formed from their inception onward. But they were not. Someone had to figure out how to use that thing called a movie camera to tell stories visually and then get those stories in front of the masses. Joe and Nick Schenck *did* that and because of them, audiences have been having their minds blown since the first cowboy pointed a gun directly at them from a silver screen.

Starting as employees, then owners, of a small Chinatown pharmacy in New York, Joe and Nick parlayed that business into a bar and then a major amusement park before finally taking a flyer on this new-fangled form of entertainment called "flickers," an art form aimed squarely at the working class. Tickets were cheap and silent films had no language barrier, and while the cultural elite dismissed the business as "lowbrow," Joe and Nick knew better.

FLASH FORWARD TO 1994—ONE OF THE SCHENCKS GIVES ME MY START in show business. No, it wasn't Joseph or Nicholas, of course; it was their great-nephew George Schenck. George had co-created a TV show called *The Great*

Defender, for which he and his partner Frank Cardea (along with co-creator Frank Ranzulli) hired me as a staff writer.

Over lunch, George would tell me stories about how as a boy, he and his sister would go over to swim at "Uncle Joe's" house, a massive Holmby Hills mansion, how they'd get lost playing hide and seek in its rooms too numerous to count. He also recalled his mother whispering about "that woman," who turned out to be a young Marilyn Monroe, who would apparently visit Uncle Joe several times a week.

THE BOOK YOU ARE HOLDING IS A WHIRLWIND TALE, A ROLLER-COASTER ride through Hollywood history. Its cast of characters includes names such as Chaplin, Keaton, Valentino, Talmadge, and Monroe, lest we forget Hitler and Luciano. It's got chills, thrills, romance, comedy, intrigue, and danger; it's equal parts *The Last Tycoon* and Horatio Alger, except this story is *real*.

Joe and Nick's is an immigrant story about two guys who not only achieved the American Dream in spades, but also helped *sell* that dream around the world.

Hell, somebody should make a movie out of this.

Terence Winter
Producer and Writer, *The Sopranos*,
Boardwalk Empire, The Wolf of Wall Street

INTRODUCTION

SOME COMPELLING FACTS ABOUT THE SCHENCK BROTHERS

- Joseph and Nicholas Schenck were the most powerful brothers in Hollywood history, more than twice as powerful as the Warner brothers. In fact, it has been estimated that the Schencks were the most powerful brothers in any industry. They held controlling interests in three major studios: Metro-Goldwyn-Mayer (MGM), Twentieth Century-Fox, and United Artists (UA). But chances are you've never heard of them because they preferred to run their global empire behind closed doors. Nick was Louis B. Mayer's *boss*.

- They created the Motion Picture Academy and the Oscars.

- They laid the cornerstone for the Hollywood studio system. They were the ones who painted the screen silver, creating a glorious world-changing product that is truly an American original. Like jazz.

- Nick lived in a Gatsby-like mansion—thirty rooms, twenty acres—on Long Island's North Shore, was happily married to a former showgirl named Pansy, and took a yacht to work each day, his office sitting atop the Loew's State Theatre in Times Square. About Nick Schenck, legendary director John Huston once said, "Nick Schenck has been for decades the ruler of rulers. He never gets his picture in the papers, and he doesn't go to parties, and he avoids going out in public, but he is the real king of the pack."

- Joe lived in a nine-bedroom, ten-bathroom Italian Renaissance–style mansion known as Owlwood in the enclave of Holmby Hills overlooking Sunset Boulevard. It was there that, after a failed marriage to Norma Talmadge, he lived the life of a swinging bachelor, becoming in 1947 Marilyn Monroe's mentor and special friend.

- For nineteenth-century Europeans, Joe and Nick were large men. Joe grew to be five-nine, stocky and powerful, and Nick was five-ten, both looking down upon the relatively diminutive men with whom they'd compete.

- While Joe was a genius at finding stars, Nick's forte was location, location, location, and he oversaw real-estate acquisition. Nick, as Marcus Loew's partner, helped create a mammoth theater chain, with many of the venues extravagant palaces like the Loew's Kings Theatre on Flatbush Avenue in Brooklyn.

- Joe joined what is today known as the "mile-high club" very early in aviation history. He and actress/singer Lili Damita might not have been a mile up, but they were up.

- Joe did four months and five days in the fed pen for tax evasion—one of his deductions involved a ménage à trois—but was quickly released after allowing the USO to use one of his houses in Palm Springs.

- Everyone thought MGM studio head Louis B. Mayer was a dictatorial leader, the boss of bosses, but those closest to him knew that he made no decisions without first "checking with New York," and that meant Nick.

- When silent-film star Roscoe "Fatty" Arbuckle was arrested for the alleged sex-crime death of a starlet, Joe paid his legal bills.

- Joe was silent-film legend Buster Keaton's first producer and best friend. If you took the star power of Adam Sandler, Will Ferrell, Seth Rogen, Kevin Hart, and Zach Galifianakis and put them into a blender, you still would not match the comic brilliance and influence of Buster Keaton. Not only was Keaton a major influence on the above-referenced celebrities, he completely changed physical comedy, and performed some of the most innovative and dangerous stunts all by himself—even more dangerous than many of the stunts Tom Cruise does with the benefit of modern rigging and technology. (Luckily for us, all of Keaton's feature films for Joe Schenck are on YouTube. Start with *The General*. You'll be amazed.) Keaton and Joe Schenck were lifelong friends. The men married sisters, film star Norma and her less-talented sister Natalie.

- Nick was a charter board member at Technicolor, Inc., a pioneer in color film.

- They helped turn back an attempted Nazi takeover of the industry during the mid-1930s and turned around an attempted shakedown by the Mob.

- While everyone else in Hollywood hired publicists to get their names in the papers, Nick hired a public relations specialist to keep his name out.

So, there you have it. Joe and Nick were great men. Flawed, of course, but great. This is a story about the early days of American cinema, with its heaping helpings of glamour and sleaze, stories of hungry immigrants who didn't just live the American Dream, they created a "dream factory." Joseph and Nicholas Schenck's story is a classic tale of rags to riches, arriving on the boat from Europe, surviving on the Lower East Side and then East Harlem, selling newspapers on a corner, working in a pharmacy, owning pharmacies, buying and operating amusement parks, booking vaudeville acts, managing theaters, producing pictures, running studios, and wielding incredible power.

Their story is also a history of the twentieth century in America: war, jazz, prohibition, sex, Great Depression, more war, organized crime, gambling, Red Scares, and blacklists. In its telling, you'll glimpse New York's Lower East Side at the turn of the twentieth century, Hollywood in its infancy, the swinging scandals of the 1920s, the lush fantasy of Hollywood's Depression period, the propaganda machine of the war years, and the paranoid malaise of the 1950s.

The Schencks were the Godfathers of the Moving Image. Their influence, and through them the influence of the cinema upon the twentieth century, cannot be overstated. From the earliest frantic days of flickering silents to the 1950s when TV invaded American living rooms, virtually every neighborhood in the country included its own picture show.

By the 1930s, there were only six major studios in Hollywood, all of which were integrated conglomerates that owned the talent and produced, distributed, and collected the tickets at their own theaters: MGM, Twentieth Century-Fox, Paramount, Columbia, Warner Brothers, and RKO. Disney and Universal were also players on a smaller scale. At one point the Schencks controlled about a third of the motion picture business, which was the fourth largest industry in America. Nick was the eighth richest man in the country and Joe wasn't far behind. Nick was head of more than one hundred corporations. (Nick was once asked, while under oath, to name every corporation he ran. He said, "Give me a break." He was the highest-paid theatrical manager in the world.)

Joe owned vast real estate in Arizona and California. With Jacob Paley, Joe owned the once gentiles-only Del Mar Race Track and a resort in Lake Arrowhead. With Sid Grauman, he built and operated Hollywood Boulevard's plush Roosevelt Hotel. Joe controlled the Federal Trust and Savings Bank and was a major stockholder in the Bank of Italy, which became the Bank of America. Mega-publisher William Randolph Hearst liked to hang out with Joe because he felt Joe played in the same league. And Hearst knew few who did.

But the Brothers Schenck held power in a way not adequately measured in money or social prominence. They were Influential with a capital I. The world formulated its vision and opinion of the U.S. through their product. Joe wrote that Hollywood was twenty times more important than all the U.S. embassies around the world. American pictures globally dictated how people thought, what they did, how they dressed.

Even domestically their celluloid concoctions set a specific silvery social tone, a lifelike depiction of the America of our dreams, with strong nuclear families in which Father knew best, and a basic fairness to the world. Good guys won. Crime didn't pay.

And everyone did their best to fall in line. In 1941, a poll indicated that more than a third of Americans went to the picture shows at least once a week. Around the world, our collective imagination was taken by the hand and guided to a happy place by motion pictures.

Despite this A-list influence, the Schencks were largely unheralded outside of the industry. With so much power, they didn't require fame. As a young man, when he ran an amusement park, Nick had been a popular public figure—but as a film/theater mogul he became shy, living in luxury on Long Island with his faithful wife and talented kids. By all accounts domestic bliss. He succeeded in keeping his nest private. At work he was "The General," a man feared by an entire industry—at night he was Papa Bear.

Joe, through carelessness, became known in later years for his outrageous self-indulgences, in a gambling casino, with starlets on either arm. But a lot happened before Joe became Hollywood's number-one swinging bachelor mogul. He'd loved and married a woman who didn't love him back, an actress who married her producer for job security. Burned, Joe fell in love a second time, and again it was an actress using him. This one even had a "manager" who steered her from one powerful man to another. After that, Joe gave up on romance. That man with a starlet on either arm was heartbroken, occupied in an endless attempt to fill the inner void left by Norma Talmadge and Merle Oberon.

Like twin Citizens Kane with bookend Xanadus, the Schencks had the world of show business covered. Despite the physical distance between them, these giants remained close and were said to talk on the phone three times a day.

Though the Schencks worked as a team, they were not identical twins, and their differences came with entertaining ironies. Joe, the older, learned to speak English without an accent. Nick's Jewish-Russian accent hung on his entire life. Joe was a nonsmoker; Nick always had a Pall Mall between the fingers of his right hand. Nick, most agreed, was the good-looking one—yet he was the family man. Joe, to put it nicely, looked like he could be your tailor, stocky with heavy jowls, a blobby nose, and sparse hair—yet he was the "swinger." Joe was a people person and could spot star quality in a performer, yet it was Nick, who normally excelled in the dry world of real estate and board meetings, who had the penchant for show business and could even be a bit of a ham. If they bickered—and how could they not, being brothers?—

they didn't do it in public, and everyone knew if you feared one, you'd better fear the other as well.

Acquaintance Howard Dietz once described Joe as "a philosopher who had a comic sense. He was not opinionated, and he gave good advice, such as, 'If four or five guys tell you that you're drunk, even though you know you haven't had anything to drink, the least you can do is lie down a little while.'"

Nick wanted others to see him as a simple man. He said his three greatest joys were being a dad, staying in shape, and going to the racetrack. Sam Marx, an MGM executive, told a story about Nick taking him on a walking tour of his waterfront Long Island estate on a Sunday morning. He showed Marx his chicken coop, where one chicken had been picked on by the others, bloodied and rendered featherless. Nick said, "Marx, you look at that and you realize that this is the way you must behave in the world . . . You must not let others pick you to pieces."

While Joe was generally beloved in Hollywood, Nick was feared and loathed (known as "Nick Skunk" behind his back). Stories of Nick's complete lack of sentimentality made the rounds. It was said Nick took out a million-dollar insurance policy on star Rudolph Valentino, and then, after Valentino died, refused to share the money with members of Valentino's family. Another story says that after the death of MGM executive Irving Thalberg, Nick made moves to limit compensation to Thalberg's widow, the MGM star Norma Shearer. Nick felt Thalberg already had too much money, a brilliant but whiny employee who against Nick's wishes had been given a piece of the pie.

Joe and Nick visited each other regularly. In later years, they flew, but back in the day they'd cross the country on the Chief, L.A. to Chicago, and the Twentieth Century Limited, Chicago to New York. Sometimes, at the train station, a small photo op was arranged. One time in 1932 Joe and Nick traveled west together and were met at the Pasadena train station by the boys from the press and a small gathering of UA and MGM top brass, which included Louis B. Mayer and Irving Thalberg appearing uncharacteristically subservient.

It is impossible to tell the story of Joe and Nick Schenck without excavating many of Hollywood's juiciest scandals and most important events, such as the:

- *lurid* Fatty Arbuckle affair, in which the film star allegedly killed a woman in a hotel suite by puncturing her bladder, and Joe paid for his defense;

- *murder* of Thelma Todd, mistress to both Joe's close friend director Roland West and alpha gangster Lucky Luciano;

- *formation* of the Academy of Motion Picture Arts and Sciences and *invention* of the Oscars;

- *industry's* panicky metamorphosis from silence to sound;

- *creation* of the Agua Caliente Resort, Casino, and Racetrack (a stick in the eye of L.A.'s exclusive WASP-y country clubs);

- *Mob's* attempted takeover of Hollywood;

- *plan of Hitler's* to control Hollywood and transform it into a pro-Nazi propaganda machine;

- *prison sentence* given to Joe Schenck for perjury;

- *birth* of United Artists, MGM, and Twentieth Century-Fox;

- *Red Scare,* commies in Hollywood, the Waldorf Conference, and the Schencks' role in the creation of the Hollywood blacklist;

- *warfare* at MGM between Nick and Louis B. Mayer;

- *coming* of devil television; and

- *strange* "suicide" of TV's Superman, George Reeves.

THIS LAST ITEM INVOLVED LONGTIME SCHENCK ENFORCER EDDIE Mannix, an iron-fisted Irishman who'd first faithfully worked for Nick as a youthful and enthusiastic bouncer during Nick's amusement-park days.

Mannix and Howard Strickling (who'd been a publicist for Metro since 1919) became respectively general manager and publicity director at MGM. They were called "the fixers," and it was their job to smooth over anything that might put the studio in a bad light. They had, under their collective thumb, doctors, reporters, cops, DAs, judges, whatever it took. Gay performers were provided beards. In the case of untimely deaths, the fixers got to the scene before the police. Stars were kept out of jail, and names out of the paper. Among the suppressed scandals were the suspicious death of Jean Harlow's husband, Paul Bern; the murder of Ted Healy (creator of the Three Stooges) by actor Wallace Beery and others; the murder of comic actress Thelma Todd; Judy Garland's drug addiction; and Loretta Young's illegitimate baby fathered by a married Clark Gable.

Joe and Nick Schenck survived it all and, though "progress" stomped and kicked dirt on the fantasy worlds they created, they retired fabulously wealthy men. Theirs and the story of Hollywood are one and the same.

LOOKING AT OLD-TIME HOLLYWOOD MOGULS, THE FIRST THING YOU notice is how similar they were. Such a small club with so much power. Jewish immigrants, driven out of Europe by anti-Semitism, who'd scraped their way up from poverty—not that they practiced their religion. In fact, their Jewishness was seldom discussed as they dedicated their energies to being all-Americans (i.e., Christian/secular) and no longer identified with their European birthplaces.

Nicholas Schenck was born in Russia but after he came over on the boat, he seldom returned to Europe. New York, and later Miami Beach, were all he needed. (Brother Joe was more adventurous, once sailing his own yacht from California to New York through the Panama Canal and regularly hitting European hot spots.)

Carl Laemmle, head of Universal Pictures, was born in Laupheim, Germany, and came to America when he was seventeen. In 1906 he purchased his first nickelodeon (a coin-operated machine that showed moving pictures). He invested in theaters, distribution, and production until his business became Universal Pictures. Universal City, opened in 1915, was at that time Hollywood's largest studio, and Laemmle is generally credited with being the first to use the "star system"—that is, recognize that customers were more apt to watch a picture if they already knew and liked the players.

William Fox (born Wilhelm Fuchs), who was the Fox in Joe Schenck's conglomerate Twentieth Century-Fox, was born in 1879 in Tulchva, Austria-Hungary. He started with one penny arcade, expanded to fifteen theaters, and eventually formed the Fox Film Corporation.

Adolph Zukor was born in 1873 in Ricse, Austria-Hungary, an orphan who spent his childhood unloved, a fact that left a void that could never be filled no matter how much power Zukor accrued. He came over on the boat at sixteen with $40 sewn inside his vest. As a kid, when he wasn't boxing or playing baseball, he had his nose in a dime novel, and those simple adventures with their strong sense of right and wrong, and clear delineation between hero and villain, became the basis for Zukor's contribution to motion pictures. A boyhood friend of Marcus Loew's, they met as cutting-and-sewing co-workers for a furrier. Zukor started his own furrier business, became wealthy quickly, and invested that money in nickelodeons, calling his flickers "Automatic Vaudeville." (Early films were called flickers because of primitive projection systems and the rapid alternation of light and dark frames in the film.) Zukor never lost his thick European accent or mastered English. He bought into a 125th Street arcade in Harlem to show flickers, and then built an arcade of his own downtown on 14th Street. This evolved into film production: *The Prisoner of Zenda* and *Tess of the D'Urbervilles.* In 1914 he merged his company with that of theater producer Jesse L. Lasky to form Famous Players, which used a distribution company called Paramount. Zukor didn't like the terms he had with Paramount and by 1915 took over that company so that he was both making and distributing his own pictures—Paramount Pictures. His early partner was Cecil B. DeMille.

Samuel Goldwyn was born Shmuel Gelbfisz (Goldfish) in Warsaw, Poland. He married Jesse Lasky's sister, formed a series of smaller studios, one of which was Goldwyn Pictures, later to become the G in MGM. Goldwyn was known for his malaprops, a mangling of the English language worthy of Bowery Boy Slip Mahoney: "I'll give you a definite maybe." "I never liked you and I always will." "We're overpaying him, but he's worth it." "A verbal agreement isn't worth the paper it's written on."

Harry Cohn was born in 1891 in New York City—his parents came over on the boat—and started in the picture business as Carl Laemmle's secretary. In 1924 he formed Columbia Pictures.

Louis B. Mayer was born in 1885 in Minsk, Russia, and grew up in

Canada. He worked for a brief period as a scrap metal dealer before switching to film exhibition and distribution. In 1924, when the big merger came, he became the second M in MGM, and managed the largest studio in history.

Lewis Selznick was born in Europe, in what is now Lithuania, although he later claimed to be from Ukraine. A former jewelry dealer, he came over on the boat at eighteen, and in 1914 organized the World Film Corporation to distribute independent pictures. He got along with Marcus Loew, hated Nick Schenck, and agreed to distribute, through his Select Pictures, Joe Schenck's first picture with Norma Talmadge. He wasn't well liked by anyone. By 1925, he'd gone out of business, stomped out by the big guys who liked his kid David but weren't sorry to see Lewis go.

The Warner brothers (Harry, born 1881; Albert 1884; Sam 1887; and Jack 1892) were very poor and came over from Poland in 1895. They started with one projector and a traveling tent show. By 1918 they were making their own pictures. Harry and Albert stayed in New York and handled finances; Jack and Sam moved to Burbank and supervised production.

So, demographically, the Schencks fit right in with this tiny group of ambitious men who would give birth to and control a world-changing industry.

Could we lower the lights please . . .

FADE IN. Exterior. Morning. Birds chirp. The world is bright, brown, and dry. CAMERA is coming through the gates of a showy Spanish stucco mansion called Owlwood built on six acres in Holmby Hills near Bel Air, home of mogul Joe Schenck. The large, manicured grounds are graced by mature oak and magnolia trees. The home neighbors Sunset Boulevard, a three-wood from the thoroughly Protestant L.A. Country Club. A tumbleweed crosses the driveway, left to right. The legendary silent-film star, Buster KEATON, now old, his stony face held in place by age, approaches the front entrance on foot. Rings the bell. A butler answers and holds the door open. KEATON steps inside. He still demonstrates the appropriate awe. He'd had a small role in *Sunset Boulevard*, and shivers at Owlwood's mustiness, shivers because life, not quite a decade after Billy Wilder's masterpiece, has imitated art. It was true what they said: In Hollywood you outlive your fame and slowly die.

KEATON (to butler)

He up?

BUTLER (flat, expressionless)

Yes, sir, Mr. Keaton. Very lively today.

KEATON

Good, I feel like playing cards.

BUTLER

Go on up. He's expecting you.

INT. We get our first glimpse of Owlwood. KEATON looks to his left as he heads for the stairs and sees the den. Everywhere is complex plaster and millwork. We see the back of a couch facing a yawning fireplace. Above the fireplace is a gigantic portrait of the actress Norma Talmadge.

Keaton is old but still athletic and takes the stairs both deliberately and lightly, turns down a hall, and enters Joe's bedroom, where Joe lies upon a large bed propped up by pillows. Keaton pulls a fresh deck of cards from his pocket.

JOE

You still owe me fifteen bucks from last time.

KEATON

Nickel a point, quarter a box.

JOE

Okay. Pull that bed table over so I have a surface.

KEATON

I know.

Keaton wheels the bed table over Joe's bed and pulls up a tall chair for himself. He cracks open the pack, shuffles the cards, deals, and the men play gin rummy as they talk.

KEATON

So, you shtup Marilyn Monroe in this bed?

JOE (laughing at Keaton's "Yiddish")

No, always downstairs. This is, was, my marital bed.
I had it moved here from the house on Adams.

KEATON

So, what was it like?

JOE

My marital bed? You married her sister.
You must have some idea.

KEATON

Not Norma. Marilyn!

JOE

Oh. She's a good kid.

KEATON

How'd you find her?

JOE

Some party. I couldn't even tell you whose house,
typical party.
But she wasn't typical. She walked up to me like
she was an old friend.

She says, "I'm named after your wife."

KEATON

Norma Jean named after Norma Talmadge!

JOE

Yeah. She tells me this story. She's from L.A.
She's about twenty. Her mom used to work for me, film cutter.
Cute. Marilyn's mom you'd figure she's cute. Right away we had a connection, you know, Buster?

KEATON

Yes. Were you thinking paternity suit?

JOE (laughs)

No, I was a good boy back in those days.
When Gladys worked for me, I mean. I was not a good boy when I met Marilyn.
But I wouldn't be surprised if Marilyn thought about it. She told me she didn't want to call me Daddy, ha! She just wanted to call me Uncle Joe.

KEATON

Isn't that code?

JOE

Sure. So what? She wasn't like that.
She told Harry Cohn to take a hike,
which is why it didn't work out for her at Columbia.
She liked me because she liked me.

KEATON

And you gave her a career at Fox and made her a star.

JOE

Are you kidding me?
She's a star without me. She has it.
She and cameras. She's gorgeous in person,
of course, but a regular kid. Cameras turn
her into a goddess. Too much maybe. She is
a thing now, not a warm-blooded person.

KEATON

She's great in *Niagara*.

JOE

So great in *Niagara*. I had her checked out by one of
Eddie Mannix's boys, a private dick, just to see
what her story was. Because the things she said were
intriguing but vague. She'd mention an orphanage, but
she had a mom and Mom was still alive so why the
orphanage?
Detective found out Gladys had mental problems, spent
time in the sanitarium, and not a nice one.
So, that's like living in hell.

KEATON

That's tough. She gets no respect. She looks like a
dumb blonde, so . . .

JOE

Don't get me wrong. I don't think she's an
intellectual, but she's a thinker.
And she comes by her problems honestly.
She's drawn to intellectuals. (Smiles.) I don't know
what the deal is with that fucking DiMaggio.
I hate that fucking dago.

KEATON

Ever since *Confidential* ran that story, everyone
knows how you feel about DiMaggio.

JOE

Good. She said she was named after Norma, so, I asked her if she needed a job. She said, and I quote, "somewhat desperately," you know how she sounds. So, I hired her as a party girl. She hung around the swimming pool looking good and during card games she lit cigars and wiggled away whenever men tried to pinch her ass.

KEATON

And she was last to leave.

JOE

Damn right. She stayed for a few months.

KEATON pulls out a silver cigarette box and a cigarette holder that appears a good six inches longer than it needs to be.

KEATON

Ashtray?

JOE

Ummm, let me ring.

JOE pulls a rope above his shoulder and the NURSE appears.

JOE

Mr. Keaton needs an ashtray.

NURSE (a sourpuss)

Doctor said no smoking.

JOE (angry)

I'm not smoking. I don't smoke.

I've never fucking smoked.
Buster is smoking!

NURSE
Yes, sir.

NURSE gets the ashtray and makes a show of opening the windows to let in the furnace-like breeze. NURSE exits.

KEATON (smoking)
You remember coming over on the boat?

JOE
The yacht? I sold the fucking . . .

KEATON
No, immigrating. Coming over on the boat.

JOE
Sure.

KEATON
Your family was poor?

JOE
No, my father had a good job. We came over because we are Jewish. Russia was making it tough on us, the czar, Alexander the Third, was brutal. He wanted the Jews to disappear. Our shtetl was under siege. . . .

CHAPTER ONE

YOUNG MEN OF GREAT BUSINESS ACUMEN

On Christmas Day, 1876 (or thereabouts), a baby boy named Ossip Schencker bowed in bare, gray Rybinsk, Yaroslavl, a medium-sized city about one hundred miles north of Moscow, in the heart of rye country on the confluence of the Volga and Sheksna rivers in Czarist Russia. (The date is best guess. There was no such thing as a birth certificate in Rybinsk, or any other kind of documentation. Even his mother wasn't sure when Ossip was born. Usually she said Christmas Day, an immigrant trick to ease assimilation—but the year kept changing. He kept growing younger. He didn't know when he was born, only that he was a teenager when he came to America.)

Rybinsk's number-one landmark was the Savior-Transfiguration Cathedral, which took thirteen years to build and was completed twenty-five years before Ossip was born, but he was never inside. No Jews allowed. In Russia, many doors were barred for Jews, who were not allowed to pursue their dreams. They were forced to live and work within their own restricted communities called *shtetls*.

Father Hyman (later Herman) made a decent living buying timber and selling it as wood fuel to the steamboats on the Volga. He made extra by selling vodka to the river boats. (Ossip's mother was named Elizabet. Later she added an h.)

About four years after Ossip made his debut, the curtain rose on Nikolay Mikhail Schencker. Later it was Nicholas. But always Nick. (His birthday was November 18, 1880, according to naturalization registration papers filled out years later. Again, not necessarily accurate.)

The plan was to sail the family to America as quickly as they could. But it was expensive, so they went in pairs. Older brothers George and Louis came across to America on the boat in 1889. George, who had a fiancée named Mary back in Russia, left Russia for America at age sixteen, but returned to retrieve Mary, a fantastic love story. Together they went back to America and were married. Louis lived and worked in the mill town of Passaic, New Jersey.

In October 1892, Elizabet kissed Ossip goodbye at the pier in Hamburg, Germany. "Go to America and become a doctor," she instructed.

Ossip came over with his sister Enni (later Annie), steerage passengers aboard a steamer. A precocious boy with a knack for math, he was Ossip Schencker when he arrived at Ellis Island, and Joseph Schenck when he left. Nick came over two years later with their mother.

Ossip and Enni arrived at immigration, a pair of innocents carrying their worldly possessions in a suitcase. Ellis Island was one long line, the queue going this way and that way, the floor made of white tile. If an immigrant was suspected of having a bad heart, an H was chalked onto their back. If suspected of being mentally handicapped, they were marked with an X. Brother Lui (now called Louis) was supposed to be there to meet them but for reasons long forgotten did not show up.

Back in those days Ellis Island was plagued by what were called boarding-house sharks. They would set up newcomers in disgusting rooms and fleece them of most of their cash in exchange. Joe and his sister had only been in America for a matter of hours when they were broke and living in a hellhole on the Lower East Side. For the rest of his life Joe had nightmares of dank yellow wallpaper bespeckled by squished cockroaches.

Joe and Annie eventually made it to Passaic, and Joe took a job at a wire factory making four bucks a week. He also went to night school where his poor English had him behind in all classes except math.

After a few months, Joe learned enough English to ask for a raise, his boss said no, and Joe quit. He threw his belongings into a straw suitcase, walked ten miles from Passaic to Orange, New Jersey, and took a job at a bicycle factory for seven-fifty a week. With his new wages he saved and took a night course in pharmacy.

He'd already realized he wasn't the kind of student who would excel at medical school, but he'd seen so much suffering in Russia that he wanted to help people, and learning to be a druggist seemed like the next best thing.

Eventually, both parents and all eight kids were in the U.S. The family lived in the heart of a teeming ghetto, in a tenement on Rivington Street on New York's predominantly Jewish and Italian Lower East Side where the flowered wallpaper was faded but stain-free.

Nick briefly attended fifth grade in a public school on the Lower East Side, but his family needed the boys to earn, so for three years Joe and Nick sold newspapers out of a burlap sack around their broadening shoulders at a location with maximum foot traffic, on opposite corners at Bowery and Canal. Extry! Extry!

It was a competitive market. There were fifteen newspapers on sale in New York. Thousands of poor newsies worked the corners of Manhattan, from the Battery to Inwood. Poor because they were barely compensated by newspaper moguls like Joseph Pulitzer and William Randolph Hearst. The boys had to buy the papers they sold at a reduced price, but if any of those papers went unsold, the paper wouldn't buy them back. Moms used the unsold newsprint as a tablecloth. Sometimes Joe and Nick sold papers in the morning, and merchandise door-to-door for the rest of the day.

(The plight of young paperboys at the turn of the twentieth century was the subject of the 2012 Broadway musical *Newsies*. A filmed-live version of the show can be seen on Disney+.)

The brothers were smarter—and a few years older—than the average guttersnipe and appreciated the necessity for turf control. One time, another paperboy tried to share Joe's corner.

"This is my corner, pal," Joe said.

"Free country," the kid replied.

Joe whistled with two fingers in his mouth and two larger boys appeared out of nowhere.

"Get lost," Joe said.

And the kid left. He flipped Joe off over his shoulder, but he left. The brothers had to share their profits with the goons, but they worked the best spot for selling newspapers, and that was the key.

Still, it was a penny-ante job, a job for kids.

IN 1897, THE SCHENCK FAMILY MOVED FROM THE LOWER EAST SIDE UPtown to Harlem. It was about this time that Joe had his first love. She was an Irish girl named Betty who lived on well-to-do Gramercy Park in Manhattan. Joe later explained that he was eager to fall in love and so was she, so they decided to fall in love with each other. They went out every Sunday to Betty's friend's house on 68th Street to make out. Betty's family didn't care for Joe's ethnicity, so the pair met on the sly. Joe told Betty that he was trying to save his money so on Sundays she had two choices: walk uptown and have an ice cream soda or take a streetcar uptown and skip the soda. She couldn't have both because Joe only had ten cents to spend.

One day Betty met Joe with sad news. "I can't see you anymore," she said.

"How come?" Joe asked.

"I've met a boy who can take me on the streetcar and buy me an ice cream soda, too," she said. Joe learned a lesson that day, one he'd never forget.

JOE EARNED HIS HIGH SCHOOL DIPLOMA BY ATTENDING NIGHT CLASSES, while working during the day. In 1899, he took night courses at the New York College of Pharmacy and became a licensed pharmacist.

While Joe was still a year shy of his pharmacy degree, he and Nick answered an ad in the very paper they were selling and took jobs at a "pharmacy" on the Bowery in Chinatown. It was called a pharmacy, but it was little more than a wooden shack so rickety that it shook when the el train rumbled overhead, a disreputable joint where Chinese men came to buy their gum opium. The dank shack also functioned as a sort of hospital where those wounded in the raging Chinese gang wars came to be sewn up and numbed—and sometimes to die.

Joe and Nick were on their first day on the new job when two men were brought in bleeding and screaming. An agent of the Ming Tuck Tong Society, wielding a hatchet, had attempted to dispatch a pair of infidels. The horribly wounded men were dragged into a back room where blood poured from them until they died. Relatives showed up not long thereafter and took the bodies away.

The boys' boss was suddenly in their faces. "Boys! When the police come, you know nothing. Understand?"

Joe and Nick nodded, eyes wide.

The boss handed them a pair of mops and gestured weakly at the pools of blood.

It was a tough job, but Joe and Nick came to see themselves as angels of mercy, giving solace to the men wounded in the Tong Wars. The brothers learned to compound prescriptions of all sorts.

There was a place on Pell Street around the corner called the Pelham Café. Sometimes Mike Salter, the proprietor, would come running into the pharmacy, sweaty and desperate.

"Quick, boys, I need a Mickey Finn!" he'd yell. Today they might call it a roofie—a knockout drink. It was one way to get rid of belligerent drunks: make them pass out before they busted up the place.

Joe and Nick would roll up their sleeves and go to work. A Mickey Finn in those days was made of calomel—a sedative when taken in large quantities, now known to cause mercury poisoning—and jalap, which came from the root of a Mexican climbing plant. Both drugs were also laxatives, another deterrent to causing trouble.

The joint on Pell Street is also important to our story because waiting tables there, and sometimes making the Mickey run, was a small, dark teenager with sad eyes and the name Izzy Baline. Izzy sang, "Come on and hear! Come on and hear! It's the best food in the land!" He was the singing waiter, and sometimes, when there was a break in the action, he'd get up on Salter's small stage and make the drunks cry with songs that dripped sentimentality, "In the Sweet By and By (We Shall Meet on That Beautiful Shore)" and "The Mansion of Aching Hearts." When the drugstore closed, Joe and Nick stopped by Salter's for a beer, and they became good friends with little Izzy.

For years, according to Joe, the brothers got no more than four hours of sleep a night, what with jobs and classes and wearing out their Russian-English dictionary.

Brother Louis was first to become an official pharmacist (he'd make it his career), and after receiving his degree worked at the Bowery drugstore with Joe and Nick. No matter the hour, there was at least one Schenck rolling up his sleeves and mixing concoctions.

Not all pharmacies were as ramshackle as the Bowery shack, and after a year the boys moved up. Joe took a job at Hornick's Pharmacy at 111th Street and Third Avenue in Upper Manhattan and convinced the druggist, "Doc" Hornick, to hire his brothers Louis and Nick as well.

According to legend, it was Joe's knowledge of chemistry that made the concoctions so popular. He knew, for example, that the active ingredient in Bayer Heroin (which came in white pill form, just like the same company's aspirin, and was marketed as a cough suppressant) was the same as that in the sticky black opium they'd sold on the Bowery. Plus, syrup for making cola fountain drinks contained cocaine. Pair the two (an ancient speedball) and you had a cocktail that kept customers coming back for more.

Doc Hornick paid the boys $15 a week and, because they were so good for business, gave them commissions on any new business they brought in. Nick loved to tub-thump, i.e., hit the streets and "drum up business." Before long they were making $40 a week, an insane sum for their age. This enabled the brothers, for the first time, to save money.

Around that time, Nick befriended a popular singer in her early twenties, a physically impressive woman with, as they said, a lot of "these and those." Her name was Eva Tanguay. Daughter of a Canadian doctor, she would soon be called the "I Don't Care Girl" and "The Girl Who Made Vaudeville Famous." She was known for her ribald "bottoms-up" humor, bawdy yet unashamed, that seemed to be single-handedly dragging entertainment out of the stuffy Victorian Age. Her popular songs all implied sexual emancipation: "Go as Far as You Like," "I Want Someone to Go Wild With Me," and "That's Why They Call Me Tabasco."

Nick's relationship with the young comedienne was a bit of an eye-opener—for him, anyway. Tanguay liked and trusted Nick so she lent the Schenck brothers $1,500 as a down payment on their first drugstore. With Tanguay's loan, the Schencks bought a controlling portion of Hornick's. The brothers had only been working there for two years.

(A half a century later, Joe Schenck's Twentieth Century-Fox would make a biopic of Tanguay, starring Mitzi Gaynor and George Jessel, called *The I Don't Care Girl.*)

JOE AND NICK WERE YOUNG MEN NOW AND SUDDENLY FLUSH—BUT what to do with their money? There were two ways to go in America if you were an enterprising Jewish man. You could stick to one of the limited fields that Jews were allowed to pursue in America, or you could be a vanguard—circumvent social barriers by inventing your own business. That was a game for scofflaws with courage.

The Schencks went conservative for a time, but then switched to risk, dare, and adventure. Future decisions involved innovation—and products to which patrons might become addicted.

One day, when Joe went wandering during his lunch hour, he discovered something both innovative and potentially addictive. Motion pictures had been projected on screens for seven years—almost always as a novelty and at first only to publicize Thomas Edison's invention of the film projector—but Joe Schenck had never seen one, not until . . .

FADE IN. Exterior. Establishing shot of the BOWERY THEATER marquee. Joe, in a suit and ill-fitting bowler hat, pays for a ticket in the kiosk out front and walks inside with a bounce in his step. He sits with about fifty other customers. In quick succession we see a female singer, male tap dancer, a juggler, a ventriloquist. EMCEE takes the stage:

EMCEE

Now a special attraction: the miracle of *moving pictures*!

Lights go out. Screen lights up. First title card reads: "Ladies, please remove your hats." (This is a time when a milliner's creations are judged by altitude.)

With the other astounded folks in the theater, Joe sees a photograph projected on the screen, a photograph that moves—moving images of angry ocean waves crashing against a rocky shore. Audience members duck and lift their feet so as not to get wet. Then an explosion of hysterical laughter at being fooled. Joe pulls his head away from the show and scans the audience around him, faces lit up by the flickering screen, showing a narcotic-like excitement. Joe understands that it is some sort of scientific process, but his first thought is . . .

JOE (speaking to himself)

Somebody's going to make a million dollars out of this.

FADE OUT.

JOE AND NICK BECAME REGULAR PATRONS OF MOVING PICTURES. THEY went to see them all, not that there were that many in 1901 and 1902. They were all very short, two or three minutes each, usually showing one scene, something alluring, funny, or historically important. Joe later recalled, "I was impressed by one picture called *The Eruption of Mount Pelee*, which turned out to not be a Martinique volcano at all but rather a beer barrel exploding in the July New Jersey sun."

The brothers kept tabs, almost subconsciously, on what audiences liked and didn't like. There were picture makers out there who didn't understand how people thought or how entertainment worked. There were some naughty subjects—*When the Husband Came Home*, *Love in a Broker's Office*—that repulsed women. Scenes depicting a woman cheating on her husband caused a grumble of dissatisfaction and more than a few walkouts. "It's not right," one woman complained. Scenes that focused on villains and offered no comeuppance were similarly rejected. Audiences wanted winning good guys and losing bad guys. Crime did not pay. All lawbreaking and immorality needed to be *punished*.

WITH THE 111TH STREET STORE THRIVING, JOE AND NICK BOUGHT the Bowery drugstore for $600 (about $21,000 in today's money), fixed it up, made it a tad less drafty, and sold it for $3,500 (about $122,000 today). Soon thereafter, they took on investors and bought three more drugstores. It looked for all the world like Schenck Bros. Pharmacy was to become their vehicle for reaching the American Dream. But Joe and Nick were restless.

One sizzling summer Sunday in 1903 Joe and Nick took the Third Avenue trolley uptown to the Harlem River, where there was a breeze. In a world before air-conditioning, finding a breeze was a key summer activity, and this spot by the river, the highest point on Manhattan, was perfect. It is the current site of George Washington High School, at the corner of West 192nd Street and Audubon Avenue, in an area then known as Upper Harlem, now as Washington Heights. Children swam in the water and, because the river was narrow, waved at the kids from the Bronx doing the same thing on the other side.

The Schenck brothers noticed, however, that while everyone was enjoying the "cool," there was nothing else to do. Everyone was just sort of milling around waiting for the sun to set so they could go back to their oven-like apartments.

"These people look thirsty," Joe said.

The brothers took out a lease on a one-story building near the trolley station at the Harlem River at Fort George that could only be accessed through an alley. In the building they put a saloon in the front and a dance hall in the back. For entertainment, they hired an orchestra and a then-unknown singer named Nora Bayes, who would go on to co-compose the famous song "Shine On, Harvest Moon" which she performed with the Ziegfeld Follies.

They called the place the Old Barrel—but the grand opening fizzled. No one wanted to walk through the spooky alley to get to the bar. The brothers tried putting a sign at the mouth of the alley that looked cheerful and safe. The sign said, "Beer and Dancing in Rear." Still, no one came.

Nick eventually came up with the winning idea. "The sign shouldn't have words," he suggested. "It should have a picture of a mug full of beer."

Joe said, "I know a guy that paints signs. He also paints landscapes on those big mirrors that go behind the bar."

The artist produced a huge wooden cutout in the shape of a beer schooner overflowing with suds. They lit the sign so it was visible from a great distance at night. The sign also brightened the alley, and did the trick. The bar–dance hall was busy for the rest of the summer.

While running the Old Barrel, Joe and Nick asked customers pointed questions, such as, "Would you come up here during weekday and Saturday evenings if there were rides like those at Coney Island?" Everyone said yes.

Joe's aptitude for math led him to an important decision. A hundred people could be drinking beer or dancing at the same time. Drugstores could handle, what, about six customers at a time? Why not leave the drug biz and become full-time barkeeps? Nick, the conservative one, liked the idea but suggested they hang on to one of their drugstores just in case Joe's new obsession fell through. He also said that they should expand their thinking. They wouldn't be just barkeeps. They would dedicate themselves from then on to amusements.

"We will provide all the things that people like to do to have fun," Nick said, and Joe eagerly agreed. Early in 1906 the brothers formed the Fort George Amusement Company and leased a chunk of elevated land at Fort George. Paradise Park was constructed on a shoestring budget. Just as legend had it that Joe's knowledge of chemistry led to the brothers' success as a pharmacist, it was Nick's carpentry skills that led to him designing and building winning amusement parks. ("He was forever tinkering with tools," went the press release, and there may have been some truth in it.)

They'd gotten as far as a merry-go-round and some of the buildings that would form the midway when Nick made an observation that halted activity.

"The land is too high!" Nick said. He counted for a moment and added, "Fifty-six steps from the trolley stop. Fifty-six stairs just to get to the entrance. That's harder than walking down an alley."

"But not spookier," Joe countered. Joe admitted that he'd been too excited about how cool the breeze was up there to worry about accessibility. "Well, all we can do is finish construction and hope for the best." This didn't make Nick happy, but he had no helpful suggestion. They couldn't afford to move the hill.

When Paradise Park opened—with a Ferris wheel (one of the first in the world, and the largest in the Northeast), and shooting galleries, to go with the merry-go-round—New Yorkers getting off the trolley down below were so excited that they—the younger ones, anyway—took those stairs two at a time to get to the park.

"After the opening," Joe later recalled, "when we found that the public didn't mind those steps, we put a turnstile in—quick—right at the fifty-sixth step and charged them ten cents admission."

Even after the opening, construction continued. Along with chemistry and carpentry, the Schenck brothers understood show-business dynamics, and used their intuition to determine what the customers wanted. Soon there was a toboggan slide, a restaurant, and a skating rink in the winter. There were two music halls, the Trocadero at the south end of the park at 190th Street, and the Star at the north end, approximately 192nd Street. A hotel was built on the property, the Fort George Hotel and Casino.

For the first few weeks, Paradise Park featured several places to buy beer, including the Old Barrel, but—as Joe later put it—"a few inebriates" discouraged families from coming. Ironic in that selling beer was their first idea regarding the park, but they banned alcohol—didn't sell it, didn't allow it brought in—and instead emphasized how much fun kids had at the park, how it was perfect for the entire family. Business boomed.

It was during the first year of Paradise Park that the Schencks received a visit from oversized New York Police Lieutenant Charles Becker, representing the corrupt NYC Tammany government.

"I could point out to you, sirs, that your park has several technical violations of the law," Becker said.

"This the skim?" Joe asked.

"Call it what you like."

Joe paid the man. Nick found the shakedown distasteful, but Joe went out of his way to befriend Becker, who after all was only doing his job as a collector for the crooks in charge. It was upsetting to Joe when a few years later Becker was one of five to be busted for plotting the murder of degenerate gambler Herman Rosenthal, who couldn't pay his tab. All five went to Sing Sing and fried in the lap of Old Sparky.

"I felt bad. I liked the guy," Joe later said.

Becker introduced Joe to professional gamblers and asked him if he ever played poker. Joe said no, but he was willing to learn. To put it mildly, Joe loved gambling, and once he started, he couldn't stop. He dropped every cent the park had made him for the summer in record time. For the rest of his life, whenever he was physically able, he gambled, still trying to win back the 1906 Paradise Park profits.

It was a long winter, but the spring of 1907 finally came, Paradise Park reopened, more popular than ever. Not an hour after the gates opened, an older man named Marcus Loew came to see Joe and Nick. The brothers' lives would never be the same.

CHAPTER TWO

MARCUS LOEW

On May 7, 1870, Marcus Loew was born in a wooden shack on the corner of Fifth Street and Avenue B on Manhattan's Lower East Side, then America's most squalid slum. (Loew would later build the Loew's Ave B Theater at the spot, capacity 1,750, to commemorate his birthplace and childhood home.) His stepfather, a restaurant waiter, and mother were from Austria and Germany, and had come to America only a few years before.

The Loews were desperately poor, cold, and hungry, so much so that beginning at age six Marcus was a newsie. Loew went to school only sporadically and worked full-time by the age of nine. He took a job as a mapmaker when he was ten but was fired for attempting to organize a strike.

At age twelve he worked in a factory where he handled furs and made dress trimmings, turning a crank for eleven hours a day, making $4.50 a week. He learned the fur business—first how to cut animal pelts and sew them into women's garments, then more lucrative skills involving distribution and marketing—and decided to become a furrier when he was eighteen.

Loew's time cutting furs brought benefits that lasted a lifetime: He made a friend at work named Adolph Zukor. The two men, future legends, appeared to be opposites: Loew a ray of sunshine in everyone's life, gloomy Zukor with a perpetual black cloud over his head. They cut furs side by side at a Manhattan furrier and talked all day. They were intellectually compatible and emotionally complementary as they discussed ways to get to the top of the hill. Loew learned that Zukor was a wounded soul, an orphan who'd graduated from hard knocks with a grim disposition—like an undertaker, some said—that led some to call him "creepy" behind his back. Loew saw past the icy demeanor and trusted Zukor as a man of honor and a superior businessman.

In 1884, at age fourteen, Loew decided to be a newspaper editor, and briefly succeeded, writing his own editorials, and selling his own advertising to merchants on Manhattan's East Side. But it was temporary. By the end of his teens, he'd twice started companies that went out of business. He declared bankruptcy at age twenty, and thereafter dedicated his life to do his part in creating the entertainment industry as we know it.

Loew had suffered with rheumatic fever as a boy, and it left him with a weak heart. He had an oddly latitudinal forehead, large staring eyes, sloping shoulders, and as an adult a hefty dominant mustache over a receding chin. He looked like a man with only a puncher's chance of growing old.

He also looked like someone who could be pushed around, but that was an illusion.

In 1897, when Marcus Loew was twenty-seven, his twin sons David L. and Arthur Marcus were born. (David worked for Loew's Inc. until the mid-1930s when he launched an independent film production company. Arthur became an actor, producer, and writer. Arthur's son, Marcus's grandson, Arthur Loew, Jr., was born in New York City on December 26, 1925. He produced films during the 1950s and '60s, most notably *Penelope*, starring Natalie Wood.)

Adolph Zukor, Loew discovered, was not just a man with a keen business mind, he was also a visionary. When Zukor saw an eight-minute picture called *The Great Train Robbery* (1903), he became one of the first to envision much longer pictures that went beyond hastily assembled scenarios—waves crashing on a shore, or scantily clad women dancing around a room—pictures that told stories in pantomime with beginnings, middles, and ends, capable of evoking all of the emotions, stimulating the greatest intellect, and instilling passion in the chilliest heart.

Loew's rise to great wealth and power initially was linked to his ability to make smart friends. In addition to Zukor, Loew befriended dramatic stage star David Warfield. Warfield owned an apartment building that was leaking money. Loew agreed to take over management of the building in exchange for a piece of the action, turned the business around, until both Warfield and Loew had some throwing around money—$40,000 that would be invested in 1900 in a penny arcade on New York's Union Square. The arcade returned his investment in seven months.

Warfield later said, "As I look back on those old days, the outstanding trait of Marcus Loew was his honesty in every sense of that word. I believe that was the secret of his phenomenal career that established so many theaters that even Marcus himself did not know their number."

In December 1904, with a $500 investment ($17,500 in today's money), Loew first exhibited motion pictures in a penny arcade on 23rd Street in Manhattan. He hired a staff of three—a manager, a cashier, and a penny boy—combined salaries $30 a week.

The moving images, which one saw through a viewfinder while cranking a handle, involved the flipping of a series of cards to create the illusion of motion. The most popular of these early pictures was one depicting Harry K. Thaw's murder of famous architect Stanford White atop Madison Square Garden (the original MSG, the one on Madison Square with a roof garden).

Loew bought an Edison projector. Loew's first real cinema, lucrative and packed with customers watching moving images projected on a screen, was in East Harlem at Third Avenue and 118th Street and had a seating capacity of three hundred. His next move was out of town—Covington, Kentucky (suburban Cincinnati, Ohio)—where he opened a 110-seat theater on the second floor of a downtown building.

Loew's trademark combo of film and vaudeville began in Covington when he hired a down-and-out actor to take the stage and recite Rudyard Kipling poems, "Gunga Din" and "Mandalay." The act was a hit. Singers, comedians, acrobats, jugglers, etc., joined the show.

Convinced that the formula—motion pictures mixed with vaudeville acts—would work everywhere, Loew converted his penny arcades in New York into theaters. He bought property at 23rd Street and Seventh Avenue where he designed a theater that resembled a train car, scenery on both side walls. The screen showed the view from the front of a train as it traveled a scenic course through the Alps and other spots of decidedly European beauty. Loew himself would put on a conductor's outfit and shout out orders to the "Operator Motorman" who would start the show through the miracle of the "nickolette" machine.

He next put in a small theater above the Hippodrome in Times Square, and it was here that he fully realized film's potential. During his first week, he sold out fifty showings of his flickers.

So, he thought bigger. Loew's next purchase was the Royal Theatre, on Willoughby Street in Downtown Brooklyn, seating capacity two thousand.

There was already a theater there, built in 1903 and known as Watson's Cozy Corner, which included a vaudeville theater upstairs and a saloon downstairs.

Loew began operations at the Royal by showing classical Italian plays, which didn't do well. After he converted the theater into Brooklyn's first cinema, supplementing the show with vaudeville acts as he had in Cincinnati, it sold out dozens of shows every day. He raided competing arcades, hired their best talent, acquiring in the process future Loew's Inc. treasurer Dave Bernstein from a theater on 14th Street. When Bernstein joined Loew, he brought his pianist Harry Carroll with him. (The piano player was doubly important, expected to accompany both the live acts and the moving pictures.) S. H. Meinhold was brought in from Connecticut to manage Loew's theaters.

The year 1907 featured some major milestones in the history of the moving image. Bell & Howell invented their film projection system. *Bronco Billy* became the first "Western." *Variety* published their first film reviews. The first feature-length film was made in France. And the top producer of American films was Vitagraph in Midwood, Brooklyn, a mass producer of gimmicky short subjects, still a few years away from caring about the quality as well as the quantity of its product.

BY THE TIME MARCUS STRODE CONFIDENTLY UP TO JOE AND NICK Schenck on Memorial Day, 1907, he owned penny arcades, nickelodeon parlors, several small theaters, and one large one. At that meeting he shook hands with Joe and Nick and said, "I would like to put up a concession at your park."

"What did you have in mind?" Nick asked.

"I have something that looks like a railroad car. It's all dark inside and it doesn't move—but I have one of those moving-picture machines inside."

The brothers' eyes lit up.

"The patrons will get the illusion that they are traveling because of the scenic pictures I will show."

He installed his railroad car, which became one of the park's top attractions, and—to further endear himself to the Schencks—he invested $10,000 in Paradise Park. Loew now had a piece of the brothers' amusement park and supplied both motion pictures and vaudeville acts, both of which drew customers to Nick's merry-go-round and Ferris wheel.

Loew and the Schenck brothers began to socialize, with many outings—

often to the Harlem Casino, or Ratner's Dairy on Delancey—feeling more like a job interview as Loew interrogated the Schencks regarding their future.

FADE IN. Interior. Afternoon. Ratner's kosher restaurant, just opened on the Lower East Side of Manhattan. Date: 1907. The place has only been open for a couple of years but doesn't look it. There is sawdust on the floor. At the counter are customers, all men talking at once, about a quarter of it in Russian. The topic is the "Kosher Butcher Strike" in East Baltimore, where Ratner has a cousin. The butchers want more from the stores that sell their meat. They deserve more because everyone knows the kosher meat is better than the whatdoyoucall gentile meat.

PORTLY CUSTOMER

I am not comfortable discussing
butchers in the dairy.

Laughter. That's the cacophony at the front of the dairy. CAMERA takes us away from the noise, to the back room where there are booths and round tables, about three-quarters occupied. At a corner table we see Marcus Loew and Joe and Nick Schenck. They speak in soft tones, in contrast to the yelling up front. They are conspicuous by their attire, businessmen. Their shoes are well polished. On the table in front of them sits a batch of Ratner's onion rolls and a plateful of sour pickles straight from the barrel. A waiter, Ratner's pimply teenage son, comes by for their order. The men order cheese blintzes, gefilte fish, salmon-in-aspic, kasha varnishkas, and some matzo ball soup. Nick is the only one smoking, and he smokes constantly, so that when he speaks smoke sometimes comes out his nose. He flicks his ashes in no-look fashion, the ashes falling some in and some near a glass ashtray on the table.

LOEW (hitting ascending notes)
So, vaudeville has a future?

JOE
Sure, sure, but you lease more theaters, it's hard to keep everyone happy.

NICK
You don't need us to tell you about the theater business.

LOEW (mouth full)
Business is business. I like Paradise Park. Well run. Makes money.

NICK
You too, Marcus.

LOEW (working his mustache with a cloth napkin)
You guys want to work for me, Joe booking acts, Nick managing theaters?
Nick and Joe exchange glances.

JOE
Let's shake on it.

THUS, JOE BECAME THE BOOKER, HEAD OF THE PEOPLE'S VAUDEVILLE Company, which Loew founded in 1904. Nick became manager of the theaters. It was a combination that made the Schencks wealthy men, and Loew's power and wealth became almost unmeasurable.

Till death they did part, Marcus Loew and the Schenck brothers were a cohesive team. It was later said that Loew and the Schencks agreed on everything, except gambling. Marcus didn't like the fact that Joe and Nick spent their free time at the racetrack.

"I would never bet on anything that eats but can't talk," Loew said.

NOT LONG AFTER LOEW HIRED JOE AND NICK, HE INTRODUCED THEM to Adolph Zukor. The men assembled in the dimly lit backroom of Shanley's Grill Room, a Times Square tablecloth joint at Broadway between 43rd and 44th streets. Zukor remained the flickers' number-one proponent. He hyped film both as a moneymaker and a burgeoning field of artistry. They would sell out houses for a time side by side with vaudeville, but eventually flickers would be a show on their own until they dominated the entertainment industry.

The men agreed that they should be *making* motion pictures. Even if Zukor's vision was mere fantasy, he was right about one thing: Good pictures would outsell hastily slapped together pictures.

"One day, photoplays will run as long as stage plays," Zukor said.

The others argued, saying no one would have the patience to sit still staring at a screen for that long.

"It is not a novelty," Zukor insisted. "It is only a novelty because we treat it that way. Pictures can be used to *move* an audience."

What Zukor was suggesting was that the new technology, moving images, be injected with a strong dose of show business. Nick and Joe got the idea. Pictures, if made by someone who was really good, could be every bit as addictive as a drugstore concoction.

(Years later, when Marcus ran Loew's Inc. and Zukor ran Paramount, they would return to Shanley's. They had remained close friends. Loew's son married Zukor's daughter. They had mansions near each other on Long Island. They were at a corner table in the Grill Room having a reunion when who walks in but future mogul Louis B. Mayer, then an up-and-coming producer. They greeted him with a quick nod and then ignored him.)

OVER TIME NICK AND JOE LEARNED THAT THEIR NEW PARTNER, MARcus Loew, was frustratingly superstitious, refusing to walk under ladders, distrusting all doctors, and believing it bad luck to sign anything on a Friday. (Although the last one sometimes served as an excuse to take long weekends.)

By 1909, Marcus's business had expanded to include twelve vaudeville houses operating as the People's Vaudeville Company, which evolved into Loew's Enterprises, which evolved into Loew's Inc. Joe was general manager,

Nick in charge of real-estate investments. The Schencks and Loew invested together (and sometimes separately) in nickelodeons, vaudeville/flicker theaters. For a time, the Schencks had a theater in Hoboken, New Jersey, on their own, but it was eventually absorbed into the Loew's chain. In 1910 the ever-restless Schencks sold Paradise Park and turned their ambitions to a bigger and better amusement park, this one atop the cliffs of New Jersey, just across the Hudson River from Harlem. (See Chapter Three.)

The toughest part of running a vaudeville circuit was moving the acts from theater to theater with a minimum of repetition. Some could be repeated without complaint. Audiences, for example, repeatedly enjoyed Hadji Ali, the Egyptian Enigma, a master of controlled regurgitation who would drink water and then kerosene. The Enigma would vomit, light the kerosene as it spewed forth, and put the fire out with the water, which always came up last. Brought the house down.

ADOLPH ZUKOR WAS BRIEFLY LOEW'S PARTNER, BUT IN 1912 HE TOOK his money out of Loew's company and put it into his own, called Famous Players. With studios in an old armory on West 26th Street, and using talent recruited from the legit stage, Zukor's first pictures, including the first film version of *Snow White*, were made so early that, in classic Bowery fashion, he hired goons to watch the door of his studio while scenes were being shot, to keep out any representatives from Thomas Edison who might try to use force to enforce Edison's patent rights. Zukor's studio is still there, now known as Chelsea Television Studios and home of the Rachael Ray and Sherri Shepherd talk shows.

IN 1911, NEW YORK NEWSPAPERS RAN STORIES ABOUT A YOUNG SONGwriter and singer who was writing hit after hit, the first being a snappy march called "Alexander's Ragtime Band." Ads for his hits—eight cents apiece—ran large in the *Evening World*. His name, the papers said, was Irving Berlin. Joe decided Berlin was perfect for his vaudeville circuit and ordered an assistant to summon the composer to his office.

When Berlin walked into Joe's office, Joe just about exploded.

"Izzy! Izzy Baline! Is it you?"

"Hey Joe, can you whip me up a Mickey Finn?" Berlin said and both men roared with laughter, hugged, and then roared with laughter again. Look how far they'd come. Obviously, Joe and Izzy had lost track of each other for a few years, but reunited they were to be close friends for life. Berlin was immediately booked at the Winter Garden Theatre. After shows, he and Joe went out together looking for girls. If one got serious with a girl, they later claimed, the other would sabotage it. They were having too much fun together.

During the summer of 1913 Joe Schenck and Irving Berlin went to a Broadway theater to see a pantomime troupe just brought into town from England by promoter Fred Karno. One sketch was called "A Night in an English Music Box" and featured onstage was a man in the process of getting drunk, teetering slightly at first, then staggering and *almost* falling in increasingly elaborate ways until the audience was in hysterics.

"Who is that guy?" Joe asked.

Berlin stuck his nose in his program. "Guy's name is Charlie Chaplin," he said.

After the show, Joe and Irving went backstage and introduced themselves. Chaplin knew who Joe was, Loew's booker.

"How much is Karno paying you?" Joe asked.

"Sixty a week."

"I can do better. Come see me," Joe said.

"I'm leaving for Philadelphia with the act, but I'm back in New York after the engagement. Okay if I come see you then?" Chaplin said.

"Sure, sure," Joe said.

Back on the street Berlin said, "Joe, I can see dollar signs in your eyes."

It was the middle of the following week when Berlin walked into Joe's office and found Joe pulling a long face.

"Whatsa matter, Joe? You lose at poker last night?"

"Yeah, ten thousand. But that's not what's bugging me. I have received a telegram from Philadelphia. Charlie Chaplin signed with Mack Sennett. There goes a million bucks."

BY 1912, A FEATURE STORY ON LOEW, WHO WAS NOW IN HIS EARLY forties, estimated his wealth at $37 million, and still a "swell fellow"—that is, nice. The Schenck brothers, the story said, were millionaires as well. Joe was thirty-six, Nick thirty-two, both now regularly getting their names in the papers. Loew was a family man, the press reported, with a beautiful wife and handsome teenaged twin sons. Joe and his pal Irving Berlin were vigorous bachelors with a penchant for showgirls. (Nick's marital status went unmentioned. Unlike the others, Nick knew how to function under the press radar. It was around this time that Nick was married without publicity to a Brooklyn cop's ex-wife named Annie about whom next to nothing is known.)

Marcus's niceness wasn't an act. Even in private he put scruples over profit. He paid out-of-work vaudevillians, and secretly gave money to charities. Here was a man who would go on to build palaces, and then allow the public to use them at a reasonable price. Indeed, one of the reasons Nick and Marcus made such a good team was that—professionally, anyway—Nick didn't particularly care who he angered and was willing to do the tasks that Marcus was too nice to do, like threatening theater operators with repossession if they were tardy paying the rent.

Nick was a product of the Bowery and did not hesitate to use bully tactics to protect his considerable turf. His best goon was Dave Bernstein, who technically was Marcus Loew's treasurer. The unwritten part of Bernstein's job was to "discourage competition." If a competitor wanted to build a theater in a town where a Loew's was already present, Bernstein wouldn't beat around the bush. He'd lead with the bad news.

"Hey, I'm with Loew's and I'll tell you right now, you don't need the headache. If you build a theater in our town, we will fight you and fight you and we will win. Do I make myself clear?" Nobody was confused.

Nick didn't want anti-Semites working for Loew's, and—like a modern-day episode of *Undercover Boss*—was not above misrepresenting himself to test gentiles on the payroll. One day Nick wanted to get a line on the prices at various vaudeville houses on his circuit during the Jewish holidays. One of the theaters he called was on East 86th Street in the Yorkville section of Manhattan. He asked to speak to the manager and a man named Keough came on the line.

"What are your prices there during the Rosh Hashanah?" Nick asked.

"During what?"

"Jewish New Year. Do you have a holiday scale or the regular daily prices?"

"It all depends. We look them over carefully when they come up to the box office window. If an Irishman appears we charge him the regular prices, but if it's a Jew we soak him holiday prices."

"Well, you low-life Irisher. You're fired!" Nick reportedly replied.

Nick wasn't the only Schenck brother combatting anti-Semitism. Joe recalled a time when he was a young man seeking a loan in a big WASPy New York bank. When the banker, who turned him down, thought Joe was out of earshot, he called him a "kike." Years later, when Joe was flush, to put it mildly, he returned to that bank, found the anti-Semite banker, and asked for a $100 million loan. The guy was practically kissing Joe's ass. He was "happy to do business."

"Well, the kike doesn't want to do business with you. Fuck you," Joe said, and walked out.

WHILE NICK SHOWED SIGNS OF CONTENTMENT, WILLING TO OPERATE an amusement park and manage Loew's theater empire forever, Joe was more impatient. Joe's days as a vaudeville booking agent were numbered. Nick had the amusement park in the summer. Joe wanted to strike off on his own, do his own thing, probably something involving motion pictures, the wave of Adolph Zukor's future.

Booking motion pictures onto vaudeville shows was appreciated by audiences but loathed by old-time stage producers like Florenz Ziegfeld and David Belasco, both of whom were shouting that pictures were a fad, soon to be a thing of the past.

Joe, when asked, said something very different: "Pictures will kill vaudeville," he said, borrowing Zukor's prediction.

Some thought Joe was nuts. Joe loved to tell a story about his friend Al Lichtman, who once rented an office by coincidence directly across from Joe's office. Surreptitiously watching, he called Joe on the phone.

"Joe, I've just come across a marvelous invention that I can get cheap. I thought maybe you'd like a piece of it."

"What is it?"

"You won't believe this but the inventor, who has just arrived from Europe, has put it on my telephone and I can see you now clear as can be."

"I'm busy, Al."

"But I'm serious, Joe. This is the greatest invention since moving pictures."

"Okay. If you can see me, what kind of tie am I wearing?"

"Striped. Black and white."

"What color is my suit?"

"Dark gray."

"And now I am going to do something. Tell me what it is."

"You're running your fingers through your hair. You're rubbing your chin. You are making an obscene gesture."

"Boy! That really is an invention. I'll be right over. Where are you?"

"Look out the window." Lichtman waved. Joe laughed. "But, Joe, there is a serious side to this. Twenty-five years from now you'll be more likely to see somebody over the phone than you will be to find a theater playing a moving picture. They just won't be making them."

It was a funny story, but obviously Lichtman's warning went unheeded.

Joe wasn't a judgmental guy. He'd prove it throughout his life. He mingled well with men of all stripe, as is practically necessary for a guy who enjoys high-stakes gambling. On August 28, 1912, Joe's name was in the papers in an unflattering way. A major trial was underway regarding illegal gambling throughout New York City. The bust included arrests of men known as "Gyp the Blood" and "Lefty Louie." Joe's name got into it because one of the suspects, the police commissioner's secretary, Winfield Sheehan, had been lying low as a houseguest at Joe Schenck's home. Sheehan was spotted going to work in "Schenck's forty-horsepower motorboat, the *Tanguay*, which is named after a popular vaudevillian." (Sheehan survived the scandal and had a second career as a VP at Fox Film Company. In 1921 his job was to tour Europe and steal ideas from French and German filmmakers.)

As the Loew's theater empire expanded, Joe became the number-one booking agent for vaudeville acts in the world, arranging the bills in 127 theaters in the U.S. and Canada. The Loew's empire began in the East but spread until Joe's territory covered the land. For Joe, routing vaudeville acts coast-to-coast became all-consuming, yet he was master of a well-oiled machine. A network of venues was in place and ready for the motion picture takeover.

When interviewed, Loew always mentioned the Schencks. "My greatest talent is my ability to surround myself with the best men for the job. And for me that's Joseph and Nicholas Schenck. Nick is a wizard in every respect, who has been with me since I started, an accomplished showman. Joe is the most powerful and important booking agent in the world, a specialist in his line."

MARCUS LOEW—ENVISIONING A WORLD IN WHICH EVERYONE WHO went to the pictures felt, for a few hours anyway, like a Vanderbilt—engineered a transformation in theaters, which in a decade went from railcars to palaces. Right up until the stock market crash an extraordinary amount of money would be spent by Loew's Inc.—and other theater chains—to build cinemas that resembled Versailles in Paris, or a cathedral in Spain. Loew's strategy was always build, build, build. The first palace opened on April 16, 1915, at the corner of East New York Avenue and Douglas Street in Brownsville, Brooklyn, never one of New York City's most scenic neighborhoods, then predominantly Jewish. For the opening, an "immense throng" showed up. After SRO tickets were sold, a crowd was turned away. In the fuss, the show started late. Irving Berlin performed. The Moller sixteen-rank pipe organ sounded direct from God. Andy Rice performed "Rice and Old Shoes: The Story of a Jewish Wedding." Lucy and Ethel Baker performed "character singing." And the crowd was thrilled by the Jungman Family, a clan of "sensational wire walkers." Nick and Joe occupied a stage box, accompanied by Judge Benjamin Hoffman; Joseph Vogel, the theater's manager; and Marcus and Caroline Loew. (Vogel was a Loew's lifer, and eventually rose to the top.) Afterward, Loew took the stage. "I've long realized the need for a luxury theater in Brownsville and am glad my vision has at last been realized."

Loew had theaters; now he needed his own pictures to show in them—so, in 1919, Marcus assembled a picture-making studio. He purchased for $3.1 million four-year-old Metro Studios, a company originally formed as a consolidation of four tiny production companies out of Jacksonville, Florida, that cranked out cheap short subjects to be shown before and between the features on a double bill. For his new studio, Loew built new facilities in Hollywood, California, on Cahuenga between Willoughby and Waring avenues. (Current site of Red Studios Hollywood.) Metro would now make its own features, including in 1921 *The Four Horsemen of the Apocalypse* with Rudolph Valentino, a major hit that put Metro on the map.

One producer at Metro was Louis B. Mayer, a hard-featured man in dandy clothes, who could be seen riding around Hollywood in a tin lizzie (when horseless carriages—automobiles—were still the exception rather than the rule) and telling anyone who would listen that he wanted to be the best producer in the world.

HUMANS BEING WHAT THEY ARE, ANIMALS, THE INDUSTRY WASN'T very old before some picture makers gave their photoplays a drenching of prurience. Violent and sexual films for an adult audience inflamed the public's notion that show business was unwholesome.

On June 28, 1919, Marcus Loew spoke before the convention of the Motion Picture Exhibitors' Association at the Hotel Statler: "Unclean pictures are the greatest menace to the business. Any exhibitor who makes a few dollars one week by showing an immoral or vicious film will give twice as much later on to undo the loss that his business has suffered. The man who cares only for the profit and nothing for the character of the productions he shows is ruining business for honest exhibitors."

Thunderous applause.

CHAPTER THREE

PALISADES PARK

AH, PALISADES AMUSEMENT PARK—A LITTLE PIECE OF HEAVEN atop the cliffs of Jersey. It became the thing that gave Nicholas M. Schenck the most joy, right up until the birth of his daughters. In February 1910, with Loew's help, Joe and Nick purchased land atop New Jersey's two-hundred-foot Palisades Cliffs, which stunningly overlook the Hudson River and Manhattan. At night the river view was dotted with excursion boats and pleasure craft lit by the romantic moon.

The thirty-eight-acre site had belonged to Bergen County Traction, the local trolley company. It was called Park on the Palisades, a picnic area with tables, benches, and a couple of concession stands. The trolley company hoped the park would increase the number of people who rode their trolleys on weekends. By 1908, there was a merry-go-round and a couple of other rides.

Before Westerns became a part of the American tapestry, talented cowboys—along with Native Americans in traditional garb—toured from town to town, ropin' and ridin' and hootin' and shootin'. The biggest of these was William F. Cody's "Buffalo Bill's Wild West Show"—featuring real-life Western legends like Wild Bill Hickok, Annie Oakley, Sitting Bull, and Geronimo. When in Jersey, the show was held at the clifftop park.

Joe and Nick first checked out the property in 1909 with the object of building a complex of cold-water flats. The thought of building cheap housing on the site angered locals, including one Rev. McCleary who warbled: "Here is nature in all its sublime simplicity. God is here."

One day, when the question of how many cold-water flats might be practical to build, Nick Schenck looked out over the site and his eyes glazed over. He saw in the mists of his imagination a place of danger and intrigue and mystery, a place of carnival music laced with screams of terror and explosive laughter, where every young man would have a myriad of opportunities to prove to the girl on his arm that he had heart. He saw a place where no one rested, an exciting place, one with thrills and spills galore, ferries taking Manhattanites from 131st Street to the Fort Lee pier directly below, Bergen County Traction bringing them up by the trolleyful.

Following Nick's vision, no one mentioned apartment buildings anymore. Nick and Joe formed the Palisades Realty and Amusement Company and bought the place. Although Joe and Marcus had a piece, they concentrated on Loew business while Nick built an amusement wonderland.

Nick had till the end of May, opening day, to execute his vision, so he rolled up his sleeves and went to work. He grew the park into the world's most famous "Fun Center," installing five new death-defying (and sometimes deadly) rides. He even got out there with a hammer and nails and helped with construction.

On May 28, 1910, the bright and shiny Schenck Bros. Palisades Amusement Park was ready. The grand opening coincided with the once-every-seventy-two-years visit of Halley's Comet, which caused hundreds to line Riverside Drive and gaze skyward. Along with the show in the sky, they saw the lights and rides atop the cliffs. Man, it looked like fun over there.

The original sign over the entrance read "Schenck Bros. Palisade Park," and sometime thereafter was replaced by one that read "Palisades Amusement Park." Newspaper ads for the opening discussed the "aeroplane coaster" built by "American Inventor Nicholas M. Schenck." The ride was two miles long and took "numerous aerial flights." (Note: Nick did not invent the roller coaster. A similar ride had existed at Coney Island since 1884. When it came to promoting his park, Nick took his lead from carnivals where fun was more important than the truth.)

To ride the Automobile Race customers climbed into one of three autos at the top of a 1,900-foot incline behind a barrier. When the barriers were lowered the cars coasted down the incline like a large-scale Soapbox Derby. The primary appeal of the ride was the real automobiles, horseless carriages, which were new to the world. Hardly anyone had one, and most people had never been in one.

But the most popular of the new rides was the Big Scenic Coaster, commonly called "the big ride," which functioned much like a modern roller coaster. The ride traveled through the park's natural forest, skipping across the tops of majestic oaks, then plummeting back to earth on a steep incline. It lasted three minutes and zipped past the entrance so people just entering the park could hear the passengers scream.

Other rides included shoot-the-shoots, switchbacks, a gigantic Ferris wheel, whirligigs, and merry-go-rounds. To enter the park, guests had to pass through large rustic turnstiles. It was a fantasy city, with multiple spires, towers, and domes bright with thousands of incandescent lights. There was an "electrical fountain" where lights that changed color under the water threw into the air a succession of rainbows.

Eventually, the park had more than just rides. There would be a ballroom, a Loew's vaudeville theater, picnic grounds, a Curtiss aeroplane, a dirigible airship, and forty acres of wooded hills and parkland. There was a series of "Dancing Pavilions," each decorated in an artistic fashion, what today we'd call themes, with smooth dance floors. Kick off your shoes and have a ball. Dance contests were held every Tuesday and Friday night.

On special occasions, daredevil high diver Arthur E. Holden would break his own high-dive record by an inch or two. Holden earned his initial fame in 1896 when he dove off the Brooklyn Bridge and survived. By the summer of 1915, Holden's record was up to 112 feet. Every time, Nick was afraid Holden would break his fool neck.

Nick was at the park every day, thinking of new ways to please the public, and making sure things ran smoothly. He employed thousands and, it was said, knew them by name and always had a cheery word as he made his daily rounds. One of Nick's favorite employees was Mary Robinson McConnell, who married James Leigh Gish, and had two daughters, the future screen stars Lillian and Dorothy Gish.

During the early days, security was an issue. Youthful ruffians were robbing and harassing the park's paying customers. One day, Nick caught a group stealing spools of copper wire from a storage shack in a remote corner of the park. The delinquents ran but Nick trapped one inside the shack and locked the door. Nick let the kid sweat for a while and then let him out.

"What's your name, kid?"

"Edgar J. Mannix, Mr. Schenck. You can call me Eddie."

"You know who I am, Eddie?"

"Everyone does. You run this place."

"How old are you?"

"Nineteen."

The kid thought he was about to go to jail. But Nick had a theory. Why put the kid in jail? He'd get out and be back. The only way to keep him from stealing from Nick and his customers was to hire him.

So, Nick told Eddie Mannix, "You work for me now."

"Yes, sir," Mannix said.

"And make sure the next time your hoodlum friends come here, they pay their dime and ride the rides," Nick added.

It worked out better than either of them could have dreamed. For Nick, the move paid dividends for the next forty years, and Mannix had a life beyond anything he could've dreamed when he was a smash-and-grab kid.

Even at that first meeting, Nick saw something mixed with the fear in Mannix's eyes, a gleam—street smarts. Turned out the kid had a history of running a policy bank for the mob and a knack for keeping numbers in his head. He also had no morals.

Eddie didn't have a lot of formal education—elementary school in Fort Lee, New Jersey, and one year of middle school in Hackensack—but the street smarts Nick sensed were formidable. As Mannix matured he became barrel-chested and learned how to handle himself. As a bouncer at Saturday night dances, he could single-handedly take care of five "rowdies" at once. Mannix's first job at the park was as ticket taker, but he quickly outgrew it. He was good at math, and an expert troubleshooter. He became the Palisades Park bookkeeper and head problem-solver. Whether the glitch was mechanical, logistical, social, or under the heading of security, Mannix knew what to do, did it, and problems went away. Sometimes problems went away that Nick didn't even know about.

ON JULY 16, 1910, NICK GAVE AN INTERVIEW TO A REPORTER FROM PATerson, New Jersey, and discussed his park's vaudeville theater: "All-star performances! Booked by my brother Joe! High-wire, trapeze artists, the Flying Herberts, Hill and Silvanni, championship bicycle riders specializing in trick riding, and the Taiso Brothers, Japanese pole balancers. The theater itself is a thrill—under a canopy on the brink of the precipice."

Some of the park's attractions remain familiar today. Others reflect barbaric notions from a long-ago and less civilized world. For example, for a time in 1916, one of the theaters at Palisades Park featured prematurely born infants being treated in incubators. Come see the tiny babies struggling to live!

Another decidedly odd attraction was the "French Hatching Cat," a real cat of unknown heritage that sat maternally on eggs while surrounded by baby chicks. At the "shooting gallery," patrons fired at the targets with actual Colt revolvers.

It remained a world in which racism was casual and accepted. No white person had problems with that season's "Old Plantation Show" which featured, according to advertisements of the day, "genuine colored people who sing plantation melodies in the happiest fashion."

Some acts, however, had a modern sense of irony, such as Sir Joseph Ginzberg, billed as "The World's Worst Singer," a cacophonic act that long predated the Mrs. Miller and Tiny Tim warbling of the 1960s.

This was a world in desperate need of a new form of entertainment.

FIRE WAS ALWAYS A DANGER. BEFORE STEEL CONSTRUCTION, ALMOST everything was made of wood, sunbaked dry, that went up like kindling at the smallest spark. There were fires at Palisades Park in 1911 and 1913. Both times rides were promptly rebuilt, a little bit bigger and a little bit better.

In 1911, Nick installed the first electronic public-address system. Speakers were mounted all around the park. These were called "Electric Enunciators" and became an attraction themselves. Nobody had heard a voice squawking out of a box on a pole before. It was a miracle.

Once a quiet picnic area that never bothered neighbors, Palisades Park was now noisy, bright, and bothered many. In the nearby towns—Fort Lee, Edgewater, and Cliffside Park—residents bellyached about the noise and general hubbub. The most common complaint was that the screams from the Big Scenic Coaster sounded like people were being attacked. Church people groused about the park being open on Sundays. There were moral objections as well, but never specific. A place like that, the judgmental griped, where women trapeze artists wore tights, must be indecent. Petitions were passed around demanding the park be closed before another soul was soiled.

One man protested, "Our quiet park has been taken over by vandals. It has gone from a free public playground to a catchpenny imitation of the commonest features of Coney Island."

When a local group sued the park seeking damages for pain and suffering from the noise, the judge was on the park's side. Nick compromised—he really didn't want to be a bad neighbor. "I'll shut down the Big Scenic Coaster no later than ten p.m.," Nick said, and the protests quieted.

The park picked up unintentional and invaluable publicity during the summer of 1911. Night attractions included spotlights playfully dancing from the clifftops down onto the Hudson. One night the spotlights hit upon a capsized boat with three men alongside splashing in distress. The searchlight operator kept the light on them until they were rescued, a river adventure that was later made into a film called *Saved by Searchlight.*

Nighttime was magic because of the bright lights, so many lights that in June 1911 Nick held a contest with prizes going to the customer who most closely guessed the number of bulbs.

Nick hyped the contest. "You can go around and count the lights if you want to, no rule against that, but remember it took my assistants a week to get the total figure."

In reality, no one actually counted anything. The correct answer came off the top of Nick's head. "One hundred thousand and one," Nick said. "We are the land of one hundred thousand lights—and one!"

On July 11, 1912, Nick announced his latest, greatest attraction: the "first in the East" Balloon Farm, for the manufacturing of dirigibles, airships, and all sorts of air balloons from toys on up. Nick hired a dirigible out of Toledo, Ohio, to fly over the park. The farm covered three acres, with a factory for construction projects, and parking space where balloons could anchor. Nick himself was the head of the new balloon company. Head designing engineer was Frank Goodale, holder of the altitude record, billed as "The World's Youngest Boy Aeronaut," although he was twenty-two and had already been flying for five years.

The farm was hurriedly set up and running to maximize the 1912 "ballooning season," which was during peak autumnal foliage.

THE ONLY THING CONEY ISLAND HAD THAT PALISADES PARK DIDN'T was the ocean, so Nick built "the world's largest saltwater pool" (four hundred by six hundred feet, a full acre) with marbleized concrete sides and bottom. It opened on June 1, 1913.

Standing at poolside, Nick spoke to reporters: "My pool is the Eighth Wonder of the Amusement World! A new highlight of the cleanest, neatest, and best conducted park in the world. Unlike other pools *with their risk of contagion*, the Palisades Park pool is *safe*. It includes all the charms of a *pure*-water lake, with waves, diving island and various depths, and at the same time overcomes the greatest of all dangers of swimming pools:" Pause. "Unsanitary conditions! This pool is perfect for those who are returning from vacation and are used to taking a morning dip in the sea. Come to Palisades Park and swim in my inland sea."

"How did you make it safe, Nick?" a cooperative reporter asked.

"I have personally incorporated into this pool devices for the safety of the public," Nick said.

"Devices?"

"Yes! Devices that owners of elaborate swimming pools elsewhere would do well to take advantage of." Nick thrust his chin forward as if he'd answered the question. He parried further by first lowering his voice and bowing his head slightly, then telling a story about a poor girl in Maine who caught typhoid fever and died from germs in her millionaire dad's pool. "Those germs were washing off of some swimmers and making a new home on other swimmers," Nick said. "But not at Palisades Park. Palisades Park is safe!"

"Where do you get the water, Nick?" a not-so-cooperative scribe blurted.

Nick practically winced. "Well, I don't get it from the Hudson River," he lied. "That water contains sewage and other means of uncleanliness. And we don't take water from the ocean. You would have to go miles and miles out to sea before you could get water that was pure."

"So where . . . ?"

"We get our water from, uh, the Hackensack reservoir! It is well filtered and supplies thousands of people in the suburbs with drinking water." The suburbs, after all, were where everything was pure. "The water starts out pure and stays pure because we change the water every single day." Another lie. "We have sanitary dressing rooms and bathrooms adjoining the pool, which will accommodate six hundred people. Five hundred feet long and one hundred fifty feet wide." (In later years, Nick would drop this lie and replace it with another, that yes, he was lifting the water from the river but continued to insist he refilled his pool every day.)

"How did you get the water into the pool?"

"They said it couldn't be done," Nick exclaimed in pure carny barker form, with just a touch of a Russian accent. "I had hydraulic engineers look at the project and they said it was impossible. At first, we wanted to pipe the water right up the side of the cliff but the wall of the Palisades was too rugged." He shook his head in awe of the ruggedness. "So, we came up with a pipe pattern that had angles and curves and installed a gigantic pumping station at Edgewater that was powerful enough to lift millions of gallons. Now we have an ocean on top of a mountain!"

Emptying and filling the pool every night was certainly an impossible task, no matter where the water came from, but none of the scribes wrote that. They wrote exactly what Nick wanted them to write.

One reporter, interested only in feeding Nick another softball question, observed the pool in person and noted that it was slightly narrower at the deep end.

"That enables the wave-making machine to operate," Nick explained. "At the narrow end the water is twelve feet deep which is sufficient for diving."

"How does the wave machine work?"

"There are two platforms, each half the width of the pool, and, by means of machinery these platforms are literally pumped up and down on the water much as a child would slap the water in a bathtub with the palm of his hand. The alternating up and down motion of these platforms on the surface furnish artificial waves as perfect and enjoyable to disport in as any waves tossed up by nature on a beach."

"What about the shallow end, Nick?"

"The shallow end begins at ankle deep and grows deeper, very gradually. All around the shallow end are fountains of water in various forms and sizes, which are not only for the beauty, but serve as shower baths where the children and the feeble may enjoy the spray."

"There's an island in the middle . . ."

"Yes, an artificial island with its own diving tower. Divers can choose from springboards and platforms at a variety of heights. Almost any height."

"When is the pool open?"

"Day and evening. People can enjoy a swim in our *pure* water after a hard day at work. Not only that, they can paddle about through the artificial waves by artificial moonlight! Our pool is the biggest and the best, safe, and hygienic swimming pool free from all dangers of contagion," Nick said, repeating his key point.

The message worked and—weather permitting—the pool was packed—capacity was either six thousand or ten thousand depending on the level of

Nick's persistent hyperbole—with men and women wearing "fashionable bathing costumes." The shallow end, with its gradual incline, was like the beach where waves crashed down and then withdrew. This end was always most crowded with lounging and playing customers, some neither children nor feeble.

There were customers who swam and played in the Palisades pool every day. Swimmers repeatedly asked Nick to keep the pool open longer each day, but he explained that this was impossible. Refilling the pool with fresh water took *fourteen hours*. Employees were under orders not to roll their eyes when the Boss said stuff like that. (Of course, there were actual considerations toward hygiene. Every once in a while, a horse-drawn cart clip-clopped up to the pool and workers shoveled in more salt.)

ALL OF NICK'S SAFETY TALK WAS LOST IN THE WINDS OF TRAGEDY ON Sunday night, July 6, 1913, when disaster struck the Aeroplane Coaster. Despite the carnival noisiness, the crash was loud enough to be heard throughout the park. Then came the cries of the injured, sending chills through the customers.

The ride was equipped with electric lights along its track, but there were no lights underneath it, so first responders had difficulty climbing up the wooden structure to the spot where two trains were grotesquely tangled together.

Hundreds of people rushed toward the accident to see. Among them were three doctors, Dr. E. P. Helstern and two others, who happened to be enjoying the park at the time of the accident.

Horrible minutes passed. The whole area was lit brightly by "calciums" taken from Loew's theater. When the rescuers finally reached the accident scene, they had to use axes and sledgehammers to get the trains apart. A crowd of thousands stood below and watched as rescuers lowered the dead and injured. An "army of volunteers" helped, taking stretchers from the ground beneath the ride to nearby horse-drawn vehicles for transport to the North Hudson Hospital.

Two dead, nineteen critical. The dead were Arthur Olson of the Bronx, a customer at the park who lingered long enough to give a statement, and Frank Leclair, a motorman on the ride, whose head was crushed.

The accident occurred when one train, containing sixteen passengers and running on a third-rail electric system, took the second of two "dips," an eighty-foot drop, but failed to climb the opposite incline. It stopped and then slipped back to the bottom where the car following, driven by Leclair, slammed viciously into it.

Rushed reporters spat out inches of copy within a squeak of deadline. They led with the things they knew for sure—like Nick Schenck was the guy who not only owned the park but "built" the Aeroplane Coaster. They dropped the word "invented" but still, it was Nick's ride.

The reporter from the *Hackensack Record* got Nick to say a few words: "Are there any theories as to what might have happened?"

"I don't know how the accident occurred. I fear the system has been trifled with, someone must've trifled with the electric devices."

"Could there have been negligence involved?"

"I have no comment on that. That's it." Nick pushed the reporter aside and walked away.

Some thought the issue was the motorman on the first car, a fellow by the name of Barney Cohen, who apparently did not give the car enough juice to surmount the incline, so it slipped backward.

Another report said Cohen was blameless, that a fuse had blown, and the first car had no power. Some witnesses said Cohen purposely stopped the first train so that a passenger could retrieve a hat that had fallen on the tracks.

And there was intrigue: The man who'd been posted at the top of the second incline, a Michael Carrado, was not available for comment. "He disappeared after the accident and we still haven't been able to find him," said a source inside the park. "Although Mr. Schenck says he knows where he can find him, and he doesn't choose to be interviewed. As you might imagine, he's pretty upset."

Nick's counsel for what he knew would be a slew of suits was former New Jersey state senator E. W. Wakelee. Coincidentally, Wakelee was in the park at the time of the accident and was in on the rescue team. He began representing Nick's interests immediately: "No comment until an investigation has been made," Wakelee said.

The *Record* lauded the Aeroplane Coaster, calling it "the most thrilling ride of its kind in the world." The drops were the highest and steepest in the world. The ride had been the park's number-one attraction, so popular that the Panama Exposition Commission paid Nick big bucks to build a duplicate for the 1915 San Francisco Exposition.

On July 15, 1913, a coroner's inquest was held to determine the cause and manner of Arthur Olson's death. It was held at Cella's Park Hotel in Fort Lee and presided over by Coroner Charles S. Robertson. One of the first to testify was Dr. Helstern, who treated some of those injured, and secured a statement from Olson at North Hudson Hospital before he expired.

Dr. Helstern testified, "Olson sat in the front seat of the car that passed the block signal and crashed into the car ahead that was stalled at the second big dip. The switchman picked up a woman's hat that had fallen onto the track, and when the motorman said something to him, he stood over, opened up a box near the signal, and threw a lever. This threw on the white light and the switchman said, 'Go ahead.'"

Councilman Charles Tuite testified that he also remembered that the switchman picked up a hat and threw it in the car near the motorman. The motorman on the stalled car told the jury that the block signal had worked all right for him just before the accident. Henry Ulrich, the park electrician, said the ride had been out of order possibly half a dozen times during the season.

Then it was Nick Schenck's turn to testify. He said that, yes, he had employed Michael Carrado as a watchman, and that he was not expected to pay attention to the signals. "His only duty was to watch the car ahead to see that it got out of the block before allowing another car to enter. I was so exasperated on the night of the accident when I learned what Carrado had done that I believe I would have shot him had I seen him. Yet, two days later I took him back to work in my park and am not now trying to put blame on him, but simply stating facts." Nick went on to testify that when more than two cars were running the watchman was always on duty. "It is an added precaution," Nick said. "It was the disobedience of the rules that caused the accident, and not due to any defect in the coaster itself."

The jury disagreed.

The Schencks were going through a tough stretch. To add to their professional trials, on November 7, 1913, Joe and Nick's dad died at age seventy-one. The family gathered at their mom's Harlem home and went through the five stages of mourning, from *aninut* to *shiva*, before returning to work for Marcus Loew and at Palisades Park.

DURING MAY 1915, THE DREADNOUGHT BATTLESHIP USS *UTAH* DOCKED across the river from the park. With it were many other fighting ships lined up for miles. Nick had a set of bleachers set up where, for no charge, park visitors could sit and look down on the river, the boats, and the great city on the other shore. In honor of what is today known as "Fleet Week," when the Navy visits New York en masse, Nick announced that all sailors in uniform would be given free admission and free rides. He then put on a fireworks show, much rarer then than now, rockets exploding in air one hundred feet above the park. One rocket was launched over the *Utah*, where it burst into a sparkling American flag. The men on deck cheered loudly.

On June 9, 1915, the eleventh annual outing of the Hudson County orphans was held. Representing the population of eight New Jersey orphanages, the kids were loaded into two hundred automobiles and driven to Palisades Park where Nick made them all his guests, and they were allowed to ride the rides, see the circus and the vaudeville shows. He threw in all the ice cream, sandwiches, and candy they could eat.

Sure, Nick was aware that the resulting publicity for his charitable acts was pumping up business, but he genuinely enjoyed watching the sailors and orphans having a good time on his dime.

Nick was the King of Fun, and had a knack for creating memories among his happy customers. On opening nights each spring, there was an evening dance, and Nick would get out there and dance with crazy legs, grinning like a showbiz pro.

One Saturday night, a contest was held for Charlie Chaplin imitators, doing the "funny walk" to various tunes. The contest attracted close to one hundred contenders in costume, faux mustaches securely (and sometimes not so securely) in place.

In 1915, Nick installed at Palisades Park the first public astronomical observatory in the U.S., with three massive telescopes. At night customers could gaze at the stars. In the daytime the most popular usage was to watch pedestrians across the Hudson in Manhattan.

That summer Nick placed a story on the newswire, bragging about the number of women who are swimming in his "natatorium" (pool). He was quoted as saying, "Every day finds them disporting in the surf with the same abandon as is pictured by artists of nymphs in a fairyland."

For those women who did not know how to swim, Nick promised that the park's two instructors were always on hand to teach anyone interested how to swim or dive. The instructors were "particularly efficient, as they have studied aquatics from a scientific standpoint, and were two of the first men in the country to master the Australian crawl."

During the autumn of 1915 the AAU held the finals of the Hudson County amateur swimming championships at the park pool. Nick called it "the largest gathering of aquatic experts ever gathered in New Jersey."

In 1916, Nick added a show called "Tangoing on the Hudson." Tim Brymn's Broadway Banjo Band played "weird yet enchanting" syncopated melodies. On September 2, Nick held a press conference: "Although it has been customary to close Palisades Amusement Park on Labor Day, this year, because crowds have been so big, I've decided to keep the place running for an additional month!" Grown men cheered. "Strike up the band!" Nick said.

Tim Brymn and his band, also in boaters, launched into "They Go Wild, Simply Wild, Over Me."

ON MAY 25, 1917, THE NOW TWENTY-SIX-YEAR-OLD EDDIE MANNIX WAS first mentioned in the newspaper. Eddie stood in for Nick at an amusement park press conference and huckstered the massive, miraculous—and imaginary—task it was to empty then refill the swimming pool every day. Though the park opened early in 1917, the pool wouldn't open until Memorial Day as usual. So, "aquatic enthusiasts" would have to wait a few days to get wet.

The most popular new attraction was the "Monkey Speedway," in which monkeys sat at the wheel of tiny automobiles on a track and "raced" at sixty mph. Mannix made much of how funny it was to see the monkeys, who would have "encouraged Darwin" had he seen how skilled they were behind the wheel. (It might've been funny, but there must have been some sort of wagering involved as well.)

Another new attraction would be considered horrifying by today's standards. Maybe not as bad as premature babies, but unnecessarily anxiety inducing. It was called "An Aerial Attack on New York" and depicted with "great realism" an attack by bomber planes, so intense that the Manhattan skyline "crumbled and fell."

Also in questionable taste was the appearance at the park of Daisy and Violet Hilton, who were Siamese twins connected at the hip by flesh and bone and could dive into the swimming pool in a jerry-rigged swimsuit. The Hilton twins went on to have a bit of a show business career. They appeared in Tod Browning's MGM horror film *Freaks* (1932), and twenty years later starred in their own grindhouse biopic, *Chained for Life*.

There was much excitement one day at Palisades Park when Joe's picture-making team, Comique, arrived to shoot Fatty Arbuckle scenes. The results are in the picture *Reckless Romeo* (1917), giving us a rare view. Scenes show the Ferris wheel, the saltwater pool with visible waves, the high diver plummeting from an incredible height, and one brief shot that shows the view from the top of the cliff of the Hudson and Manhattan across the way.

WELL AFTER BOTH SCHENCK BROTHERS HAD MOVED THEIR PRIMARY concerns to motion pictures, Nick was still thinking of ways to get fresh customers to come to Palisades Park. When the saltwater pool opened for the season in 1925, one little kid came to the park every day for weeks, and all he did was swim laps. The kid looked great in the big saltwater pool. Tiny, but great. Nick, the story goes, had an idea.

Nick invited the press for a tour of the park looking splendid in his boater hat and cane in his left hand, cigarette in his right. He used the cane to gesture and point as he roamed the park, guiding customers, talking up his devices, and working up interest in coming attractions. Nick's daughter Marti remembered those days fondly, the way her father always had "incredible energy and an enormous sense of fun."

On this day, Nick knew all about the kid and his swimming prowess but played it for the scrum of reporters like he was just encountering him for the first time.

"What's your name, kid?"

"Johnny Devine, Junior."

"How old are you?"

"Six."

"How much do you weigh?"

"Fifty-eight pounds."

"How long have you been swimming?"

"Since I was two."

"Do you think you could swim all the way across the Hudson River?"

"I don't know, Mr. Schenck. It's awfully far but I bet I could," Johnny said. That got an "awww" and a reptilian smile from the press.

"If you can swim all the way across the river, I'll give you anything in the park you want," Nick said.

"I want all the hot dogs and waffles I can eat and I want to ride the Motor Parkway for an hour straight."

"You got it, kid. You got it, Johnny Freckles. And I'll even throw in a silver loving cup."

After an adequate time to build up the event in every New York and New Jersey newspaper, at 3:30 p.m. on Tuesday, September 1, 1925, Johnny Freckles, already shivery and a little blue in the lips, stood on the 132nd St. pier in Manhattan.

Nick, clearly enjoying the spotlight, looked eight feet tall next to the child.

"Okay, Johnny Freckles, dive in!" Nick said enthusiastically. Johnny did, a sailor's dive with frog legs, and twenty-five cameras captured the moment.

The kid could swim of course, that was the whole point, but he was small, and the current was strong. The tide shifted, further complicating his efforts.

Nick watched with binoculars.

"Where's he headed, Boss?" Eddie Mannix asked.

"Looks like he's swimming out to sea. We better get across." Nick and Mannix jumped on a boat.

Using a sidestroke and scissors kick, Johnny Freckles took a suspenseful thirty-seven minutes to make it across, and when he finally reached the Jersey side, he was well downstream from the amusement park, so he had to be picked up and taken to the park where both Nick and Joe Schenck gave him his silver cup and allowed him free rein over Fun City. Then came the hot dogs and waffles. (The original schedule had eating then riding, but Nick reversed the order. He didn't want the kid to throw up.)

As the grinning little boy accepted his trophy near the pool, a reporter shouted out, "Do you think you'll ever swim the English Channel?"

"Maybe. When I get big," Johnny said.

Nick barked, "Remember to do what Johnny Freckles does, come to Palisades Park and swim in our one-of-a-kind ocean wave pool!"

Johnny jumped in the pool and swam slowly back and forth to the photographers' delight.

It had cost Nick a few bucks to make it happen, but Johnny Freckles had given the park a million dollars in free publicity.

The stunt bent reality in a couple of ways. The kid really was six, but he was a known swimming attraction before he ever got to Palisades Park. He was the son of a Philadelphia swimming instructor, had his own trainer, a fellow by the name of John Fitzpatrick, and had already swum across the Delaware River when Nick had his "inspiration."

NICK CREATED ANOTHER PUBLICITY BONANZA USING THE NEW MEdium of radio in 1924 when New York station WHN spoke live on the air to an army pilot who was flying a biplane over Palisades Park.

"We can hear Charlie Strickland's music coming from the dance hall," the pilot said. The amusement park crowd cheered wildly.

In 1926, Nick built Palisades Amusement Park its own radio station, WPAP, with studios in a building shaped like a radio just outside the ballroom.

That same season Nick built his first new rides in years: the Skyrocket and the steel Cyclone. The Skyrocket reached one hundred feet in the air, while the Cyclone added thrills by coming dangerously close to the cliffs.

In June 1927, aviator hero Charles Lindbergh flew the *Spirit of St. Louis* up the Hudson River. When he passed Palisades Park, a fireworks display greeted him. A few weeks later the park was abuzz with little rascals and their stage moms as Hal Roach came to the park to cast his latest *Our Gang* comedies.

Along with pumping up interest in his park, Nick was also head of the damage-control department. Sometimes, as we've seen, bad things happened. In 1924 a man died of a heart attack while diving off the top platform into the pool. During Nick's last season at the park another diver died after hitting his head on a diving board. In 1926 a woman fell out of her car on the Skyrocket and died. The next season another fire destroyed the Skyrocket and several other rides. In May 1928 two sheds used to store the park's fireworks exploded, killing one employee.

Nick remained the head spokesman and cheerleader at Palisades Park long after brother Joe began producing motion pictures (see Chapter Four). Nick's interest in the park didn't wane until the late 1920s, when circumstances forced him to dedicate all of his time to Marcus Loew's entertainment empire.

In 1929, Nick decided to replace the three feet of old sand that had for years provided the "beach" for the saltwater pool. The old sand was sifted and found in it were five necklaces, seven cigarette cases, eight cigarette holders, six pairs of sunglasses, four rings (one with a diamond), four combs, a set of dentures, a $5 gold piece, and about $25 in change.

BY THE 1930S THE PARK HAD LOST ITS LUSTER. FOR ONE THING, IT WAS the Great Depression and far fewer could afford fun and games. Nick stopped giving away hideous Kewpie dolls at the game booths and rewarded winners with groceries.

On the positive side, the George Washington Bridge was completed in 1931, making it far easier to get to the park from New York by automobile.

Nick sometimes used his position at Loews Inc, to publicize the park. MGM star Jean Harlow rode the Scenic Railroad while photographers snapped away. In 1932 Olympic gold medalist Johnny Weissmuller opened the pool. Weissmuller became a household name only three weeks later when his first picture, *Tarzan the Ape Man,* opened.

On May 18, 1934, the Schencks sold Palisades Park. When Nick stopped patrolling the park with his boater and cane, striding along his brightly lit midway, riding the rides with the customers, beloved by his people, something in Nick died. He never again sought out the limelight.

CHAPTER FOUR

EVELYN NESBIT

THE MADNESS OF THE FLICKERS BEGAN IN APRIL 1896 AT THE KOSTER & Bial's Music Hall—formerly the Manhattan Opera House but now a vaudeville theater on West 34th Street in New York. For the first time a paying audience saw moving pictures projected on a screen. The first motion picture was called Thomas A. Edison's Latest Marvel, the Vitascope. *(Today, a plaque in Herald Square commemorates the event.)*

ON AMUSEMENT PARK MONEY PLUS LOEW'S SALARY, NICK AND JOE were living a rich man's lifestyle. Though Nick was the one who would later be well known for taking his boat to work, it was Joe who first took to the water. Yachting became Joe's primary passion. He purchased a boat, and—accompanied by friends—took it on a series of trips, one the length of Long Island Sound, and another to City Island and back. Joe became the "rear commodore" of the Beechhurst Yacht Club, sailing out of Whitestone, Long Island.

But it was on a bigger boat, a steamer ship on the Atlantic, in fact, that Joe met his destiny. He'd sailed to Europe to scout vaudeville talent during the summer of 1913 and during his return trip observed a woman on the promenade deck with a flow of shiny copper-colored hair and a familiar face.

"Who is that woman?" Joe asked a crewmember.

"Sir, that is Evelyn Nesbit."

Joe's eyes widened. Evelyn Nesbit Thaw. Famous, notorious, repeatedly scandalous, hounded by death and intrigue, and in her late twenties unbelievably beautiful. As was true of most "scandalous" women of the era, her life choices stemmed from desperation. She was the so-called Girl on a Velvet Swing, the girl from Pennsylvania who worked as a model as a teenager to help her family after her father died, who first gained public attention in 1901–02 as the sixteen-year-old girlfriend of up-and-coming eighteen-year-old actor John Barrymore. When the young actor impregnated the teenager, she was "sent away" to a Jersey boarding school where she received an abortion disguised as an appendicitis operation. She then launched to superstardom on June 25, 1906, when, during the opening of a new show called *Mam'zelle Champagne* on the roof of Madison Square Garden, her millionaire husband, Harry Thaw, after beating Evelyn for not being a maiden when they married, shot and killed famous fifty-two-year-old architect Stanford White, who'd "outraged" Evelyn when she was sweet sixteen.

"You won't love her again!" Thaw said as he snuffed White. Perhaps not his exact words.

Thaw was twice tried for the murder and finally acquitted after an insanity defense. His mother began a publicity campaign emphasizing Thaw's defense of his wife's virtue and pointing out that White had been a serial deflowerer, a man whose penthouse apartment came with wall and ceiling mirrors and the previously mentioned velvet swing. Thaw was twitchy and disagreeable so they sent him to the Matteawan Hospital for the Criminally Insane.

Evelyn had been steadily in the news since the initial scandal, and her reputation as a "bad girl" was a large part of her appeal. She was the sort of woman that rich men paid good money for, married or not.

It was easier then than now to be a bad girl. Almost any role outside of wife and mother was construed by many Americans as halfway to whoredom. That said, Evelyn was a bad girl among bad girls. She worked at it, a then-novel push toward notoriety and stardom now routine for young Hollywood actresses who court publicity on TV shows like *TMZ* with bad behavior. And she became truly legendary. (Joan Collins, Elizabeth McGovern, and Gretchen Mol have all played her on film and TV.)

During the spring of 1912, Evelyn was the third party in a divorce filed by Mrs. Linda Lee Thomas, from her husband, millionaire banker Edward D. Thomas, who once made the gossip columns when he and Evelyn were too rowdy and got the boot from the Hotel Knickerbocker's grill room.

Evelyn loved to travel. She went to the Nile and saw the pyramids, and then on to Paris, where she could get lost among a sea of beautiful women. Trouble brewed when Mrs. Thomas realized that her husband had traveled to those same places at the same time.

Sixty days later Evelyn was in the papers again, this time because Thaw, apparently issuing press releases from his padded cell in Fishkill Landing, said that he'd heard that Evelyn—still his wife, after all—had given birth to a child during his hospital stay, and that the child was now going on two years old. Thaw pointed out that Evelyn had never mentioned a child during her rare visits to Matteawan. He hadn't seen her in over a year, and before that there was a three-year gap between visits.

Thaw's mother said, "If the baby exists, my son must be the father."

The hospital superintendent disagreed: "Any suggestion that patients are having sex in the hospital is unreasonable in the extreme."

Everyone correctly assumed that the kid was real, and Thaw wasn't the dad.

That summer Thaw fought for his release, claiming he was once again perfectly sane, and the matter ended up in court. Evelyn was called to testify, but she didn't do much. She merely identified her husband's handwriting on a series of somewhat paranoid letters he'd written while institutionalized. Thaw's hearing didn't go his way and he was sent back to Matteawan for three more years. Frustrated, he planned his escape.

The following year Evelyn was sued by a New York jeweler for failure to pay for jewels delivered to her while her husband was in the Tombs, the NYC jail, awaiting trial. Evelyn's defense was that she was broke. She declared bankruptcy to get the bill collectors off her back.

She'd had a minor stage career, but when Joe saw her on deck, she had not made a stage appearance in nine years. As she returned to America in August 1913, she had a showbiz comeback on her mind. Her new boyfriend, and future husband, was dancer Jack Clifford, and the couple was working on an act.

Joe approached her on the promenade and introduced himself as a film producer. He later claimed he didn't know much about her past, just that she was enchantingly attractive. She quickly filled him in on her story, and he knew instantly she would be great in moving pictures.

"I am in constant fear that Thaw will escape from Matteawan. If he does, he will seek me out," she emoted.

Joe patted her hand. By the time they sailed into New York Harbor she'd agreed to star in a picture that Joe would produce.

Joe even had his title: *The Threads of Destiny,* an "intense drama of the unseen side of Russian life." When disembarking, Nesbit was told that her worst fears had come true. Thaw was on the loose. He'd escaped two days earlier.

"Don't worry, I won't let anything happen to my star," Joe said.

Joe quietly rented studio space in Fort Lee, New Jersey, convenient to Palisades Park. Joe wrote a scenario based on stories that Nesbit had told him on the ship. He brought in Joseph W. Smiley to direct. The film co-starred Nesbit's real-life small son Russell Thaw, the kid conceived while dad was in a padded cell. Production was completed in two weeks. (This film has been lost and little is known about it.)

Joe Schenck and Evelyn Nesbit made a second picture in 1917 called *Redemption*, which told Nesbit's real story, just with a few names changed for legal reasons. Newspaper ads read, "A photo-drama of Life Depicted With Relentless Truth." It opened at the George M. Cohan Theater in New York to such anticipation that customers paid premium prices. Two bucks!

But that was it for the partnership. Nesbit was not a gifted actress, but it was her instability that caused Joe to cut her loose, and she went on to have a quiet but painful life, nomadic and marred by alcoholism and drug addiction.

Joe made $200,000 on the Nesbit pictures, millions in today's money. He later told a reporter, "It's strange how events that appear to have no connection with you often set the course of your destiny. While I knew my life was going to be dedicated to moving pictures, it was really Harry Thaw's escape from Matteawan that decided me to get into picture production as quickly as possible."

He said he talked it over with Marcus Loew and Nick. They agreed. It was fate.

BUT NOW JOE HAD A FORMULA IN HIS MIND. IN 1915, BETWEEN THE two Nesbit pictures, he asked his friend director Roland West, "If you see any young girl who looks as if she has real acting ability, let me know."

Two weeks later, West came to Joe. "I've just seen a girl in a picture called *The Battle Cry of Peace*. She can't be more than nineteen or twenty, looks like a dream, and she certainly can act."

"What's her name?"

"I don't know. But we can find out."

Joe went to see the picture and there learned that the actor's name was Norma Talmadge.

CHAPTER FIVE

NORMA

On May 2, 1894, Norma Marie Talmadge was born Presbyterian in Jersey City, New Jersey, to an unemployed alcoholic father named Fred and a stage mom named Margaret (Peg). That birthdate is only a probable, as Peg made variant statements about her daughter's age, aware from the start that actresses have an all-too-brief shelf life before entering the showbiz purgatory of middle age. Peg even told reporters that Norma had been born in Niagara Falls, a more scenic entrance into the world, and also a provable lie.

Dad drank and wasn't around for long. One Christmas morning, when Norma was small, Dad went out to "buy food" and never came back. If the Talmadge women believed in the unreliability of men, this was why. It was also the thing that made Peg run her daughters like a business: desperation.

Peg, Norma, and her two younger sisters, Constance and Natalie, moved to Brooklyn, where they lived at a series of addresses, on 59th Street in Sunset Park until Norma was six, St. Marks Avenue in Prospect Heights until she was eleven, and then on Fenimore Street in East Flatbush, which is where Norma lived when she entered the fantastic world of show business.

To make ends meet, Peg washed clothes, sold makeup, taught art classes, and rented out rooms. Norma and her sisters attended and graduated from Erasmus Hall High School in Flatbush. While a student, Norma helped pay the bills at home by posing for color slides illustrating songs featured in "the pits of nickelodeons."

In 1909, Peg Talmadge took fourteen-year-old Norma on a streetcar from their East Flatbush home to Vitagraph Stock Company at East 15th Street and Locust Avenue in Midwood, Brooklyn. The Vitagraph complex was built in 1897, the first modern motion picture studio in the world. First try, Peg and Norma were unceremoniously tossed out, but Peg tried again. This time Norma was noticed by scenario editor Beta Breuil, who cast her in her first film, *The Household Pest* (1910), as a girl who gets kissed under a photographer's cloth.

Norma—cute as the dickens, of course—attracted attention with her emotive face and was further mentored by the studio's top leading man, Maurice Costello. She was paid $25 per week whether she worked or not, but she usually worked. Soon thereafter sister Constance found work at Vitagraph as well. The third Talmadge sister, Natalie, wasn't interested in being in front of a camera.

Still only sixteen, Norma next appeared in *In Neighboring Kingdoms* with portly funnyman John Bunny. She starred in a series of pictures with leading man Antonio Moreno. Her work first gained strong public attention when she appeared in *A Tale of Two Cities*, a three-hour serial shown in theaters in one-reel increments over the course of eighteen weeks. (Norma must have been making Vitagraph a bundle. When they built their West Coast studio in 1913 in the Los Feliz section of Los Angeles, the street outside was renamed Talmadge Street. That L.A. facility, like the Brooklyn Vitagraph, was bought out by Warner Brothers. In 1948, it was purchased by ABC TV, and is still the home of the daytime soap *General Hospital*.)

She played clumsy waitresses and reckless women heading for a fall. By 1912, Norma had appeared in more than one hundred films, and had received on-screen credit in forty-one of them. By 1913 she was ranked the forty-second most promising young actress by *Photoplay*.

Constance was also doing well, nicknamed the "Vitagraph Tomboy." In 1913, Peg and the girls moved to an apartment in Midwood two blocks from Vitagraph.

On January 31, 1914, the Brooklyn newspapers first mentioned Norma by name. *The Vavasour Ball* was just out, a two-reeler (twenty-minute short) in which she co-starred with Vitagraph vet Leo Delaney.

In 1915, Peg negotiated a new contract for Norma at the National Pictures Company in Los Angeles, eight features at $400 per week. That August, the Talmadges made their first trip to California, where Norma shot her first film for National, *Captivating Mary Carstairs*. The shoot went poorly, the film flopped, and the studio soon went under. So much for Norma's $400 per week.

Her daughters might've been delicate flowers, but Peg was big-boned, heavy-footed, and relentless. In days she'd negotiated a new contract for Norma, this time with the Triangle Films, where D. W. Griffith was making pictures at Fine Arts Studios on Sunset Boulevard. Griffith signed Constance as well and made her a star by casting her as Mountain Girl in *Intolerance*. Over the next year, Norma starred in seven pictures for Triangle. She lunched at the Dirty Spoon across Sunset with swashbuckling star Doug Fairbanks. When the contract ran out, Norma returned to New York, where fate, in the form of Joe Schenck, was waiting for her.

(Vitagraph expanded internationally rather than domestically and was severely wounded by the First World War, so much so that the Warner Brothers bought them out in 1920.)

RETURNING FROM HIS SCREENING OF *THE BATTLE CRY OF PEACE*, JOE summoned Roland West and said, "Find the girl from that picture and offer her seventy-five dollars a week."

A couple of days later West walked into Joe's office. "Joe, I've got bad news. That girl wants four hundred. She says she won't sign for a penny less."

"How old is she?"

"Twenty."

"No twenty-year-old is worth that much," Joe said, and that appeared to be that. But destiny was determined to get Joe and Norma together. By this time Joe was producing Fatty Arbuckle pictures (see Chapter Six), and Arbuckle invited Joe out to a restaurant in Long Beach, Long Island, called Healey's.

"There's an actress I want you to meet," Arbuckle said. "I think maybe she'll be a big star someday."

Of course, she was Norma. Joe, stunningly smitten with hat in hand, identified himself as the producer who'd offered her seventy-five a week the previous year.

"You should have signed me at four hundred," Norma retorted. "Now my price is a thousand. That's what I get at Triangle Pictures."

"I'll beat that," Joe said. "I'll give you the thousand a week, your own production company, and twenty-five percent of the profits on your pictures."

Norma blinked three times. "Do you really mean it?"

"I always mean what I say."

Joe sounded confident, but later admitted he had no idea where he was going to get the thousand bucks a week to pay her. He was an excellent businessman and made a lot of money, but he was also careless, a well-known soft touch on Broadway where guys down on their luck would hit him up for a grand or two. He took after Marcus Loew in that sense. (Joe's generosity continued after his move west, and years later it was said that there were a hundred Hollywood old-timers on his private charity list.) He was also a degenerate gambler—horses and cards, mostly, although he'd bet on anything—and sometimes lost money faster than he made it.

He ran his business like a traveling bookie, going from handshake to handshake. Friends were amazed at how Joe could keep track of his investments in his head. He was always buying a piece of this business or a chunk of that real estate and nothing seemed to be written down. Some were winners, some losers. Joe once told a reporter that in those days he'd have $200,000 one day and $200 the next. His nickname on the sidewalks of New York was "Easy Come Easy Go Joe."

But Joe had two things going for him: a cockeyed confidence and a strong character. He was a man who kept his word. He really did always mean what he said.

Regarding his offer to Norma, Joe later said, "I was skating on thin ice, but I made those promises to Norma for two reasons. I knew I could borrow enough money to make a picture with Norma and that picture was bound to make money. My other reason was I was wishing to become closely associated with her, no matter how much it was going to cost, because I knew from the moment I first laid eyes on her that I loved her."

The showbiz team of Joe and Norma quickly gained the attention of Lewis J. Selznick, general manager of World Pictures in Fort Lee, and father of David O.

"You make 'em, I'll distribute them," Selznick said. The men shook hands. (Selznick, Joe would later learn, was said to have had the first casting couch in the photoplay biz. He was nicknamed C.O.D. by the starlets who dillydallied in his intimidating office. Years later, Constance Talmadge asked that his name be removed from the credits for her pictures.)

Joe promised Norma the "best of everything." In his way of thinking, she would always get both the trolley and the ice cream soda. And he delivered so much that Norma complained to a friend—mildly—that she now had to worry about things like safety deposit boxes. Back in the old days, before she met Joe, she kept her jewelry in a brown paper bag covered by vegetables in the icebox.

"Insurance companies won't touch picture people," Norma added.

Joe had earlier attended a New York stage performance of *Panthea* starring British stage star Olga Petrova. It was perfect for Norma. He was trying to scrape up enough money to buy the photoplay rights when he received a nice dividend on his Loew's stock and was back in the black.

To direct the picture, Joe recruited "Megaphone" Allan Dwan, for $1,000 a week. "Dwan knows lighting," Joe said. "He'll show Norma to her best advantage."

Then Joe met Peg Talmadge, who brought the term "battle-ax" to mind. Margaret Dumont could've played the part if she mastered the Flatbush accent. Peg told Joe that she did not wish for any of her daughters to marry. "Especially Norma," she added.

Joe responded by asking Peg how much Norma's sister Constance was making at Griffith's Triangle Pictures, and maybe she might want to have her own production company as well once her contract was up. Peg softened on the topic of marriage and moved herself and her daughters into a suite at the fancy Algonquin Hotel, where Joe was a regular visitor. He said he needed to consult with Norma regarding the *Panthea* scenario and casting. Peg, no fool, knew the real reason. Joe was coming a-courting.

According to Peg's retelling, Norma was singing to herself and merrily skipping around the Algonquin apartment. She was galloping like a pony when Peg confronted her unnatural happiness.

"You are in love with Joe Schenck, aren't you?"

"Oh, Mother, I am hopelessly in love with him," Norma reportedly said with a swoon.

Peg still didn't want Norma married, but she also knew a gift horse when she saw one and didn't want to offend Joe. She later admitted that she had a practiced routine she performed to discourage her daughters' suitors. She found one aspect of every man that she could use to embarrass him. With treacle on her lips, she cloyingly combined motherly kindness with ridicule. With Joe it was his derby hat. Joe's forehead was too large for his hat, and it always slipped askew at the slightest movement, yet he insisted on wearing it anyway. When Joe was visiting, discussing scenarios and casting with Norma,

Peg never left them alone. When Joe left, she'd say, "Don't lose your hat, Joe." Joe was no fool either and after a while switched to a soft gray lid that stayed in place.

To make *Panthea*, Joe rented out a large warehouse on East 48th Street in Manhattan. He would eventually purchase the property and house three production companies in it. At the time Joe was living in a small apartment at 72nd Street and Broadway but while making *Panthea* he took to sleeping on a cot at the studio.

Now, according to Joe, Peg knew his motives for spending so much time with Norma, but as far as he knew, Norma hadn't figured it out. Joe considered himself an expert at reading the most poker of faces, but he couldn't read Norma. But that all ended one day when Joe invited Irving Berlin to the studio to meet his new star.

"Joe, that woman is crazy about you," Berlin said.

Joe lit up. "Irving! Are you kidding me?"

"On the level, Joe. The sooner you propose the better, and I'm all for it!"

ON JULY 4, 1916, PEG WENT OUT TO DO SOME SHOPPING AND JOE dropped to a knee and proposed. Norma tearfully agreed. Norma, who barely knew her own father, took to calling Joe "Daddy." Neither had the courage to tell Peg about the engagement. Again, cupid (a.k.a. Irving Berlin) came to the rescue.

On October 20, 1916, Berlin took Peg to the theater. "Norma is shooting night scenes, won't be home till late," Berlin told her.

With the coast clear, Joe and Norma drove to Stamford, Connecticut, and were married by a justice of the peace. That done, they sped back to New York and Norma was in her own bed asleep by the time Peg returned from the theater.

For weeks the marriage remained secret. On November 4, 1916, a reporter printed an item regarding the marriage license taken out by Joe and Norma in Connecticut. Peg was asked for comment and denied it was true.

"Norma will not be marrying for some time to come," Peg said.

The big reveal came on Christmas Day, at a private screening of *Panthea*. The consensus was that the picture would make "barrels of money." When the lights came up, Peg was beaming with joy.

She approached Joe and said, "Joe, you wouldn't make a bad son-in-law at that."

"Peg, I'm glad you feel that way," Joe replied. "I've been your son-in-law for over two months."

Peg swooned. Her knees buckled. Joe gathered her with a strong arm around her abundant waist.

"I'll get the smelling salts," Norma announced.

But when Peg's eyes fluttered back open, she smiled, and suggested everyone head uptown to the Claremont Inn on Riverside Drive to celebrate.

Many were cynical about the marriage. "That's one way to get ahead," they said, marry the boss. Close friend Anita Loos saw it differently, and once wrote that she rejected the notion that Norma married Joe just for career advancement.

Loos, a giggly woman who with husband John Emerson would write silly scenarios for Constance Talmadge pictures, wrote, "Joe was no Rudolph Valentino. I could understand being in love with Joe, because I've always been a pushover for power that's governed by gentleness."

Panthea director Allan Dwan disagreed. He told a story about the marriage's immediate aftermath. Although Norma was always on time for shooting in the morning, on this morning she was late and didn't arrive at the studios until 10:00 a.m.

Dwan found Norma in her dressing room crying.

"What's the matter?" he asked.

"I'm married to Joe Schenck," she replied.

"Since when?"

"Since last night," she said through her tears.

Norma, Dwan felt, had apparently given up romance in favor of her career by marrying her boss and benefactor, a move exploited by snarky gossip columnists. Dwan felt Joe was all set up to be the last to know.

Perhaps reality was somewhere in between. If Norma was so unhappy to be Joe's wife, she didn't let on past that first morning following what might've been a disappointing wedding night.

On opening night for *Panthea*, Joe and Norma were too nervous to attend any of the screenings. Norma recalled that they were scared "half to death." Joe had sunk a boatload of money in the picture. As for Norma, her entire future rested on how *Panthea* was received. (A plot summary and cast list for *Panthea,* and other films billed as "Joseph M. Schenck Presents," appear in the Appendix.)

On the day of the release, they boarded a train at Grand Central, although Norma later couldn't remember where they headed. She did remember that they were still on the train when telegrams began to arrive. *Panthea* was a smash.

They took the moment of glory to publicly reveal their marriage, Norma telling a reporter, "Two people were never more in love. I call him Lambie, and he calls me Child."

Joe said he married Norma because she wouldn't sleep with him otherwise, and Norma, clutching his arm, cheerfully winked.

Panthea set a record by opening simultaneously at two Broadway theaters, the New York and the Rialto, which were only a few yards apart. The *Brooklyn Chat* gushed, "Throughout the picture, the wonderful work of Miss Talmadge is the outstanding feature. No screen star has ever risen to such superb heights or shown such dramatic power as she. Her work is superb, the last word in wonderful acting."

When Joe and Norma returned to New York, a scribe asked Joe how he could tell a winner from a loser when he was reviewing story ideas.

"The box-office winner gives you a lump in the throat. If the film is a dog, it does not," Joe replied.

At first Joe and Norma lived in an apartment building on Park Avenue in the East Fifties, then later bought a big house on a hill in Bayside, Queens, a 5,273-square foot mansion overlooking Little Neck Bay that had been built in 1905. He kept the apartment, however.

A regular houseguest in Bayside was Irving Berlin, who one morning looked at Norma across the breakfast table and snapped his fingers. "Norma, you have just given me an idea for a song," he said.

He left the rest of his breakfast and moved with long strides to the piano. Within an hour he'd written "A Pretty Girl Is Like a Melody," a song that soon thereafter would become the theme song for the Ziegfeld Follies and would go on to be the basis of an extended song-and-dance number in the MGM picture *The Great Ziegfeld* (1936), a sequence that won Seymour Felix an Oscar for Best Dance Direction.

About Norma's success in *Panthea*, Peg later commented, "It was wonderful for all of us. Another milestone—another memorable mark in the history of her career. Now little newcomers with shaky knees and wide eyes were standing on the edge of her charmed circle and asking in tones awed and fascinated, 'Is that Norma Talmadge?' Norma had at last ascended the topmost wrung of the ladder."

Joe and Norma's union still brought nothing but smirks from columnists hungry for "items." One scribe penned, "The readers of this department will surely unite in congratulating Joseph M. upon acquiring such a bewitching little wife, and the fair Norma upon choosing a husband so wisely."

Joe and Norma seemed happy. He never missed an opportunity to show Norma off in public. On one train trip west, Joe and Norma got off in Chicago, dressed to the nines, and walked the red carpet at the premiere of *War Brides* at the Studebaker Theater. After the picture, the Schencks caught the next westward train and continued their trip.

JOE RAPIDLY ESTABLISHED HIMSELF AS A FILM PRODUCER, DEVELOPING a formula that would keep his star/wife on top for years, scenarios in which she could suffer much, triumph, and wear a variety of enviable costumes. In real life and on the screen, Norma always wore the latest thing, fresh from the dress designers of New York and London. Many of her films featured clothes designed by New York couturier Madame Francis. (Norma's fashion sense earned her a ghosted monthly advice column in *Photoplay*, a job that grew until she was giving under her byline all sorts of womanly advice such as how to buy Christmas presents and adjust for the high cost of living.)

When Norma's sister Constance joined Joe's troupe in 1919, the formula for her was similarly simplistic, as her plots were variations on Shakespeare's *The Taming of the Shrew*, with the shrew in this case being a spoiled and rambunctious "modern girl." To write them, Joe brought the team of John Emerson and his effervescent wife Anita Loos from California and installed them in an apartment on East 75th Street. Their task: Make Connie queen of comedy. (By design, Norma starred in dramas, and Constance in comedies, a line that avoided competition between them.) Emerson and Loos worked for Joe until 1920 when Loos decided to write plays for the legit stage. (She went on to write the book for *Gentlemen Prefer Blondes*, which in 1953 became a star vehicle for Marilyn Monroe.)

WITH A WIFE/STAR, HER FUNNY SISTER, AND A FILM DISTRIBUTOR ATtached to his business, Joe felt it was now time to borrow serious money. He went to Attilio Giannini, a former U.S. Army surgeon in the Spanish-American War, now president of the Bank of Italy, a small bank on Broadway. Giannini had been concentrating on lending money to Italian immigrants working in the fur and import trades—catering to clients the bigger banks didn't trust.

Joe and Giannini shook hands.

"Nice to meet you, Joe. I have read about your success as producer of the Talmadge picture."

"Doc, I hear you are a pretty open-minded fellow," Joe said. "So, I'd like to borrow a lot of money."

And that was how their friendship began. That initial loan was $100,000, which Joe used to improve his 48th Street studios and set up a production schedule. Joe bought the building next door on 48th Street, knocked out a wall, and enlarged his studio space. The press called it "a Super Studio," still ramshackle and crude, but huge—now taking up much of the block between First and Second avenues. When Eddie Mannix wasn't at Palisades Park helping Nick, he was on 48th Street, helping Joe. With three pictures being made at once, directing traffic was the biggest part of Mannix's job.

Giannini invested in pictures and Joe, after a while, invested in the bank. In time, the Bank of Italy changed its name to the Bank of America, and Joe became a directorate. Giannini later recalled, "Joseph Schenck was the first man who really established a solid contact between the banking business and motion pictures. I loaned Joe money time after time, and he always met his loans."

Joe also brought Giannini business from other film and stage producers. Giannini boasted that he made money on every loan: "And Joe Schenck started it all."

After high school, Norma's youngest sister, Natalie, showbiz decidedly not in her blood, attended business and typing classes and took a job working behind the scenes at Norma's studio as a financial and executive secretary. Without talent, "Nat" sullenly pondered her future security and, taking after Mom, obsessed over the bottom line. It was while working in her dingy office at Joe's 48th Street studio that Natalie would meet her future husband.

Panthea had only been out for a couple of months when Joe began to bill Norma as "one of the biggest stars of the screen world." Joe and Norma toured most of the Loew's theaters in the New York City area, so that theatergoers who went to see *Panthea* could see the star in the flesh. Norma didn't say much but waved elegantly and moved on to the next picture show.

Joe always knew that Norma wasn't going to come cheap, so he indulged her. That spring, she and Joe went to Palm Beach, Florida, to start work on a picture. Before she left New York, Norma bought $5,000 worth of hats, gowns, beach costumes, and bathing suits.

A newspaper asked Norma to write her autobiography for their readers. Norma (or more likely Peg) wrote, "I am twenty years of age and therefore much too young to write an autobiography. However, my short life has been a stage of many interesting and I might well say happy occurrences, and of these I am quite willing to make you my confidant. I was born at Niagara Falls, where I spent the first ten years of my childhood amid most pleasant scenes. Indeed, when I am in a pensive mood, my earliest and fondest recollections go back to the days I spent at the most historic and beautiful spot in the whole world, the objective of all globe-trotters, the origin of the slogan, 'See America First.'" The lies kept coming. She didn't attend ancient Erasmus Hall in gritty Flatbush, but rather "one of those private boarding schools where men are barred from the premises."

She continued, "At school, I had great fun. Pillow fights, night parties, secret smuggling of love letters and private theatricals. These were but a few of the many happy events of my boarding school days."

She told how, when she was fourteen, she went to the picture show, caught the acting bug, and applied for a job the next day. "I was literally jostled onto the screen, for when I reached the studio, numerous stagehands were vigorously shifting scenery and I was caught in a whirlpool of white overalled humanity and scenic flats, with their backgrounds of gorgeous ornamentations, embracing interior sets, and pushed into the heart of studio activity. I was only a little girl then and therefore had to put on a long skirt to make me look older, and I was so excited I got all tangled up in its folds. But I felt quite at ease when a woman scenario writer was so kind as to notice me and help me get an extra part. They seemed to like me, for I was put in stock at once at a salary of twenty-five dollars per week."

She said that she'd made many pictures but considered her marriage to Joe her greatest achievement. She was happy to be "under the control of the two greatest theatrical men in the business: the first, my husband, and the second Lewis J. Selznick, whose rapid rise in the field of motion picture production is the talk of the amusement world."

The October 1918 issue of *Motion Picture* magazine ran an article in which they used poetry to describe the screen's greatest stars. About Norma, they wrote: "She is scarlet poppies in a white field, sable, and ermine, a studio tea in Greenwich Village." Joe asked Norma what that meant. She shrugged. (Sister Constance, the perky comedienne, was described as "April showers, a college campus, a ride in the sun, kiss in the dark.") The magazine (and others of its ilk) ran Norma's and Constance's pictures in what they called "full-page portraits," which later became known as pinups.

FOR THREE YEARS, JOE AND NORMA PRACTICALLY PRINTED THEIR OWN money. In 1919, Joe discontinued his deal with Selznick and his pictures were distributed by First National, which meant more screens. For Joe, work was going great. At home, it was another story. . . .

It wasn't until about 1920 that Joe get his first inkling that all was not well in the big house atop the Bayside hill. Joe got up one morning and entered the sun deck where breakfast was served and looked out over the bay. Norma's furball Pomeranian, Dinky, had already had his breakfast and was underfoot. Joe felt like a million bucks. Norma was going on location for a few days while he was remaining in New York to take care of business. It was to be their first extended separation, a fact that weighed more on her than him. In fact, he was oblivious.

Joe remembered: "I was so happy that I failed to notice that Norma and Peg, already seated at the breakfast table, were not quite so joyous. I remember they gave me an odd look. I was too happy, too engrossed in how well business was going."

Dinky leapt into Norma's lap, where he seemed to spend most of his time.

Joe didn't notice anything wrong until Norma burst into tears and, carrying the dog like a football, fled the table, hurt because she thought Joe wasn't going to miss her.

"And to make matters worse," Joe remembered, "I ate two big lamb chops after she left crying. I should have realized what a precious thing I had in Norma's love—but it was the old, old story. Too busy."

He tried to make up for it with larger gifts. Joe bought Norma the deed to a $1.5 million apartment building built by financier A. C. Blumenthal at Wilshire and Berendo, convenient to Hollywood and Downtown L.A., eleven stories, forty-six luxury apartments, eight rooms apiece, spectacular hardwood floors, servants' quarters, and service elevator. Joe renamed it The Talmadge.

SOMETIME IN 1927, AT A STAR-STUDDED PREMIER AT GRAUMAN'S CHINESE, Norma Talmadge, it was said, accidentally stepped in wet concrete out front, thus starting a tradition of leaving hand- and footprints in front of the theater. It is demonstrable that Norma was *among the first* to leave her mark on Grauman's walk, but at least eight other stars claimed to be first.

CHAPTER SIX

ARBUCKLE AND KEATON

THE HEFTY BUT NIMBLE ROSCOE CONKLING ARBUCKLE WAS THE youngest of nine children and reportedly weighed sixteen pounds at birth. He was born on March 24, 1887, in Smith Center, Kansas, but his family came west when he was one. He was in vaudeville at eight, and intermittently worked on the stage for eighteen years, until 1913, specializing in acrobatic comedy, singing, and general clowning.

As the story goes, in 1913, Arbuckle weighed 250-plus pounds and was working as a plumber in Echo Park, L.A. He answered a call to unclog a drain for Mack Sennett, who made the Keystone Kops pictures. Sennett saw the plumber's comic potential, gave him the nickname Fatty, and put him to work in his "Fun Factory" as a pratfalling "kop." At first Sennett paid Arbuckle $3 per day. Four years later, when Arbuckle and Sennett parted and Arbuckle signed with Joe Schenck, he was making $5,000 a week ($150,000 a week in today's money), a salary in the industry second only to Chaplin's. To put it in perspective, the average American worker in 1913 made less than $14 a week.

At first, Arbuckle appeared in hundreds of shorts but always in bit parts. He never used his bulk for a laugh, never getting stuck in a doorway, but rather got laughs by exhibiting his remarkable agility despite his girth.

Even though he wasn't featured at first, he was a human sponge when it came to the photoplay-making process. He often spent breaks asking questions of the crew and the director, wondering why things were done the way they were. He appeared with some of the biggest stars of the day, including Mabel Normand and Charlie Chaplin, whose experiences Arbuckle also culled. By 1914 he was assisting in the direction of his own two-reelers. He now starred in his own pictures, often with his stage name referenced in the title: *Fatty Again* (1914), *Fatty's Reckless Fling* (1915), etc.

In 1915, Vitagraph's overweight screen star John Bunny died. The business, apparently, only had room for one obese star at a time, and Arbuckle's career was launched by Bunny's death.

On January 1, 1917, Arbuckle's contract with Keystone ran out and he went to work for Joe. Keystone comedian Al St. John also made the switch to continue working with Uncle Roscoe. To celebrate Arbuckle's signing, Brownie Kennedy's roadhouse in Mishawum Manor, Massachusetts, hosted what was later referred to as a "wine and girl" party. The stars of the event were twelve "party girls" who were well paid for their evening's work. In attendance were Joe Schenck and fellow moguls Adolph Zukor and Jesse L. Lasky. Someone didn't like the sounds that were coming out of the party room and peeked inside through a transom. The spy saw Arbuckle and a couple of the girls standing on a long table doing a comical strip tease. There was much laughter.

Middlesex County district attorney Nathan Tufts learned of the party and contacted the moguls, saying that for, say, $100,000—$3 million in today's money—he'd see that the story went away. The story didn't go away, largely because Joe told him to take his hundred grand and stuff it. Joe turned Tufts in, and Tufts was indicted on extortion charges.

Tufts's career went down, but the moguls were embarrassed by headlines such as LAMBS ARE FLEECED and THAT MIDNIGHT ORGY. Joe probably had some explaining to do next time he saw Norma. A few years later, the story of the Brownie Kennedy's orgy would gain resonance when another "wild party" ruined Arbuckle.

FOR ARBUCKLE, JOE DEVISED A PRODUCTION SCHEDULE. THEY WOULD crank them out. He called Arbuckle's production company Comique and installed it on the top floor of the 48th Street facility, now the largest studio in the East. Norma worked on the ground floor, Constance on the second floor, and Arbuckle up top.

Comique only stayed in the building for one year before moving west. Norma and Constance went west in 1922, although their production companies kept New York offices in the Loew's State Theatre building.

After all of Joe's acts were out of the 48th Street building, he rented it to Lewis Selznick. (Eventually the building was converted into a parking garage and torn down in 2009.)

Arbuckle's Comique two-reelers were released through Adolph Zukor's Famous Players Pictures, which would one day evolve into Paramount Pictures, and were fantastically popular. Put Fatty in little-girl curls and a dress, licking an oversized lollipop, and it was comedy gold.

The press followed Arbuckle as if he were royalty. In 1917, Arbuckle trained from California to New York, and spoke to the press at several stops along the way. According to one hyperbolic scribe, "Fatty" gained fifteen pounds on the trip because of the "many banquets" he'd attended along the route. He arrived at Grand Central Station with an entourage of thirty-five, and thousands were on hand in hopes of getting a glimpse.

Arbuckle's career received another boost in 1917, when Joe recruited into the Comique fold a brilliant young physical comedian by the name of Buster Keaton.

On October 4, 1895, Joseph Frank "Buster" Keaton was born in Piqua, Kansas, the newest member of a vaudeville family that was at the time warming up for magician Harry Houdini. Their act was called the Mohawk Indian Medicine Company. Part of the show was songs and yuks, the rest a sales pitch for snake oil.

Buster Keaton first appeared on stage at age three in Wilmington, Delaware. Buster would do something naughty, and the act consisted of his dad throwing him against the scenery, or into the orchestra pit, or the audience. No matter what you did to the kid, you couldn't make him cry. He was sometimes billed as "The Kid Who Can't Be Harmed" and "The Human Mop." One part of the act that always got a huge laugh was when Joe would grab Buster by the ankles and use him to mop the stage floor. Joe would cut that part of the act only if the stage was too rough or splintery.

The New York Vaudeville Stars opened the show, featuring the noted sax player Professor Majinel, who also emceed. The Bowery Four were on next, two comedians and a pair of chesty *soubrettes*. And there were the brassy Mullini Sisters, who played duets on their cornets. And the Keatons, a family of "grotesque comics" featuring a dad who contorted himself and the unharmable kid. Mom Myra set up the props. Then, the great Houdini.

The Keaton act was hugely popular, but there was something geeky about the abuse little Buster took, something that he didn't pick up on when he was three but would soon enough. Just because he couldn't be injured—Dad taught the boy how to fall—didn't mean he couldn't feel pain. The act hurt plenty, but that was his job. People laughed at his pain because he refused to acknowledge it. That psychological premise kept Buster ever humble. The emotional pain of being a professional masochist would stick with him for the rest of his life.

Dad Joseph was billed as "Leg-around-your-neck Charlie." His act convinced people that he had no bones, and when he did his tricks, involving jumping from chair to chair to a table, little Buster recognized the cruel tone of 1901 audiences, rooting for his father to miss his landings and hurt himself.

In some towns, where there were laws against children being in vaudeville acts, the Keatons were chased out and had to meet up with Houdini at the next stop. It was hard not to attract the authorities. The poster bragged of a "Little Boy." Even in New York City, the act resulted in blowback. In May 1901, The Three Keatons were scheduled to perform at Coney Island's Steeplechase Park but were shut down by the Brooklyn Society for the Prevention of Cruelty to Children.

As Buster matured, his father's alcoholism worsened, and the kid found himself tossed and beaten to the amusement of others by a man who was three sheets to the wind. In 1914, Buster tried to explain away the geekiness: "The secret was to land limp," he said. "And breaking the fall with a foot or hand. It's a knack. I started so young that landing right is second nature to me. Several times I'd have been killed if I hadn't been able to land like a cat. Imitators of our act didn't last long because they couldn't stand the treatment."

During the summer of 1916, Joe Schenck signed The Three Keatons to the Loew's vaudeville circuit. Joe dealt with Dad but recognized that the now twenty-year-old "kid" with the stone face was the franchise. According to Keaton it wasn't long after the signing that he ran into Joe Schenck by chance, coming out of the Rialto Theater in Times Square.

"Buster, you know I make two-reelers with Fatty Arbuckle," Joe said. "You ever think of being in pictures?"

Keaton said he had. He thought he could make pictures, use the screen to hone the audience's attention and expectations, all of which would be subverted. "I'd also like to stay put for a while. The road's got me down. I've been on the road my whole life."

Joe nodded enthusiastically. "Come with me. I'd like to show you the Comique setup," Joe said.

Joe offered a job, and Keaton took it, diving into flickers headfirst, working both in front of and behind the camera on Fatty pictures (and sometimes smiling). On March 19, 1917, shooting began on *The Butcher Boy*, the first Schenck-produced Arbuckle/Keaton collaboration. Keaton was a cornucopia of comedic ideas, but still a film neophyte. Arbuckle, less clever, knew the ins and outs of filmmaking from his years with Mack Sennett. They made a brilliant team.

It was on this set that Keaton met Natalie Talmadge, Norma's serious-minded sister working downstairs as an executive secretary. He was twenty-one and she twenty.

"I was attracted to her at once. She seemed a meek, mild girl who had much warmth and great feminine sweetness," Keaton later wrote. His opinion would change.

When *The Butcher Boy* was released on April 23, 1917, it received rave reviews and sell-out crowds. During its first week, more than three hundred theaters showed it. Buster Keaton may not have known how to take a pie in the face when he first started working with Arbuckle, but he was a fast learner. Because of the success, Joe Schenck immediately gave Keaton a raise to $75 a week.

Outside of showbiz, Keaton's obsession was baseball. Keaton was a ballplayer at heart, had the skills of a pro, and may have made the bigs if his dad hadn't beaten a vocation into him. Once in a while in the summer, he and Joe would play hooky and go up to the Polo Grounds to catch a Giants game.

Adolph Zukor was able to rent the Arbuckle/Keaton picture to cinemas for $35 a day, the same price as for Charlie Chaplin pictures. The second Schenck-produced Arbuckle picture, *His Wedding Night*, was just as popular as the first and again Joe gave Buster a raise, this time to $100 a week.

After *His Wedding Night*, Joe rented out his 48th Street studio and moved his three production companies to the former Biograph studio on 175th Street in the Bronx. Since the Biograph was already set up to be a studio, renovations were unnecessary. In addition to stages and offices, it had a kitchen, a dining room, and a room for film processing.

According to Keaton, Joe spent his time overseeing Norma's pictures, leaving Keaton and Arbuckle to their own devices. After six pictures, Arbuckle suggested to Joe that they move the company west.

"What's the difference?" Joe asked.

"It's too hard to do exteriors in New York," Arbuckle said. "Shooting exteriors is a nightmare. The light is bad, always changing, controlling the background involves shutting down whole blocks. Out west, the sun is always the same, you always know just how much muslin to hang, and there's nothing but desert, nothing unexpected to get into the frame—except for the occasional tumbleweed." Arbuckle let out a guffaw. Joe said he'd think about it.

IN 1918, THE WINDS OF WAR BLEW ACROSS SHOW BUSINESS. ON JANUary 7—with battles raging in Europe and America joining the fray—the government proposed to close 118 vaudeville theaters to save coal that could be used for the war effort. Marcus Loew and Nick Schenck, representing "Broadway managers," protested. The closing of the theaters, they argued, might save 168 tons of coal a day, worth $2,600, but cost the government $11,400 per day in tax revenue (there was a ten percent tax on theater tickets). The theaters ended up remaining open, but the theatrical men at the meeting agreed to buy Liberty bonds. Loew bought $50,000 worth and Nick $10,000. Later that summer, Nick sold "war savings stamps" at Palisades Park.

Irving Berlin enlisted and went to boot camp at Camp Upton with the 77th Infantry Division in Yaphank, Long Island. While other soldiers were whining about their aching muscles and egos, Berlin wrote a Broadway show. It was called *Yip Yip Yaphank*. The most famous song from the show is "(Oh) How I Hate to Get Up in the Morning." It tells of a group of recruits including Misters Jones, Green, and Brown, who wake to the bugle and take orders. (Much of this material was repackaged into a Broadway show, and then an MGM picture, called *This Is the Army*.) "God Bless America" was also written for the show, but not used because it was considered too somber for a comedy. The song remained unknown for about twenty years, until Kate Smith recorded it.

According to Berlin's daughter, during her dad's time at Camp Upton, Joe Schenck wrote the camp's commanding officer, a General Bell, and told him to discharge Berlin because he was much too old and delicate for the army.

"He is very high-strung and suffers from a nervous stomach," Joe wrote. "I fear the rough-and-ready army life will be the death of him."

The general disregarded the letter. Joe sent Berlin care packages, food kind to his stomach, medicine, and a hot-water bottle. But it wasn't necessary. By all accounts, Berlin thrived in the army.

On July 8, 1918, Buster Keaton enlisted at Camp Kearny outside San

Diego. He was quarantined for forty-eight hours, immunized with double doses of typhoid vaccine, and with sore arms drilled until he was ready to drop. Two weeks later, he was pushed like a sardine into a train east to Camp Mills on Long Island where he received another series of inoculations in preparation for being shipped overseas. Natalie was staying with her sister Norma in Bayside. Keaton managed to get her on the phone and arranged to see her one more time before going off to war. Soon thereafter Natalie arrived at Camp Mills in a chauffeured Packard. Keaton, impersonating an officer, climbed into the luxury car, returned the salutes of the camp guards, and went AWOL for a day, traveling with his girlfriend to Long Beach, Long Island.

"We had a wonderful day together at the beach," Keaton recalled.

At the restaurant for dinner Natalie had to pay the check because Buster didn't have enough money on him. The Packard then returned Keaton to the camp, where he again saluted the guards upon his entrance, changed back into his soldier uniform, and before the month was through was shipped off to the trenches of Europe. At first, he thought he'd be in a trench for the rest of his life—but, though it was hell, it was brief. By November 1918, the war was over.

Keaton claimed that it wasn't enemy fire that traumatized him. It was the overcrowded personnel ship, the rainy weather when everything was mud, and the threat of Spanish flu, which was killing more people than the war. The latter scared him the most, and he feared he was doomed when one day on guard duty, he got sick, very sick. As it turned out, it wasn't flu, but it nonetheless made soldiering impossible. His inner ears were so swollen that he could hardly hear. His hearing never came back entirely. Doctors blamed the hearing loss on a chronic low-grade fever. Keaton shrugged. That was what happened when you spent weeks with wet feet.

While Buster was overseas, Joe Schenck sent Joseph and Myra Keaton $25 every week to help out. Buster was forever grateful. During the spring of 1919, Buster Keaton returned stateside, disembarked at Red Hook, Brooklyn, and was taken to a hospital in Manhattan, where he was treated for a nervous disorder and deafness. From the hospital, Buster called Joe Schenck at his Times Square office and Joe came to visit. Joe was shocked by Keaton's appearance.

"You look terribly piqued," Joe said. "You've lost so much weight. I never saw you look so sick and miserable." Joe apparently did not believe in white lies. Joe then pulled out his wallet, yanked out a handful of cash, and gave it to Buster.

Although Joe had been producing for three years, he was still—officially anyway—the general booking manager for the Loew vaudeville empire. Joe still received a salary from Loew's, but Joe's "assistant" Jake Lubin did all the work. In 1919, Joe officially retired from his vaudeville job, and dedicated the rest of his days to pictures.

By 1920, Marcus Loew's studio, Metro, had a handful of stars under contract but they were all dramatic players. Nary a yuk among them. Joe talked to Marcus Loew.

"You need comedies," Joe said.

"It's true," Loew acknowledged.

"I have Buster Keaton and Fatty Arbuckle. Maybe that's a team that could make pictures for Metro," Joe suggested.

Loew signed the Keaton-Arbuckle team promptly, Comique went west, and Keaton made his first picture on his own, *The "High Sign."* Filming began January 12, 1920, on location at Redondo Beach where Keaton was tossed off a moving train, taking the painful fall deadpan and without injury.

Joe had his film crews on an efficient schedule, as efficient as possible with the notoriously deliberate Buster Keaton in charge. Although audiences were rarely conscious of it, Keaton's films were shot in a steady predictable rhythm, to the delight of the theater piano players.

Also in 1920, Joe negotiated a new deal in which Arbuckle would move from shorts to features, a format previously reserved for dramas.

DURING THE SPRING OF 1920, JOE TOOK OVER A NEW STUDIO IN HOLLYwood and called it Metro Annex. The studio was six years old and had been originally known as the Lone Star, where Charlie Chaplin made twelve shorts for Mutual Pictures. The facility featured a large stage, a lab for film development, and dressing rooms. Buster Keaton described the Metro Annex as the "size of a city lot." By this time Joe was paying Buster $1,000 a week plus a quarter of each of his pictures' net, the same deal he'd given Norma and Constance.

The planned move to Metro was not preapproved by the Talmadge girls, but they had to go along with it. Constance and Norma had been out west before, but Peg considered New York the social hub of the U.S., where anybody who was anybody chose to live. But they went. Buster and Joe were too valuable to be three thousand miles away.

As soon as Keaton heard Arbuckle was slated to make features, he wanted to make features, too.

"Comedy features are the thing of the future," Keaton told Joe. Keaton didn't know it, but Chaplin was already working on his first feature-length film. But Joe said no. Keaton was to stick to two-reelers.

On May 31, 1921, Buster Keaton—professionally frustrated and physically challenged, still using a cane because of inner-ear balance problems—married Natalie Talmadge in Joe's Bayside home. Keaton was married on his parents' twenty-seventh wedding anniversary. No member of Keaton's family came to the wedding. Attendees included best man Ward Crane, writer friends John Emerson and Anita Loos, Peg, Norma, and maid-of-honor Constance. Services were performed by City Court justice Louis A. Valente. The ceremony took place in the mansion's sunroom, called the piazza, which was surrounded by snowball bushes in bloom. Joe gave the newlyweds a Rolls-Royce.

About the wedding, giggly Anita Loos later wrote, "Peg's smile was forced; she considered Natalie's marriage as a mere substitute for stardom. I disagreed. I used to think that looking across a pillow into the fabulous face of Buster Keaton would be a more thrilling destiny than any film career." Oh my.

As soon as the ceremony was over, the newlyweds climbed in their new car and headed toward Hollywood, where Keaton was scheduled to be back on the set in three days. Days later, the remaining Talmadges boarded a train and followed the Keatons west.

In 1920, Constance had wed John Pialoglou, a wealthy Greek tobacco importer best known for his ballroom dancing, so by the end of 1921 all three Talmadge girls were married off. (On June 2, 1922, Natalie gave birth to Buster Keaton's first son, James. On February 3, 1924, Natalie had a second boy, who wasn't named right away because "Norma needed to be consulted," and Norma was on the other coast with Joe in Palm Beach, Florida. Only after Norma got her vote was the boy named Robert Talmadge Keaton. Buster later complained that he hadn't been given a vote when it came to naming the baby. The Talmadge women took care of it.)

Constance Talmadge's marriage to the Greek tobacco baron was brief, and she was soon back on the prowl. She attended a party aboard Joe's yacht and there met Irving Thalberg, who became infatuated with her. Peg was thrilled. What better way to become Hollywood royalty than to marry the "Prince of Hollywood." Plus, word was he had a bad heart. Nab him and the payoff might come quick.

Being adults, Constance and Irving had a rigorous relationship, which some felt drained Thalberg's leaky battery. But he was happy at first, drained of more than just battery fluid. Then it went bad. Constance found fidelity difficult. Thalberg had options, broke it off with silly Connie, and switched to real Hollywood royalty, Carl Laemmle's daughter Rosabelle. That, too, didn't last. Thalberg's days as a "swinger" ended when he fell in love with rising star Norma Shearer, his companion for the rest of his days. Long before Blake Lively and Ryan Reynolds, Jennifer Lopez and Ben Affleck, there was Irving Thalberg and Norma Shearer, an unmatched power couple.

Constance's lifestyle was starting to register negatively in the fan magazines. She'd been romantically linked to many men. Dorothy Gish implied promiscuity when she said, "Constance is always getting engaged, but never to less than two men at once." After Constance's divorce she was engaged to a New York millionaire socialite, an opera star, and actors Buster Collier and Clifton Webb. It's unclear how many were "at once." In 1926 she married Captain Alastair Mackintosh of the King of England's Scots Guards.

Fans didn't like that funny girl Connie flitted from man to man. With attendance at her pictures down, her production schedule slowed and, without looking back, she retired from show business before the decade was through. She married a third time, to the owner of a chain of department stores.

Constance's star may have been fading but Buster Keaton remained one of the biggest stars on the planet, breaking records across Europe, his pictures running in some houses for five months. That didn't mean that Keaton, like Constance Talmadge, couldn't give Joe a headache. Keaton and Natalie were having brawls in public, also making the papers.

One spring, Nick made a rare trip out west and while there visited Buster Keaton's new Beverly Hills home, the Italian villa, still under construction. Since they'd wed, Natalie made it clear that Buster's job was to build a luxurious house where she, sister Constance, and her mom, Peg, could all live. Whether Buster, too, lived in the house was not terribly relevant. To Keaton's chagrin, Natalie was never satisfied, so he—not a mogul but an employee who owned none of the corporation that bore his name—built the house on credit, and then spent an additional fortune having the grounds landscaped. He was deeply in debt, and still Natalie was unhappy.

Nick was impressed by the intricate carvings in the stone fireplace, and water fountain in the conservatory off the foyer, and the tiled patterns on the floor of the solarium, and a speakeasy with a pool table and a well-stocked bar. The grounds consisted of four tiers of lawn, a Venetian-tiled swimming pool, and Italian cypress trees.

Nick told Joe, "I sure hope Buster isn't in over his head." But they both knew he was. Natalie Talmadge, the only sister not to contribute to the family fortune, was also the greediest.

Joe felt relief when Natalie eventually kicked Buster out. Keaton's role in the Talmadge machine was always going to be humiliatingly marginal. Better he was out.

The situation's saddest note was that Natalie changed her sons' names from Keaton to Talmadge, and the boys grew up unaware of their famous dad.

THE SCHENCK BROTHERS WOULD ONE DAY HAVE TO GO OUT OF THEIR way to demonstrate that they weren't in collusion. But in 1921 that still hadn't come up. Loew's Theaters routinely screened Comique and Talmadge pictures. Joe, Nick, and Marcus Loew all owned stock in Metro Pictures. A state of cooperation prevailed.

The moguls, related or not, were relentlessly polite to one another. They realized they were a very small club, and in addition to making pictures that competed against one another, they competed at the card table, the racetrack, and they considered themselves good friends. Moguls never tired of patting each other on the back. When Joe invented the Academy Awards, the back-patting became an annual ritual.

In February 1921, the moguls met at ritzy Delmonico's restaurant at Fifth Avenue and 44th Street in Manhattan. Joe Schenck was there, along with Marcus Loew, William Fox, Sam Goldwyn, Carl Laemmle, Lewis Selznick, and D. W. Griffith. Adolph Zukor called the meeting and sat at the head of the table. It reminded Joe of the meeting years before, when Zukor was Marcus Loew's friend from the furrier, envisioning motion pictures as an art form. This time Zukor's question was, to be blunt: How dirty should pictures be?

All agreed not much, and then conceded to a man that they'd deliberately used sex and teasing sexual situations, sometimes insufficiently coded, to "spice up" a picture. Sex was also key to advertising. But now there were complaints.

Segments of middle America felt any suggestion of birds and bees was forbidden. The "clean up pictures" movement was led by one big-mouth priest, Brother Crafts, who said, "Motion pictures are geared toward the mortal sin known as the sex thrill."

Of course, kids and adults watched the same pictures in 1921, so there was that. All the moguls knew about that great expanse of God-fearing America—the Great Plains, the Deep and God-Fearing South, deep in the heart of Texas—was the number of dollars they made there. Why tick those people off?

Zukor suggested that they agree to ground rules, what could and couldn't be shown on film, and in this way avoid potential government guidelines reacting to Brother Crafts's rhetoric. There was a moment of chaos as men used to being in charge all talked at once.

Zukor calmed them down: "Don't worry, we have a plan. I'm going to let Jesse tell you about it."

Jesse Lasky had a presentation prepared. "I propose a code of rules," Lasky said, and handed carbon copies of a document around the table. "If everyone follows these rules the government will have no reason to step in."

The bottom line of the document was that "No picture showing sex attraction in a suggestive or improper manner will be presented." A good picture needed a love story, naturally, but only "wholesome love" could be depicted. "Avoid sensuality," the document ordered. There were other specifics. No white slavery. No nudity. No belly dancing. No unnecessarily prolonged passion. No depiction of vice as pleasurable or rewarding. No insulting of religious beliefs and no misuse of religious symbols. No salacious lobby posters. No gore.

Zukor wanted to keep the meeting secret but the story leaked to the press. Filmdom's code of conduct was in the papers the next morning. The news, as planned, stifled the movement for governmental regulation. Life went on. Pictures stayed as sensuous as before, and sometimes featured white slavery and prolonged passion—both Rudolph Valentino specialties. Some of the moguls did take greater care where they sent which picture. There was no reason to rub the church ladies' noses in it.

Joe took an active role in the "keep pictures clean" movement when he convinced the postmaster general in President Warren G. Harding's cabinet, Will Hays, to quit his job and be "motion picture czar," in charge of reassuring America that pictures were self-regulated and keeping salacious scenes off silver screens. It didn't take that much convincing. Hollywood paid Hays many times his cabinet salary.

Hays, an elder in the Presbyterian church, later said he "didn't like the odor" of the Harding administration. "If I can't whip Washington into shape, maybe I'll have better luck in Hollywood," Hays quipped, flashing large snaggly teeth.

DURING THE SUMMER OF 1921, JOE MADE PICTURES IN CALIFORNIA, but technically he and Norma still lived in Queens. Sometimes they felt they spent most of their time on the train going back and forth.

Joe leased his Bronx studios to Lewis Selznick. In California, Norma and Constance worked at the Pickford-Fairbanks Studio (named after the "first couple" of the flickers, Mary Pickford and Douglas Fairbanks), corner of Santa Monica Boulevard and North Formosa Avenue. But Joe purchased studio space in Hollywood on Melrose Avenue, a familiar location today as, after a couple of growth spurts, it became the site of Paramount Pictures, and the Talmadges again had their own space. Joe called the Melrose facility United Studios.

He felt it best to keep Keaton separate from the other production companies. Keaton's shoots were so slow, complex, and eccentric, that it was best they went unobserved. Some days, Keaton would declare a holiday and his cast and crew would pick teams and play baseball.

Joe, through Comique, purchased a studio from Chaplin at the southwest corner of Eleanor Avenue and Lillian Way for Keaton and renamed it "Buster Keaton Studios."

IN CALIFORNIA, JOE MADE NEW FRIENDS, AMONG THEM SID GRAUMAN, whose wet cement Norma allegedly stepped in accidentally. Grauman was a West Coast Marcus Loew, whose theaters were bigger and more glamorous than anyone else's. Grauman invented what we think of as the "big Hollywood premiere," with the multiple spotlights searching the sky, tasseled ropes and stretch limos, bleachers for starry-eyed fans, and a red carpet for the glamour parade of twinkling stars.

Small with a startling shock of gray hair that defied all attempts to comb it, Grauman was a good friend to have as he knew everyone in town. Joe was soon having dinner with Charlie Chaplin, Mary Pickford, and Douglas Fairbanks. Joe enjoyed the company of the married "Doug and Mary" and purchased a cottage at Laguna Beach next to theirs. It was at the beach house that Joe played his first West Coast poker. Grauman, Joe found, was not a good card player, and Joe gave him lessons so he wouldn't lose his shirt every time. But nothing worked. It got to a point where Joe felt he needed to teach Grauman a lesson. Joe and Sid played poker, just the two of them, in Grauman's "playpen" apartment. They played all night and by dawn Joe had won the apartment. Joe went home and Sid went to bed, but after a few minutes there was a violent pounding on his door. He opened it and two ruffians entered, wearing derbies, and chewing dead cigars. They flashed badges and claimed to be with the sheriff's department.

"We're here to take over the apartment on behalf of Mr. Joseph M. Schenck," they explained.

"What do you want from me?"

"We need you out of the premises."

"Umm, okay, give me a second to get dressed."

"Sorry, no." Grauman managed to throw on a flamingo-colored robe over his yellow pajamas and allowed himself to be escorted to the "cops'" automobile. He was driven fifty miles into the California wilderness and shoved from the car, which drove off. Grauman hiked to the nearest phone, which was miles away, and called Joe.

"It's a joke, Sunshine," Joe said. "I don't want your apartment. I just wanted to teach you a lesson. From now on, stay out of big-time poker games!"

Joe continued to gamble wildly, of course, and not just at the poker table. He purchased land on Signal Hill, just north of Long Beach, sank an oil well, and soon was pulling out fifteen thousand barrels of oil a day. Joe named the well the "Buster Keaton Gusher."

AS JOE AND HIS MIDAS TOUCH SETTLED IN OUT WEST, MARCUS LOEW was still improving his New York setup. On August 29, 1921, Loew's Inc.'s new Broadway headquarters opened. It was the Loew's State Theatre, designed by Thomas Lamb with seating capacity 3,316. It sat underneath a sixteen-story office building for Loew's employees. Loew's office was in the penthouse, overlooking Times Square.

The State was the first Broadway theater to have a construction cost north of $1 million. Its first manager was Joseph Vogel. The first picture shown there was Keaton's *Hard Luck*. In attendance were a slew of celebs, including Keaton and Natalie, and Joe and Norma, he in a tux, she in a flame-colored velvet evening coat. Sister Constance also was on hand but dressed in a more sedate pale blue. Theda Bara, June Caprice, and the entire cast of the Ziegfeld Follies showed up as well.

LESS THAN A WEEK AFTER THE BRIGHT TIMES SQUARE OPENING, THE industry's reputation took a dark hit from which it never entirely recovered, plummeting from glamour to gutter.

On September 5, 1921, a day party took place in suite 1219 of the St. Francis Hotel in San Francisco, occupied by Roscoe Arbuckle, actor Lowell Sherman, and director Fred Fishback. Throughout the afternoon inebriated guests came and went. There were five men and four women in the suite when the "incident" occurred. One guest was a thirty-year-old model and "starlet" named Virginia Rappe, who was best known as the cover girl on the sheet music for the song "Let Me Call You Sweetheart." At the party, Rappe fell ill, and a doctor was called.

As Arbuckle later explained, "We carried her into another room and put her to bed. The doctor and all of us thought it was no more serious than a case of indigestion, and he said a little bicarbonate of soda would probably relieve her." On September 6, Arbuckle returned to L.A.

Joe and Norma were at home in Bayside when Joe received a long-distance phone call. Norma watched Joe's face fall.

After he hung up, Norma asked, "What's wrong, Daddy?"

"Child, I'm wondering what my bank balance is. I've got a lot tied up in production."

"What's wrong? How much do you need?" Norma asked.

"I don't know—but plenty. Roscoe is in trouble in San Francisco. A girl in his hotel rooms got sick and is dying. They are talking about charging him with manslaughter. You know how he spends money. He's hasn't a cent. I've got to help him. I know he's innocent."

Joe packed a bag and caught a train west.

ON SEPTEMBER 9, ARBUCKLE LEARNED THAT RAPPE HAD DIED IN A private sanitarium. He was summoned back to San Francisco by city authorities. Joe Schenck and Sid Grauman went with him. Upon turning himself in at the Hall of Justice, Arbuckle was arrested, measured, and weighed (266 pounds), handcuffed, and put in a cell. It turned out that Rappe had died from peritonitis caused by a punctured bladder and witnesses were saying things that led police to believe Arbuckle was responsible for her fatal injury.

According to those witnesses, Arbuckle had grabbed Rappe, and saying something to the effect of, "I've been trying to get at you for five years," pulled her into a bedroom and closed and locked the door. Her screams led the other party guests to pound on the bedroom door and attempt to break it down, and when Arbuckle at last opened the door, Rappe was unconscious on the bed. When she woke, she blamed Arbuckle for her injuries. The story made newspaper headlines for months.

The press contacted doctors who gave their opinions. Bladders don't just get punctured on their own, they said.

Reporters were told that the party suite had been thoroughly trashed. One bed was broken down to the floor, mattress half off, and separated from its headboard.

THE FATAL EFFECT ON ARBUCKLE'S CAREER WAS INSTANTANEOUS. HIS name became a synonym for hideous sexual violence. The resulting scandal was bigger than Will Smith's Oscar slap, Kanye West going off the rails, or the Alec Baldwin shooting tragedy combined. Sid Grauman pulled the new Arbuckle film from his theater. Others followed. The L.A. Athletic Club revoked Arbuckle's membership.

Joe visited Roscoe in jail. "Tell me, Roscoe, are you guilty of any crime in connection with this death?"

"Joe, as God is my judge, I wished that girl no harm. The whole thing was an accident."

"You have money for a lawyer?"

"You know me, Joe. I make, I spend."

"All right, I'll pay."

Arbuckle began to sob violently.

"Please, Roscoe, don't blubber. Tell me, what does Minta think of this mess?" Referring to Arbuckle's wife, the actress Minta Durfee.

Arbuckle sniffled. "She's sticking by me. She believes in me, too," he said with a teary, bewildered grin. (Minta stuck with him for a little more than two years before filing for divorce, citing desertion and neglect.)

AT THE INQUEST, VIRGINIA RAPPE'S GOOD FRIEND MAUDE DELMONT testified that she became concerned when she realized that Virginia and Arbuckle had gone into the bedroom, and that the door was locked. She pounded on the door but got no response. She went out and fetched a hotel manager who unlocked the door. Inside they found Arbuckle, wearing Virginia's hat at an inebriated angle. Then she saw Virginia writhing in pain, her clothes shredded on the floor, and saying, "He hurt me. He did it," referring to Arbuckle. Another person at the party, Zey Prevon, heard Virginia say, "I'm dying. I know I'm dying. He hurt me." Two other partygoers signed depositions agreeing with Delmont. The autopsy did nothing to help Arbuckle's case. The coroner, Dr. Shelby Strange, found bruises on the victim's upper arms and on her legs. The bladder rupture, the doctor said, had been caused by "external violence."

Joe attended Rappe's funeral, which drew eight thousand people, just about all of them newspaper readers caught up in the horrible story. Joe mingled and listened to the conversations. Everyone was convinced that what happened in that San Francisco hotel room was "typical Hollywood."

With Joe paying the bills, Arbuckle's defense team consisted of Frank Dominguez, Milton Cohen, and Charles H. Brennan. Joe had a meeting with them before he returned east.

A few days later, Arbuckle was out on bail and trying to reach out to his employers. He sent Joe a note, reportedly in a childish scrawl, that read: "When something happens in half an hour that will change a man's whole life, it's pretty tough especially when a person is absolutely innocent in deed, word, or thought of any wrong." Then, remembering that Adolph Zukor had once had a scandal of his own involving a wild party in a hotel room, Arbuckle asked Joe to remind Zukor that he knew what a shakedown was.

Papers of the Hearst group kept the scandal alive, printing uncaptioned pictures of long-necked beer bottles with their coverage of the case. William Randolph Hearst himself later claimed that Fatty Arbuckle sold more newspapers than the sinking of the *Lusitania*.

The press, Hearst papers particularly, were looking for any angle to keep the story on the front page. Realizing this, fame-thirsty starlets sought out

Hearst reporters with possibly true—but not necessarily true—stories involving the sexual deviations favored by the picture crowd.

Virginia Rappe's self-proclaimed boyfriend, struggling comedy director Henry Lehrman, puffed out his chest and promised that, if a jury didn't punish Arbuckle, he would. Lehrman pounded a fist into his palm to demonstrate his point.

John Roach Straton, the first radio preacher, dedicated a sermon to Arbuckle and the sinful colony of Hollywood.

In Montana, where a theater owner was showing an Arbuckle picture to appease the public's morbid curiosity, a group of cowboys waited until Arbuckle's face filled the picture frame, then pulled their six-shooters and turned the screen into a sieve.

At Arbuckle's first trial, his defense predictably went after the victim's reputation, claiming she was a party girl known to get drunk and tear off her clothes, that she bruised herself by throwing herself around drunkenly. The prosecution's case failed to arrive. The partygoers who'd made statements damaging to Arbuckle now took a powder or changed their stories. One woman who'd been at the party disappeared. Somebody was getting to the prosecution witnesses. Those who showed up arrived in court with cloudy memories. They'd been drinking at that party—who knew what happened? Arbuckle remained mute. The first trial resulted in a hung jury—although when polled Arbuckle's first jury had voted ten-to-two to acquit.

Between Arbuckle's first and second trials, Joe officially became sick of traveling back and forth. One evening, he asked Norma, "How would you like to move to California?"

"I don't know, I . . ."

"I will build you a house out there that will put this place in the shade."

"In that case, let's go."

Before Arbuckle's second trial in 1922, Joe Schenck gave a speech before the First National Exhibitors' Circuit of North California in which he defended his friend Roscoe: "Wild rumors that thousands and thousands of dollars are being spent in the defense of Arbuckle are without foundation. As a matter of fact, the cost of the first trial was only thirty-five thousand dollars. I ought to know something about this matter, as I put up the money to foot the bills."

Arbuckle was sitting at the defense table for his second trial (January 11 to February 3, 1922) when he learned that Paramount director William Desmond Taylor had been murdered, yet another scandal that had Hollywood reeling.

Arbuckle was convicted—briefly—at his second trial. The judge overturned the conviction because a poll of the jury revealed the verdict had not been unanimous but rather by a nine-to-three vote.

At the third trial, the jury deliberated for less than ten minutes before acquitting him. The jury then did something very un-jury-like. They issued a public statement that read, "Acquittal is not enough for Roscoe Arbuckle. We feel that a great injustice has been done him. We also feel that it was only our plain duty to give him this exoneration under the evidence, for there was not the slightest proof adduced to connect him in any way with the commission of a crime."

The statement had no effect. Rumors that he had violated Rappe with a beer bottle persisted.

A free man, Arbuckle shook Joe Schenck's hand.

"Thanks, Joe. What did all of this set you back?"

"Don't worry about it, Roscoe. You'll be able to pay me back someday."

But Arbuckle couldn't pay Joe back, so Joe and Norma took Arbuckle's Tudor mansion on West Adams Boulevard near Figueroa. This arrangement worked out well until 1929 when the estranged Mrs. Arbuckle, the actress Doris Deane (the wife after Minta Durfee), decided she owned half of that house. Deane took Joe and Norma to court a few times before the matter was settled. According to the *L.A. Times*, the case was an aftermath of the Arbuckles' divorce action. The divorce was still pending but in the interim a property settlement was drawn whereby Arbuckle agreed to clear title to the property and convey it to his wife. Trouble was, the title to the house was in Joe Schenck's name.

The house had an interesting history. It was built in 1905 as the "Miner Mansion," and in 1917 was bought by Theda Bara, whose career subsequently tanked. Bara was released by Fox and sold the house to Arbuckle in 1919. Before the Schencks moved in, director Raoul Walsh rented it. (The house is still there, owned by the Archbishop of L.A. and used to dorm seminarians.)

On February 12, 1922, Joe wrote a message to the American public that ran in many of the country's daily newspapers. In New York, it ran in the *Times*. The message was meant to tamp down rumors that Hollywood was a cauldron of sin. Rappe's and Taylor's deaths had America buzzing. So, damage control:

"We are not rampant with vice," Joe's message read. "We are law-abiding citizens, and we rear families. And yet William Taylor's death has resulted in aspersions being cast upon this industry and upon us, for we are striving to make the world a better place to live in through the screen. And we, who have accepted that responsibility placed upon us by the public through their patronage, feel it a personal affront to assume through innuendo that we are not worthy of that honor."

Along with Joe Schenck, the message was signed by Charlie Chaplin, Mack Sennett, Louis B. Mayer, Norma and Constance Talmadge, cross-eyed film star Ben Turpin, director King Vidor, and Buster Keaton.

ON APRIL 18, 1922, ZUKOR CALLED A MEETING AT HIS OFFICE AT FAMOUS Players studios on Fifth Avenue in Manhattan. He invited Will Hays, Jesse Lasky, and Nick Schenck, who explained that he was there on behalf of himself and his brother Joe. This represented Arbuckle's producers and distributors.

Zukor told the others that because of the Arbuckle furor, his pictures had to be banned, and banned loudly. Zukor's guests didn't roll over. Lasky and Nick argued that they shouldn't be so quick to judge, that Arbuckle was an earner, after all.

Zukor explained that they really didn't have a choice. Arbuckle was guilty in the public's mind, and any use of his image from then on would be seen as exploitation. Eventually, Nick and Lasky gave in. Hays wrote up a press release, which Zukor approved: "After consultation at length with Mr. Nicholas Schenck, representing Mr. Joseph Schenck, the producers, and Mr. Adolph Zukor and Mr. Jesse Lasky of the Famous Players-Lasky Corporation, the distributors, I will state that at my request, they have canceled all showings and all bookings of the Arbuckle films. They do this that the whole matter may have the consideration that its importance warrants, and the action is taken notwithstanding the fact that they had nearly ten thousand contracts in force for the Arbuckle pictures."

Paying for Arbuckle's defense might've cost Joe $100,000, but the scandal cost Joe millions. Hays's press release put an end to an ugly practice: theaters exhibiting Arbuckle pictures to stoke morbid curiosity. In his new context, Arbuckle's moon face and bulk were chillingly grotesque.

Joe also made moves to distance himself from his friend. Roscoe, he felt, was innocent but bad for business. Joe dissolved Comique and replaced it with Buster Keaton Productions. The stockholders remained the same: Joe, Nick, Irving Berlin, and the sons of Marcus Loew. Arbuckle had owned no stake in Comique, and Keaton owned none of BKP. Though they "had their own production companies," it was in name only. Joe switched Keaton's distributor from First National to Marcus Loew's Metro Pictures.

A *New York Times* reporter in L.A. informed Arbuckle that he'd been kicked out of the business. Arbuckle visibly reddened and sputtered: "Gosh, this is a complete surprise, and I might say a shock to me. It's the first I have heard of it. I don't know what it is all about. I thought I was well-started on my comeback. You see, it's this way, Joseph Schenck of New York, who produced my pictures, will be in Los Angeles tomorrow. He will know all about this matter. And I am entirely at sea, as far as being able to explain it goes, I shall content myself with remaining silent."

Well, Arbuckle was right about one thing. Joe did know about it. It tore out his heart, but he had to go along with it. Arbuckle called Joe and asked if his blacklisting was true.

"Sorry, Roscoe," Joe said. "But you are out of pictures."

"But Joe, I was acquitted."

"Yes, by a jury. Not by the public," Joe replied. "Hays says we can't release any more of your pictures, not even the ones already in the can."

As would happen to OJ Simpson decades later, Arbuckle's showbiz career was ended by a crime for which he was acquitted.

The Christian right grew noisier. As one ranting evangelist put it, Hollywood was run by "five hundred un-Christian Jews." Now the Arbuckle scandal confirmed their worst paranoia. Hollywood was a soul-charring disease.

Arbuckle was broke. Keaton tried to get him work behind the scenes. A gloomy Roscoe was showing up at United Studios and hanging around with nothing to do.

It was widely known that Henry Ford, the inventor of the Model T and the assembly line, was a devout anti-Semite, and didn't like the idea that Hollywood was run by Jews. He believed they were all communists that needed weeding out from good Christian society. Judaism was communism turned into a religion, and motion pictures were the Jews' top method of disseminating propaganda. Ford's theories were ironic because, first and foremost, none of the moguls were even close to being communists. They were capitalists through and through. So, that part was way off base. The other thing was, since arriving in America, none of them had spent one iota of energy actively "being Jewish." To the contrary, they Americanized in every way possible, and their product almost always presented a decidedly white, Anglo-Saxon, protestant POV. The moguls knew better than to flaunt their common religion, all too aware that photoplays were a Jewish industry, perhaps the only Jewish industry in America, and their wealth and power existed completely outside the normal good ol' boy network. The moguls only had each other. The establishment felt Tinseltown would best be ruled by a Rockefeller or a Vanderbilt. W. R. Hearst, maybe. Ford's newspaper, the *Dearborn Independent*, called out Joe Schenck and Marcus Loew, referring to them as "two Jewish gentlemen who naively assert that Arbuckle must be innocent because he means a lot of money to them."

SICK OF ARBUCKLE SULKING AROUND KEATON'S STUDIO WITH NOTHING to do, Joe booked him on a "world tour" cruise and took him to San Francisco to see him off. As Arbuckle walked the plank to board his ship, Joe noticed how out of shape he was. Always big, Roscoe now sagged and dragged. He was going to seed, sluggish in his movements. Joe pulled his eyes away and looked down at his own midsection. He, too, liked to eat and appeared soft.

While Arbuckle cruised, Joe went on a diet. Though he had a Packard and a chauffeur named Robert, he walked to work each morning, five miles. During the walk he wore long woolen underwear, so he was sopping wet when he arrived. He'd shower at the studio, throw on fresh clothes, and go to work. He'd sometimes work until midnight, and then he'd walk home. He also took up golf at this time, but unlike brother Nick, he never got the hang of it.

WITH ARBUCKLE OUT, JOE GAVE NORMA'S CAREER MORE CONSIDERation. *Motion Picture* magazine had just named her the number-one "Leading Woman," based on reader votes. Her next to be released, *Smilin' Through,* was her last made in New York. Her California pictures would be bigger with better production values, often period pieces with exotic settings.

The Arbuckle scandal in his rearview mirror, Joe set about keeping his dream-house promise to Norma and bought a parcel of land on Hollywood Boulevard. Upon it he would build a mansion. It would have open fireplaces in the living room, dining room, library, and card room. The "sun parlor" would be large enough to host dances, done in Japanese wicker. Norma's boudoir would have a violet carpet, walls of pale green and tan, and French furniture of lavender inlaid with scrolls and pastel-shaded flowers. Her bedsheets would be silk and pale lavender in color. She would get both the trolley and the ice cream soda.

ON CHRISTMAS DAY 1922, ARBUCKLE WROTE AN ARTICLE THAT WAS picked up by a series of newspapers in which he begged the public to look upon him with the good will of the season. "The sentiment of every church on Christmas Day will be peace on earth and good will to all mankind," he wrote. "What will be the attitude the day after Christmas to me?"

The article had no effect on public opinion.

During the summer of 1923, Joe created a production company called Reel Comedies, Inc., for the purpose of putting Arbuckle back to work directing comedies—under the pseudonym "William Goodrich." "Goodrich" directed six unpopular shorts before Joe pulled the plug on the project.

CHAPTER SEVEN

THE DESERT MIRAGE

On February 15, 1923, two men very important to Nick Schenck's legacy first teamed up. They were producers Louis B. Mayer and twenty-three-year-old Irving Thalberg, who began their association at the top of Louis B. Mayer Pictures, supplying product to Loew's Metro. Sometimes in harmony, at others discordant, they would become one of the most powerful teams in showbiz history—till death they did part.

Thalberg, born in Brooklyn, was the "boy genius" of Hollywood known for his literary adaptations, transforming books he'd read as a bedridden kid into moving-picture art. He began at Universal working for Carl Laemmle but was hired away by Metro. Thalberg believed that pictures could be made in assembly-line fashion like Henry Ford made automobiles. Unlike other men, he had the imagination and the judgment to control the budgets and creative elements of multiple projects. He was a mass psychologist, instinctively knowing what audiences wanted, and what turned them away, a gifted diplomat, smoothly moderating disputes between Mayer and "New York"—which was how Metro's executives tended to refer to Marcus Loew and Nick Schenck. Thalberg, "The Prince of Hollywood"—alas, never to be king—preferred literary works, adaptations, complicated and dry. Mayer liked pretty girls and wholesome tales of small-town America, an America that greatly resembled the Canadian town in which he grew up. Both men could be pains in the ass, but none were better at what they did.

L. B. Mayer was born in Ukraine on July 12, 1884—although he later claimed to have been born on the Fourth of July. Mayer never knew the name of the town he'd been born in. He came over on the boat as an infant, his family settling in Saint John, on the Bay of Fundy in New Brunswick, Canada. As a heavily muscled boy, he dove into bay waters, where the changing tides are legendary, to retrieve scrap metal from shipwrecks for his junk-dealer father to sell. He quit school at twelve to help dad full-time. He reportedly had a sizeable Oedipus complex, hating his stern disciplinarian father, and clinging to his mom until her death. This mindset showed up in his relationships with employees and in the films made under his management. He was known to discipline cast members who were "disrespectful of motherhood." In 1904, Mayer married the daughter of a cantor, and the couple had two daughters.

In 1907, Mayer purchased a theater in Haverhill, Massachusetts, called the Gem Theatre, which had six hundred seats and at least that many rats. When he bought the dump, its nicknames in the neighborhood were the "Germ Theatre," a reference to the sanitary conditions, and the "Garlic Box," a reference to its predominantly Italian clientele. Despite the theater's condition, Mayer knew it was the only theater within a twenty-mile radius, and once fixed up was bound to make money. Mayer rolled up his sleeves and personally gave the house a good scrub and refurbish. He changed the name to the Orpheum and opened it to the public as a cinema on November 28, 1907.

By 1910, Mayer opened a second theater in Haverhill, the Colonial Theater, seating capacity 1,600. After becoming a U.S. citizen in 1912, Mayer moved to Boston and in 1914 founded the American Feature Film Corporation, the idea being that he would make his own pictures to show in his own theaters. In 1915, he teamed up with Pittsburgh promoter Richard Rowland to form Metro Pictures, which cranked out a picture per week. And that was where Mayer was when in 1920 Marcus Loew bought Metro.

Mayer knew you didn't need filth to heat up an audience. Chemistry did the trick. And he knew chemistry when he saw it. Mayer is given credit for "discovering" many stars, including Joan Crawford, who wisely jogged each morning past Mayer's house while braless. He handicapped stars like they were racehorses, placing them strategically in films to promote their plusses and protect their minuses. He famously critiqued swimming-pool actress Esther Williams, "Wet, she's a star. Dry, she ain't." A man of wisdom, he proclaimed that all pictures had to appeal to the "brain, heart, and crotch."

Mayer, predictably, got along with Joe Schenck, at least at first, but not with Nick. Both brothers recognized Mayer's skills as a creator and a supervisor, but Nick was suspicious of his outgoing in-your-face personality. Mayer was dramatic, hypochondriac, all wildly swinging emotions, sometimes swinging during a single sentence, and Nick was icy cool when it came to business. Nick didn't like a man who was apt to have a temper tantrum anytime things went wrong. Nick considered Mayer a loose cannon. Mayer was required to call Nick as soon as he got to his office every morning. This rule was among the many reasons Mayer hated Nick's guts. Nick didn't trust Mayer and Mayer knew it.

Marcus Loew and Nick felt they needed someone out west to always watch Mayer. The job was perfect for Eddie Mannix. Mannix's first job at Metro was to be bookkeeper (watch the money) and be an assistant to Irving Thalberg. As he had when doing the math at Palisades Park, Mannix outgrew the job and became the studio general manager. He met with Louis B. himself every morning to talk about any problems that might crop up that day. The list would make it back to New York pronto.

As it turned out, Nick's suspicions regarding Mayer were largely unfounded. LB knew how to run a studio, he had a sixth sense about quality, and spent wisely. Nick liked the system, nonetheless. Heaven forbid, Mayer should get a notion to go rogue. Mannix was always watching.

Mannix's ability to scare people was always used to Nick's advantage. He wasn't above threatening a star who wanted more money or threatening to call in "the boys from New Jersey"—that is, gangsters—if he wasn't sufficiently intimidating that day's "problem." Part of Eddie's daily duties was reading every incoming and outgoing telegram from the Metro lot. No one had the courage to complain. Everyone had heard things about Mannix, enough to know it was smart to be afraid of him. Mannix's experiences fixing things are oft-told legends, the most spectacular involving fantastic detective work. When a "high police authority" told Mannix that they knew for a fact that extortionists were in possession of a stag film called *Velvet Lips* that showed Joan Crawford having sex when she was a teenager, Mannix spent $100,000 tracking down all copies of *Velvet Lips*, including the original negative. Then, to finish the job, Mannix called in the boys from New Jersey and had the extortionists tenderized.

Mannix could not be blackmailed. At MGM, he meticulously kept a "secret ledger" which detailed all MGM secret expenditures and misadventures. Any blackmailer had to fear that Eddie knew more about him (or her) than they did about Eddie.

NICK, OF COURSE, WAS ALWAYS INTERESTED IN KEEPING BUDGETS IN check. One way was to, as Mayer usually did, emphasize that Metro was a team effort, and to accept less money was to be a good soldier. (Years later,

Mannix had a sign on his desk that read, "The only star at MGM is Leo the Lion." If someone asked for more money, he just pointed at the sign.)

Nick reacted angrily to any Metro employee who publicly intimated that company employees were well paid. When executive Al Lichtman commented to a reporter, in an attempt to laud the universally loved commissary, "This studio is the only place in the world where you can make five thousand dollars a week and free meals," Nick got Lichtman on the phone and scolded him.

Nick still had the park, he had Marcus's theaters to run, and now a studio to keep a long-distance grip on. Yet he was still exercising his visionary skills. As if he'd dreamed one night that a sepia-toned girl from Kansas might one day open her front door and enter a world of colors more vivid than life, Nick joined the board of directors of a fledgling company called Technicolor, Inc. An early attempt at color, a picture called *The Gulf Between*, was a failure. Changes were made in the process, and the first film successfully using Technicolor was *The Toll of the Sea* (1922), released by Marcus Loew's Metro. Joe observed production. Joe, Nick, and Marcus Loew attended the premiere at the Rialto in New York. Consensus was that the process was close but still impractical. For one thing, color film was very expensive, and, for another, the process—for reasons too complicated to understand—couldn't reproduce the color blue, which made shooting exteriors awkward. The process improved and by the early 1930s, shooting films in color was a viable, although still expensive, option. And years later, when color film was first used to its fullest potential, with the burning of Atlanta and the entrance to Munchkinland, it would be Nick's company that pulled it off.

Marcus Loew was envisioning the future as well. He purchased radio station WHN, in New York City, and moved its studios into the Loew's State Theatre. Along with offering fine musical and spoken entertainment, the station became an advertising wing of Loew's Inc., plugging films and promoting stars. By 1924, broadcast radio was coming into its own, and consoles began appearing in living rooms across the country. All you had to do was twist a knob or two and you could do the new dance, the Charleston, and sing along with Eddie Cantor's "Doodle-Doo-Doo."

WITH CONSTRUCTION UNDERWAY ON NORMA'S DREAM HOME, JOE REalized that he was making money so fast he had no time to gamble it away. He contemplated retirement.

"I had always worked hard," he later recalled. "And I'd had no time for pleasure. I'd thought I'd like to go in for fishing and sailing and golf and other sports, and sit back and enjoy life, just retaining enough of a financial interest in pictures and theater and real estate to make a good living and make it unnecessary to break in on my savings. I wanted to travel, too, and see the world."

Joe tried traveling. While Norma made pictures in California, Joe went to Russia in 1922 on a "business trip" to explore business opportunities in his native land. Russia, Joe felt, straggled behind the rest of the world in the production and exhibition of motion pictures. In Rybinsk he visited places he'd known as a boy. The old country was bleak, a gray edge devoid of glamour, full of suffering. The experience gave him perspective. He saw how far he had come. He remembered his mother's wish that he be a doctor, his dear mother who was in New York, practically blind and in poor health. Before he left, he told her he'd been thinking of taking it easy, and she'd been displeased. "Work hard as your father did," she said. That ate at him. He wasn't in Russia for more than a couple of days when he began to miss Norma, miss the busy schedule he maintained as a film producer, miss gambling.

He sent a telegram to an associate in New York: "For God's sake, start calling me immediately about anything just so I can keep occupied until I am ready to leave. What I said about retiring please forget. I must have been out of my mind."

He found no "business opportunities in Russia." (Elizabeth Schenck lived another nine years, and died on October 21, 1931, at age eighty-nine.)

Upon returning stateside, Joe received a panicky telegram from the Talmadges out west. Norma's long-gone father Fred Talmadge had reappeared—as deadbeat dads sometimes do when they smell money. Peg and her daughters wanted the down-and-out Fred kicked to the curb, but that wasn't how it worked out. Joe got there as soon as he could and, to the horror of Peg and her daughters, found himself liking and feeling sorry for the down-and-out Fred Talmadge. Joe gave Fred a job in the property room for Norma's and Constance's pictures. Predictably, Fred did no actual work but rather talked the electricians' ears off about Brooklyn and the Dodgers. Fred eventually decided he didn't like the climate in L.A. and returned east. (A few years later, when Fred was dying, it was Joe who was summoned to his bedside. After Fred passed, it was Joe who told Peg and her daughters the sad news, and it was he who was hurt when no sadness ensued.)

During the business day Joe delegated busy work and saved himself for broad-stroke wheeling and dealing. As the "HOLLYWOODLAND" sign was under construction, Joe purchased a twenty-percent interest in West Coast Theaters, Inc., a $30 million company financed by "Los Angeles capital." West Coast Theaters, in turn, had just bought out two theater chains and now ran one hundred theaters in greater L.A. "What is good for Los Angeles is good for me," Joe said.

LIFE TOOK ON A WHIRLWIND FEEL. WHEN NORMA AND CONSTANCE were both between pictures, Joe took them on a work vacation. He paused at the train station in Pasadena to address the press, addressing complaints by theater managers regarding "block booking." That meant, if they wanted a good picture, they had to buy a few stinkeroos as well, not that Joe ever used that word. "We want exhibitors to make money with our product, and to make money on every picture they buy." Joe and the sisters boarded the train. Joe read. Norma and Constance seemed in constant motion, somehow busy all the time, switching from car to car. In New York they spent a couple nights, so the Talmadges could visit the society touchstones. Then aboard a ship and at sea, Joe reading, the sisters flitting, and another train to Paris for shopping, where Constance shockingly told a reporter that the bob hairdo and short skirts were here forever, and then to England where Norma and Constance judged a nationwide beauty contest, in which eighty thousand photo entries were narrowed to one hundred semifinalists. The finalists lunched at the Savoy Hotel with the sisters. The winner, a twenty-year-old Irish woman named Margaret Leahy, was promised a supporting role in Norma's next picture. Returning stateside, Joe, the Talmadges, and contest-winner Leahy were met at the Hudson River pier by Buster Keaton and others. The hiccup came when Leahy got to Hollywood and was discovered to lack all acting skill. She was released from *Within the Law* and sent to acting school. She did not improve. Joe solved the issue by assigning Leahy to co-star in a Keaton comedy, giving Buster instructions to work around her and to "under no circumstances let her act."

That taken care of, Joe took the Talmadge sisters to Tijuana to see a thoroughbred racehorse named Buster Keaton win a stakes race. Norma was smitten and purchased half of the colt. Back in L.A., they learned the annual Exhibitors Herald poll had named Norma as the top box-office attraction. That called for champagne. Life was simply marvelous. Even business was a lot of fun. Back in the old days, deals were almost always made in a grimy office, in a dairy over pickles, or backstage with vermin. Out west, business was done at poolside with cocktails served. Sometimes it was hard to tell the business from the party. Joe's next big business offer came from his new beach buddies, Doug and Mary, who were in bathing suits when they made it. Fairbanks and Pickford, along with superstar Charlie Chaplin and legendary director D. W. Griffith, had been since 1919 the United Artists, a studio that was controlled by the talent rather than by "money men." The idea was intoxicating to artists, of course, most of whom had no idea how to produce a motion picture. Joe, and Doug and Mary, and Chaplin were sunburnt, sandy, and salty from the sea when out of nowhere, business was conducted. . . .

"We want you to be our chairman," Fairbanks said.

"United Artists? Why me?" Joe asked, wearing nothing but shorts and leather sandals. His big belly was tanned brown.

"You're a guy who knows how to get things done," Fairbanks said.

"What's in it for me?"

"A nice salary, a hand in producing for a new crew of talent, nothing to affect the production schedule you already have," Fairbanks added.

"And, you finally get to have me under contract," Chaplin said, and gave Joe an impish grin.

(This was quite a switch for Chaplin, who reportedly had been dead set against bringing Joe in. Earlier Chaplin had said privately and publicly that he didn't think Joe should have disproportionate power within UA because, although he personally liked Joe, he didn't believe Joe to be an artist. Chaplin changed his tune when the financial realities were explained to him. UA, without Joe, was leaking money and had fallen a half million dollars in the red. One thing Joe's pictures did was earn—guaranteed. Even the Keaton pictures, expensive as hell, pulled a nice profit. Plus, Chaplin saw Keaton as personal competition. But, once Chaplin learned UA needed saving and Joe could save it, he joined the others in inviting Joe aboard.)

"Buster, the Talmadges, they all come with me?" Joe said, "All of my crew and office staff?"

"The more the merrier," Mary Pickford threw in. (This turned out to not quite be true. UA was not interested in Norma and Constance, so their pictures were distributed by First National. Constance only made one more picture and retired.)

Joe took the gig and things at UA perked up immediately. In quick order, he recruited fresh talent—Gloria Swanson, John Barrymore, Corinne Griffith, and Rudolf Valentino. Joe was named United Artists Chairman of the Board. Hiram Abrams, another Russian-born Jew who'd earlier been an exec at Paramount, retained his position as UA president.

Joe told the press that, although the number of annual pictures produced by UA was increasing now that he was chairman, the emphasis at UA was always going to be on quality rather than quantity.

"We will never have more than fifteen pictures a year," Joe said to a reporter from *Motion Picture News*. "All of great quality. Each picture must have something *big* about it."

Theaters came next. Joe Schenck—in conjunction with Douglas Fairbanks, Mary Pickford, Lee Schubert, and Sid Grauman—formed the United Artists Theatre Circuit, which would open theaters in twenty American cities. Joe would be head of UA Theatre Circuit for the next thirty-one years until he disposed of his holdings as part of his retirement.

Soon, UA was Hollywood's best picture-making, distributing, and exhibiting organization. But not for long. Marcus Loew and brother Nick were working on some deals of their own.

IN 1924, LOEW'S INC. GAINED CONTROL OF SAMUEL GOLDWYN PICtures, which wasn't making any money, but owned a couple of commodities that would prove to be valuable. First, a forty-five-acre studio in Culver City, built around 1915 as Triangle Pictures by ill-fated Western filmmaker Thomas Ince. Although it was surrounded by Los Angeles, Culver was its own city and part of L.A. County. (And, as MGM would learn in 1933, it was directly above the Newport-Inglewood fault, making it prone to dance beneath your feet.)

When Marcus Loew acquired the studio, it looked like a desert mirage, built upon the spot where L.A.'s old and new money came together. Productive oil derricks owned by the Keck family pumped away just outside the lot. For a touch of green, there were clumps of magnolia trees. A single fig tree grew outside the front gate. "Meetcha at the fig tree," was a thing. Later, the city would grow up around the lot, and paradise was paved. Following the purchase by Loew, that land—plus 150 additional acres purchased later (from Joe Schenck)—became the site of twenty-seven stages, later soundstages, a laboratory capable of processing one hundred thousand feet of motion picture film every day, and prop rooms where art directors and costumers would have their pick of fifteen thousand items.

Joe Schenck sold the 150 additional acres to Marcus Loew for $375 per. Shrewdly, Joe charged extra for each tree on the property, claiming they would be used "as scenery." The new land became known as Lot Three, and it was here that Loew built an artificial lake. When part of the new lot needed filling, free dirt was acquired from the City of Los Angeles, which was excavating the ancient La Brea tarpits. They needed a place to dump the dirt and were pleased to do so at Metro Lot Three.

Loew's Inc. also picked up in the Goldwyn purchase one Howard Strickling, a master of pubic relations, which the new merger would absorb. Strickling and Eddie Mannix became the studio "fixers" whose job it was to swoop down upon crime scenes and scandals and wash them clean of studio involvement before the police or press arrived. If a cop saw Mannix or Strickling coming out of a murder scene as he was going in, he kept his yap shut about it. That's why so many of Hollywood's high-profile scandals remain mysterious. The truth was purposefully obscured, reality warped, leaving history uncertain.

Marcus Loew also purchased Louis B. Mayer Studios, the Metro exec's production company that, unlike Goldwyn, was making money. The merger of Metro, Goldwyn, and Mayer proved to be perfectly complementary. Metro had talent but was inefficient. Sam Goldwyn had talent and land, but lost money. Mayer made money, but his studio was small. Together, they became history's largest film factory. And it was all under the umbrella of Loew's Inc. Their pictures would have unheard of distribution in 125 cavernous downtown Loew's theaters with a potential for 150,000 tickets sold for each performance.

The Metro-Goldwyn-Mayer (MGM) merger became effective on April 10, 1924. The competing studios could only look on with envy. MGM was hogging the talent. Loew put Mayer in as studio head. Mayer and Thalberg remained a team. Mannix remained Nick's spy. Loew considered making Nick the head of MGM but Nick wished to remain in New York. L.A. gave him a headache. Mayer, to his chagrin, was told that he would have to answer to Marcus Loew and Nick Schenck, both three thousand miles away. Mayer did not go gentle into subservience, a problem that burbled under the surface for decades.

Although the first MGM pic was a small film starring Lon Chaney, John Gilbert, and Norma Shearer, the first MGM epic designed to be the biggest and greatest of all time was *Ben-Hur: A Tale of the Christ*, a sword-and-sandal scenario envisioned in an unprecedented scope. It would be an extravaganza with heartthrob Ramon Navarro in the lead, a film spectacular, the chariot races alone to make cinematic history. Turning all of that dreaming into reality created trouble immediately. Production problems were everywhere, exacerbated by the fact that shooting was in Rome and Mayer was in Culver City. The mice were very far from the cat, and they played. The screenplay was being written on the fly by the girlfriend of the director's brother. It was a mess.

During production, Joe and Norma, touring Europe, visited Italy. Norma shopped. Joe, on behalf of Nick, audited the *Ben-Hur* set in Rome. He was appalled by the dysfunction and sent Marcus Loew a two-page telegram detailing the emergency measures that needed to be taken. If all of *Ben-Hur*'s written scenes were shot, the film would run four hours, ten minutes. The costumes didn't fit. Sets were disproportionate to their backdrops—things that could be fixed quickly at home but in Rome meant long delays.

Nick insisted that brother Joe, who technically had no role or interest in MGM pictures other than as "competition," sit in on a strategy meeting with Mayer and Thalberg. Joe said keep the talent, fire everybody else, send a new team, and get your toughest taskmaster director over there pronto. And that was what they did.

They also decided to shoot the famous Roman Colosseum chariot race on a Hollywood set. Art director Cedric Gibbons spent four months, using eight hundred workers, and built a "circus maximus" at the intersection of Venice Boulevard and Brice Road (now known as La Cienega Boulevard). Just the lower half was built. The top half, which you'd see on screen, was a hanging miniature, with cardboard cutouts representing spectators in the nosebleed seats. When the race scenes were shot, stars from all studios wanted to be extras. Thousands watched an incredible show, twelve chariots and forty-eight horses racing like rolling thunder.

The production apparently took its toll on Thalberg, who had a heart attack in his MGM office and spent months on the mend before returning to work. It was a strong reminder to those who were jealous of his power that Thalberg, though formidable, was hardly permanent.

BACK IN CULVER CITY, JOE HAD A FEW FINANCIAL REALITIES TO DEAL with. Constance was on her way out, losing her cuteness and ravaged by a moral press. Even Norma's career seemed to have peaked. His real money-maker was Keaton, and Keaton, though a good friend, was a little bit crazy. Buster's mind kept telling him to hurt himself in new and legendary ways.

Joe was Keaton's friend and admitted to knowing nothing about comedy, so Joe's hands-off approach was almost always to Keaton's advantage. Keaton was a cinematic genius and left on his own created masterpieces—sometimes at his own expense. When Joe did get involved it was always detrimental to the product. Like the time Joe picked up the rights to a Broadway comedy in a poker game and told Buster Keaton to adapt it to the screen. The show was called *Seven Chances*. Buster hated the idea. Adapting lackluster scripts from the New York stage was a waste of his talents.

Joe's interventions into Keaton's career, often characterized as career damaging, even mean, were always geared to eliminate Keaton's dangerous stunts. Joe and Buster, of course, were married to sisters, and there were no doubt back-channel requests to get Buster to change the way he made pictures before he killed himself or ripped an arm off trying to grab a dump truck as it went by. No one wants a gift horse with three legs.

"Look what happened to Harold Lloyd, he blew off half his hand!" the Talmadge girls likely observed.

These attempts to save Keaton never worked, however. In this case, Keaton was fast and loose in his adaptation of *Seven Chances* and transformed the ill-fitting project into one of his masterpieces, with help from a seeming thousand boulders rolling down the side of a hill. Keaton injured a leg during filming and was hobbled for his next picture. So, Joe's plan backfired.

A DAY IN THE LIFE OF JOE SCHENCK

8:00 a.m.: Joe and Norma arrive in Pasadena on the train from Chicago. Norma limos to United Studios where she reports to the set. Joe goes to work.

11:00 a.m.: Joe signs the long-faced cowboy star William S. Hart to a UA contract. Some think the sixty-year-old Hart is washed up and raise an eyebrow. Truth is, the deal is highly favorable to Joe: Hart pays for his own productions, but Joe provides the scripts. (As it turns out, Hart only has one picture left in him—but it's *Tumbleweeds* which plays somewhere or another for the next four years. Hart had an interesting career, playing Shakespeare in New York before riding horses in Hollywood.)

Noon: Photo op with Hart and press as Joe announces the signing. While he has scribes before him he says he's going international.

"Sid Grauman and I are building a chain of theaters in the U.S. in alliance with United Artists and the German company U.F.A. We're negotiating for a Broadway site below 14th Street in New York," Joe said. He bragged about a reciprocal deal he'd made with a German film company, booked seven Doug Fairbanks pictures to the Russians for $75,000 in cash.

"The whole world is becoming Americanized through motion pictures," Joe said. "Everybody recognizes American types and scenery and wants to come to this country. The most universally spoken language is American. I don't mean English, I mean American! We could get along without our ambassadors and diplomats as long as our motion pictures are exported to all parts of the world. It is through us that the world forms its vision and opinion of the U.S. I shall resist all movements to limit the number of Hollywood pictures playing abroad."

1:00 p.m.: Lunch at Fox.

2:00 p.m.: Joe is driven to Culver City, where he and Cecil B. DeMille are honored with a party, music provided by the Universal City, American Legion, and Culver City bands. One of the speakers is Harry H. Culver, the founder of Culver City, who lauded DeMille and Schenck for their contribution to the community's business and civic life.

6:00 p.m.: Banquet for the Association of Motion Picture Producers of California, at which Joe is presented with a plaque that reads:

THREE TIMES DISTINGUISHED BY ELECTION TO THE OFFICE OF THE PRESIDENT OF THE ASSOCIATION OF MOTION PICTURE PRODUCERS OF CALIFORNIA, INC., FROM HIS ASSOCIATES, AS A TOKEN OF HIGH REGARD, SINCERE AFFECTION AND KEEN AP-

PRECIATION OF HIS EFFICIENT AND SUCCESSFUL ADMINISTRATION OF THE AFFAIRS OF THE ASSOCIATION

10:00 p.m.: All-star bridge game at the Dunes. He and bridge partner Eddie Mannix invite Irving Thalberg and Carl Laemmle, Sr., and fleece them. The casino is in the middle of nowhere twenty miles outside Palm Springs, a classy joint with a surf-and-turf menu, thick carpeting, paneled walls, and chandeliers, built so deep in a woods and far from the road that nobody can drive by and say, "Hey, there's Joe Schenck's car."

2:00 a.m.: Home.

FROM THE MOMENT MARCUS LOEW PURCHASED METRO, NICK KNEW that dealing with the wild behavior of screen performers was going to be the worst part of his job. One early "problem girl" was Barbara La Marr, a beautiful actress who started out writing scenarios but moved in front of the camera at the suggestion of Mary Pickford. La Marr was a libertine—"I take my lovers like my roses, by the dozen"—who ran away from home at age twelve, was arrested for being an "underaged stripper," and took at least five husbands in ten years. She drank, took drugs, and gave Eddie Mannix early practice in covering up sloppy behavior. By 1924 she had developed a drug addiction that left her unable to work. "Exhaustion," MGM called it. After a stint in a sanitarium, she was arrested for morphine possession. Nick instructed Mannix to keep her on the payroll, in exchange for making a few filmed "public service announcements" regarding the danger of drugs. On January 30, 1926, Mannix called Nick and told him La Marr was dead at age twenty-nine. Dope.

The cover-up occurred in two stages: "Tell the fan magazines she died from vigorous dieting," Nick said. "Then bribe the coroner to say it was TB."

"Gotcha, Boss," Mannix said, and it was done.

ON APRIL 4, 1926, THE NEW NORMA TALMADGE PICTURE *KIKI* PREMIERED. It was a comedy, odd for Norma—and an indication that she no longer had to share the spotlight with her sister whose career was on the wane. The story goes that Joe had no choice but to put his wife in a comedy as *Kiki*'s playwright, André Picard, had said he would only grant film rights if guaranteed that Norma would play the part on screen.

Norma's performance won critical raves. She was "lovable," and "at the height of perfection as a comedienne." Norma played a Paris urchin peddling papers, scraping out a living with her wits. Her character goes on to be a chorus girl, whose budding career is derailed after a clash with the show's leading lady. Ronald Colman played the leading man.

Kiki came out as the initial buzz of sound pictures made the rounds, a subject Norma touched upon while promoting *Kiki*. There was a scene in which Norma was shaking a coal scuttle while Colman was trying to speak on the phone. He ad-libbed a gesture in which he covered his ear to hear the phone better. Norma boldly said that Hollywood didn't need "synchronization or whatever it's called" for audiences to hear the action. "All they need is Ronald Colman!"

The sequence that affected audiences the most wasn't a love scene, or a comedic ad-lib, but rather the knockdown drag-out battle Norma's character fought against Gertrude Astor. The actors were into it, and it was said that Astor lost part of her hair while Talmadge had her skirt ripped off. The pair nailed the scene in one take, the last shot of the day.

But, despite reviews, *Kiki* was a bomb. Norma's fans were used to seeing her in dignified roles. They expected Norma to suffer and survive. Seeing her in a picture that reminded them of her sister Constance, the funny sister, turned them off, and the picture lost money despite Coleman's ability to make them hear.

The same week as the *Kiki* premiere, Joe and Norma joined Mayer, Fairbanks, Pickford, Thalberg and others in the formation of the Title Guarantee and Trust Company, which bought and sold huge chunks of L.A. real estate, most notably tracts of housing built in Playa del Rey on the Pacific Ocean south of Santa Monica. Joe and Mayer kept homes in the tract, Joe's at 707 Ocean Front Boulevard, Mayer's at number 609. As time went on, Mayer developed the oddest relationship with the Schenck brothers, one his pal, one his despised boss.

THERE WERE PLENTY OF HOLLYWOOD CHARACTERS THAT NICK couldn't stand, but there were few men in the picture business that Nick loathed more than Lewis Selznick. Nick knew Selznick from Fort Lee, going way back, and knew Selznick's sleazy reputation with women. Selznick's office was at the end of a long corridor that was patrolled by armed guards. He lived in a twenty-two-room apartment on Park Avenue, had many servants, a collection of Ming vases, and reportedly rented sex workers for his sons. That was the kind of thing that made Nick grind his teeth. How do you expect America to stop thinking Hollywood is infested with alley cats, when that kind of behavior came from the very top?

Selznick was head of Associated Exhibitors. As Nick's goal was to have a monopoly, or as close as possible, on the picture business, he'd taken steps to squash Selznick's company. Selznick had a plan to glom some of the profits from *Ben-Hur* by purchasing a theatrical circuit that had been promised a piece of the action. When Selznick went to Nick to discuss his new power, Nick became very angry. All Selznick was doing was making Nick lose money. For the meeting, twenty-three-year-old son David O. Selznick came along.

"What do you think I should do, David?" Lewis asked, while steam came from Nick's ears.

"I think you should drop it, Pop. It's not good business," David said. Nick looked at the boy with wide eyes. Surprisingly, the elder Selznick took his son's advice and let Nick off the hook.

"David, if you ever need a job, let me know," Nick said, with something resembling a smile. David knew there would be a job waiting for him at MGM one day.

And there was.

Soon after the meeting between Nick and his dad, David tried to get a job at MGM, but was turned down by Mayer because he hated David's dad so much, he didn't want *any* Selznick in Culver City. So, David went directly to Nick, who hired him as a reader starting at $75 per week. Selznick rapidly worked his way up until 1939, when he produced what would become MGM's greatest film, *Gone with the Wind*.

CHAPTER EIGHT

JAZZ SINGERS AND BROKEN HEARTS

ON AUGUST 23, 1926, JOE WAS IN POLAND SPRING, MAINE, HAVING A meeting with UA president Hiram Abrams when the phone rang. It was for Joe, bad news. UA's biggest star, the thirty-one-year-old Italian-born heart-throb Rudolph Valentino, was dying in a New York hospital room. He'd had surgery for a perforated gastric ulcer that hadn't gone well. Joe rushed to Valentino's side and was alone with Valentino when the star spoke his last words.

"Don't worry, Chief. I'll be all right," Valentino said.

When Joe came out of the room his face was wet with tears. A huddle of reporters watched him silently.

"Rudy has made his last picture. Valentino is dead," Joe said.

The world came to a pause. America went into mourning, women in particular. There were women who'd felt more passionate when watching Valentino on the silver screen than they did with their husbands. In New York, Italian restaurants built altars to Valentino so patrons—mostly woman—could say a quick prayer to the Great Sheik before dining. As would happen with Elvis decades later, some refused to believe that Valentino *could* die. The body was trained west and entombed in the Hollywood Forever Cemetery. Pallbearers included Joe and Nick, Adolph Zukor, Marcus Loew, Hiram Abrams, Will Hays, and Douglas Fairbanks.

On November 15, 1926, UA president Hiram Abrams himself passed away. Joe was quickly named to succeed him. Now Joe had a firm grip on UA. Chaplin may not have been happy but Joe didn't care.

HOLLYWOOD WAS A GIANT PARTY DURING MOST OF THE 1920S. SILENT films looked the same whether or not the players were hungover. Stars and creators cruised along, confident that their money train would always remain on the tracks. Stars had money, youth, and beauty—and felt they would always have money, youth, and beauty.

Ah, but that's not how it works. As the second half of the decade roared in legendary fashion, the winds of change were blowing and with them an initial shiver of anxiety in filmdom.

On August 4, 1926, Nick attended the Warners' Theatre on Broadway, where a new process was demonstrated that added a soundtrack to motion pictures. William Fox, Adolph Zukor, and Lewis Selznick were also there. The film shown at the unveiling was *Don Juan* with John Barrymore. Audiences heard only sound effects and music, but everyone was impressed. *Variety* put out a special edition announcing the coming of sound. Warners's stock skyrocketed.

The Warner brother behind the demonstration was Sam. The original idea was to give pictures a musical soundtrack only, although WB quickly figured out that the process—called Vitaphone, developed by Western Electric—could record dialogue as well.

Earlier that same summer a musical called *The Jazz Singer* had been playing on stage on Broadway only a few theaters away. WB would choose this as the vehicle to make their first "completely" sound film, with both songs and dialogue on its soundtrack. The choice was interesting because its story of a boychik who breaks his mother's heart by becoming a secular entertainer was so conspicuously Jewish, a rarity in pictures up to that point (and after) despite the common heritage of the handful of men who ran the industry. The original idea was to star George Jessel in the lead, but by the time preproduction began, Al Jolson had been cast, an entertainer whose actual show business career largely mimicked that of the character he played.

ON JANUARY 11, 1927, JOE BECAME ONE OF THIRTY-SIX FOUNDERS OF the Academy of Motion Picture Arts and Sciences, best known today as the sponsor of the annual Academy Awards. The founders met at the Ambassador Hotel in L.A. The seed for the idea was planted during a party at Louis B. Mayer's Santa Monica beach home, when it was brought up during a conversation between actor Conrad Nagel, director Fred Niblo, and producer Fred Beetson. The trio agreed that there needed to be a single organization that could benefit the entire screen community, solve technological problems, arbitrate labor disputes, and police screen content. Joe suggested an annual awards dinner, and they liked that idea, too.

Back in January 1926, Joe Schenck and Sid Grauman had gone in together on construction of the twelve-story, three-hundred-room Roosevelt Hotel built in a Spanish Colonial Revival style just across Hollywood Boulevard from Sid's Chinese Theatre. The hotel, with its leather davenports and wrought-iron chandeliers, was the epitome of swank. In 1929, the Roosevelt's Blossom Ballroom became the site of the first Academy Awards ceremony, with Doug Fairbanks as host.

Those who watch the Oscars today, a show running over three hours with song and dance and comics being slapped, would not recognize the first Academy Awards dinner. Winners had been announced months in advance, so there was no suspense. As it was the first, films from both 1927 and 1928 were considered for honors. The awards part of the evening lasted only fifteen minutes. The first Academy Award ever was presented to Emil Jannings for best actor, for his performances in two films, *The Lost Command* and *The Way of All Flesh*. Following the dinner, Jannings returned to his native Germany with statuette in hand and became part of Hitler's public-relations machine. It would be eight years before the term "Oscar" would be applied to an Academy Award, after Academy librarian Margaret Herrick said the statuette resembled her uncle Oscar.

(Joe and Sid sold the Roosevelt in 1934, and today it is reportedly haunted by the ghosts of Hollywood's glorious past. Since 1991 it has been a Los Angeles Historic-Cultural Monument, and is every bit as posh as it was. It still hosts a formal-attire "star-studded viewing gala" on Oscar night, $350 per person in 2023, with a large TV screen set up in the same ballroom where the first awards were presented.)

JOE SCHENCK'S PREVIOUS ATTEMPTS TO GET BUSTER KEATON TO MAKE pictures without risking his life had been wildly unsuccessful, but the resulting films were awesome. Joe feared it was only a matter of time before the boy who could not be harmed had his luck run out. So Joe tried another tactic, one that ended up hurting his friend Buster in ways he may never have completely understood. Joe wanted people to think money made him fire Keaton, a lie that didn't bear scrutiny. Clearly it was misguided compassion that caused Joe to end his career as a filmmaker.

Keaton's last film for Joe was *The General*, an irony because that film is considered by film historians to be not just among Keaton's best, but one of the greatest films of the silent era, loosely based on a real-life incident that took place during the spring of 1862, during the American Civil War, in which a Union spy named James T. Andrews broke through Confederate lines in Tennessee, stole a train in Georgia, and drove it north destroying tracks and bridges behind him.

The problem with the picture was that it was ridiculously expensive to make ($400,000). "It better be good," was all Joe had to say when he paid the bills.

Keaton's cut of the film was flabby. After the first two previews, a significant portion of the film was cut, thirty minutes replaced by a lone intertitle. The third preview was held at the Alexander Theater in Glendale, California. Joe and Norma attended this screening, Joe's first chance to see what had cost him four hundred grand to make. At the end, the audience stood with thunderous applause and turned to face Keaton, who took an elaborate bow.

"Bravo!" they shouted.

Joe Schenck was all smiles. "The best he's ever made," Joe said, like a proud parent.

That might have been the last nice thing Joe ever said about the picture. According to Joe's version of facts, business was slow. Best guess was that it was the title. *The General*. It referred to the name of the locomotive that was a major character, but audiences didn't know that. They knew from the poster that Keaton was in gray, and the picture was about the Civil War. "What's so funny about a Confederate general?" many might ask. Both in the north and south, the idea of Keaton poking fun at war-making was off-putting, Joe said, even though the film itself had little of that.

When soon thereafter Keaton's contract was up, UA took a pass. *The General* had been out for six months, and Joe was still hoping he'd break even on the disaster.

Joe didn't just kick Keaton out and say good luck. He called brother Nick and arranged for Keaton to be signed by MGM at a considerable raise, a studio where Keaton wouldn't have to do much, read his lines, follow his director's instructions, and collect his money.

Joe felt he'd handled the Keaton problem in as generous a way as possible. Nick would be in charge and make sure Keaton remained busy. He'd get Thalberg to think up some great Keaton *ideas*.

Joe of course was oblivious to the one thing that made the trade hellish for Keaton: He would no longer have undisputed rule over his work. He would be a cog in the MGM wheel, and he would get on and off the assembly line as he was instructed. At MGM, Buster's productions were supervised by Laurence Weingarten, which didn't help Keaton's adjustment. The men took an instant dislike to each other.

On paper, the new situation looked easy. Whereas other stars were expected to make four pictures a year, Keaton only had to make two. Nick hired members of Keaton's old crew, and gave him his own lot, off campus, as they say. He'd only have to come to Culver City once a week to pick up his check. The job would be *easy*.

It was customary for Mayer to negotiate with new talent, giving them pep talks instead of money. In Keaton's case, Mayer was left out of the loop. Nick set up a system for Keaton that was, at least in part, separate from Mayer's. Keaton in fact rarely spoke to Mayer, a thorn in Mayer's side, and always did his business dealing with either Nick or Eddie Mannix.

Mayer told everyone who'd listen just how unfunny he thought Keaton was: "He's Joe's brother-in-law, that's all he is," Mayer said.

Mayer wouldn't have said that had he gone along on a trip back east, where Keaton was to shoot key sequences for *The Cameraman* (1928). Plans were to shoot him out on the streets, but it proved to be impossible as he was mobbed by adoring fans every time he went outdoors.

Buster might've had adoring fans, and out west he had his own lot, but he would never again have his own pictures. MGM told him what to make, who to play, and how to play him. Gags written for him were stale and misused his skills. Buster put up with that for a while and began to day drink.

His troubles would only worsen with the coming of talkies. MGM became chirpy and giddy with music. Keaton would have to spar in his gravelly mumble with sharp-tongued comedians like Jimmy Durante. Predictably, his popularity plummeted. Last straw came when Keaton blew off an MGM p.r. event to go to a college football game at the L.A. Coliseum. When Keaton's MGM contract expired it was not renewed.

Like many inebriates, Keaton took no responsibility for his showbiz demise. On the way out the door, Keaton grumbled, "You studio people warp my character."

While many in the industry assumed that Joe Schenck and Buster Keaton were on the outs socially because of their business past, strangers never fully

:holas M. Schenck lived his business life in
) distinct parts. First there was the Young Nick
o ran Palisades Amusement Park with
oyish zeal, through thick and thin, always
hand to meet his public and hype his product.
thor's collection.

Then came the Old Nick, old it seemed as soon as Marcus Loew died and left him in charge of the Loew's Inc. empire. From garrulous and hammy, he became grim and intensely private. *Author's collection.*

The young, dapper Joseph M. Schenck. *Author's collection.*

The more mature Joe, at the peak of his power. *Author's collection.*

Nick Schenck during his days as owner, operator, and chief tub thumper of Palisades Amusement Park. *Author's collection.*

An early girlfriend and benefac of Nick Schenck was Eva Tangu a bawdy vaudevillian knowr the "I Don't Care Girl." She l the Schenck brothers the mo to buy their first drugst *Author's collecti*

The first entertainer ever hired by Joe and Nick was Nora Bayes, who would go on to co-compose the famous song "Shine On, Harvest Moon," which she performed with the Ziegfeld Follies. *Author's collection.*

When Joe and Nick Schenck partnered with Marcus Loew, they hitched their wagon to a comet's tail. When Loew died in middle age, Nick took charge of an empire that soon had him among the top ten richest men in America. *Author's collection.*

Marcus Loew's furrier friend Adolph Zukor predicted flickers would grow from novelty into art and became head of Paramount Pictures. *Author's collection.*

When Nick Schenck found Eddie Mannix, shown here, he was a juvenile delinquent with a head on his shoulders. Nick turned him into one of the top execs at MGM. *Courtesy Fort Lee Historical Society.*

Joe and Norma's first house, in Bayside, Quee
on a hill overlooking Little Neck Bay. It v
here that Natalie Talmadge stayed in 1
so she could be with Buster Kea
an extra night before he went off to v
Author ph

The view of the entrance to
"Schenck Bros. Palisade Par
At some point an *s* was ad
to make it Palisa
Courtesy Fort Lee Historical Soci

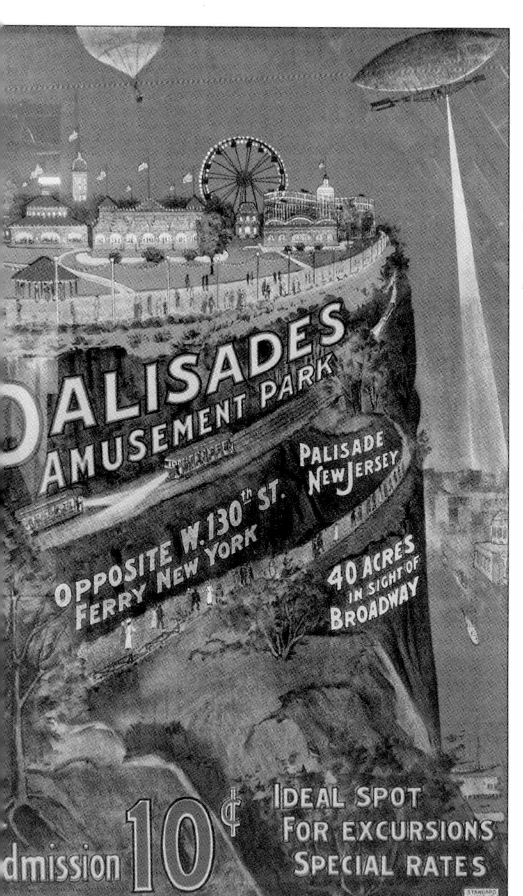

Beautiful poster circa 1910 advertising the new amusement park on the cliffs overlooking the Hudson. *Courtesy Barrymore Film Center, Fort Lee, New Jersey.*

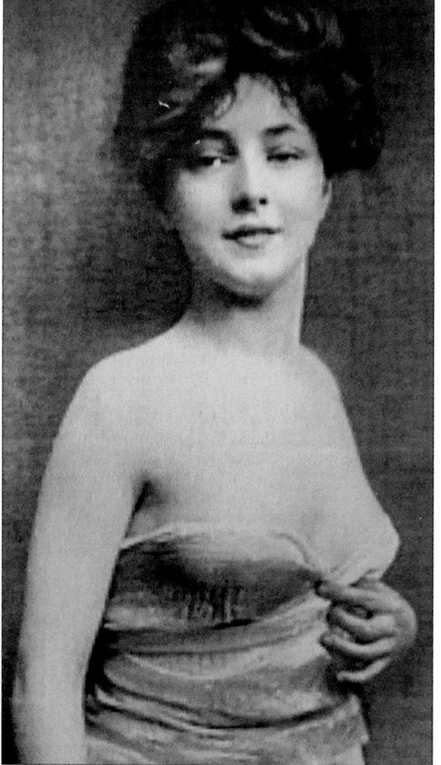

Joe Schenck met the notorious Evelyn Nesbit on a steamship crossing the Atlantic during the summer of 1913. He hurriedly shot a picture starring her and made a quick bundle. His success gave him the template he would repeat again and again in Norma Talmadge pictures. *Author's collection.*

In 1917, scenes from a Fatty Arbuckle picture called *Reckless Romeo* were shot in Palisades Park, offering us a rare view of the saltwater pool, a glimpse of the Hudson River with upper Manhattan on the other side, and daredevil high diver Arthur E. Holden doing his thing.

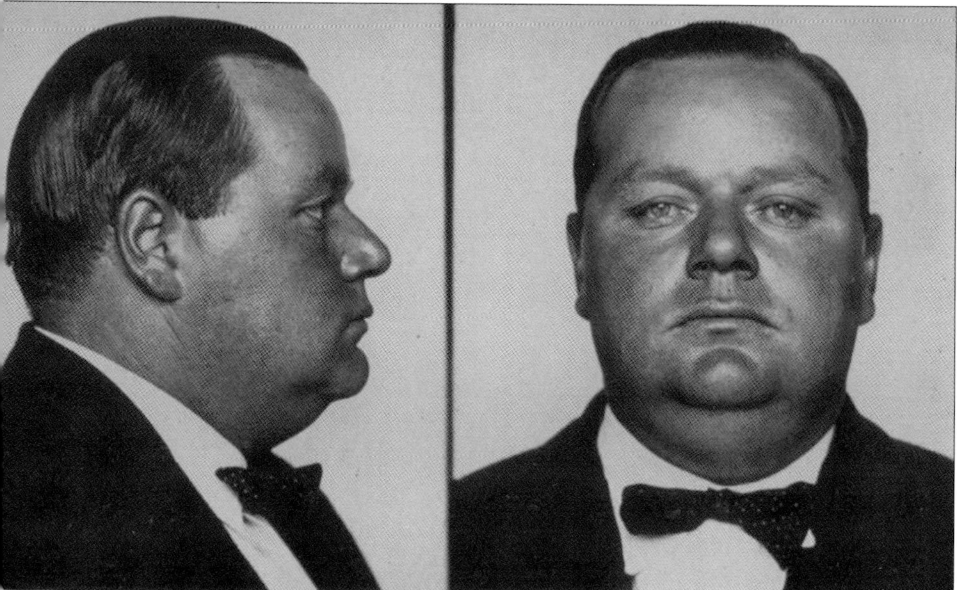

Arbuckle under arrest. Whatever happened in that San Francisco hotel room, it rendered Arbuckle forever unfunny.

ʼie scenes like this took on a new meaning after candal that all but ended Arbuckle's career. *ʼrtesy Barrymore Film Center, Fort Lee, New Jersey.*

MGM "fixer" Edgar J. "Eddie" Mannix had worked Nick ever since the day Nick and Joe caught him stealing from Palisades Park. At MGM his job was to make sure Louis B. Meyer did what Nick Schenck told him to do. *Author's collection.*

The beautiful Talmadge Sisters, Norma and Constance. Joe set each up with her own production company and during the 1920s they made a bundle for "Joseph M. Schenck Presents."
Author's collection.

Info-rich shot of a silent movie being made. That's director Allen Dwan, who helmed Norma Talmadge's *Panthea*, with the megaphone at the right. That's Marion Davies in the middle. They're making *Dark Star*, with W. R. Hearst picking up the tab.
Courtesy Barrymore Film Center, Fort Lee, New Jersey.

Actress Betty Mack (left) with Constance (center) and Norma Talmadge on deck during an Atlantic voyage.
Library of Congress.

Buster Keaton appears overwhelmed by the Talmadges, Connie top left, Natalie top right, Peg and Norma in front.
Author's collection.

Newspaper ad for Joe's first picture, *Panthea.*
Author's collection.

Buster Keaton first appeared on stage, at age three, in Wilmington, Delaware. Buster would do something naughty d the act consisted of his dad throwing him gainst the scenery, or into the orchestra pit, into the audience. No matter what you did to the kid, you couldn't make him cry. He was sometimes billed as "The Kid Who Can't Be Harmed" and "The Human Mop."
Library of Congress.

'TIGER GIRL' IN 2 NEW HOLDUP

THREE CENTS CITY & COUNTY

EVENING HERALD

LATE NEW

MARCUS LOEW IS DEA

Thousands in Labor Day Fet

THRONGS AT PARKS AND BEACHES

DRUG STORE MOTORIST ROBBED

NOTED THEATER M SUCCUMBS IN SL AT N. Y. MANS

URUGU MADE OF LE

POLICE COMB L.A. IN 'MME. XYZ' HUNT

YANK WORLD FLIERS MAKE INDIA HOP

Marcus Loew's death resulted in banner headlines everywhere, coverage most often reserved for world leaders.
Courtesy Barrymore Film Center, Fort Lee, New Jersey.

Marcus Loew, a member of the New Jersey Film Hall of Fame.
Courtesy Barrymore Film Center, Fort Lee, New Jersey.

The Loew's Kings Theatre on Flatbush Avenue in Brooklyn, New York was one of the original Loew's Wonder Theaters, opening on September 7, 1929 with a combination of motion pictures and live entertainment. It was designed by Harold W. Rambusch using design elements from the Paris Opera House and Versailles.
Author's collection.

A hambone gathering of United Artists with their plates. From left to right: Hiram Abrams, Paul D. O'Brien, Mary Pickford (with her mom), Charles Chaplin, Arthur W. Kelly, Douglas Fairbanks, and Joe Schenck, who is winking and holding his plate as a waiter might. *Library of Congress.*

A rare instance of United Artists and Loew's sharing a theater, the Ohio had a seating capacity of 3,079 and opened on March 17, 1928 on East State Street, downtown Columbus. The first picture to be shown there was *Divine Woman* with Greta Garbo. The first talkie was *The Tempest* with John Barrymore in April 1929. *Library of Congress.*

Nick, Pansy, and Louis B. Mayer sometime in the early 1930s. At least Pansy seems happy. LB can think of a thousand places he'd rather be. *Author's collection.*

n June 25, 1938, the motion picture industry pledged to cooperate with the U.S. government. On hand for a meeting in the White House with FDR were: (front row, left to right) Barney Balaban from Paramount, Harry Cohn from Columbia, Nick Schenck from Loews Inc., "motion picture czar" Will Hays, Leo Spitz from RKO; (back row, t to right) unidentified, Sidney Kent from Twentieth Century-Fox, N. J. Blumberg from Universal, lbert Warner from Warner Brothers. *Library of Congress.*

One of Joe's first girlfriends after his divorce was Australian actress Mary Maguire, who w engaged to a Nazi and might have been a spy She was cast in one Twentieth Century-Fox picture before Joe sent her on her way. *Author's collection.*

Exotic "doncer" Grace Poggi was of the women who testified at Joe's t Joe gave her a fur and claime as a business expe *Author's collect*

Joe Schenck met Norma Jeane (who would become Marilyn Monroe). Their relationship began in the late 1940s along standard casting-couch lines but developed into a sweet-natured friendshi Though two generations separated them, she only outlived him by ten months. *Author's collection.*

This promotional still of Joe Schenck makes him look like a character in a film noir, which might not have been that far from the mark.

One of the first actresses Joe Schenck signed to UA was Ukrainian beauty Anna Sten, shown here in a publicity shot for the UA production *Nana*. She went on to have a long career.

Charter member of the "mile-high club"? On October 22, 1932, Colonel Roscoe Turner completed the first-ever one-day airplane flight from Mexico City to Los Angeles, 1,700 miles in a Gilmore Lion monoplane. With him in the plane were Joe Schenck and actress Lili Damita. Upon arrival in LA, Damita was sporting the souvenir sombrero Joe bought her. *Author's collection.*

MGM publicity shot of twenty-six-year-old superstar Jean Harlow, who on June 7, 1937 died of cerebral edema, brain swelling, but the overall cause of death was uremic poisoning, kidney failure. *Author's collection.*

After his divorce from Norma Talmadge, Joe Sch fell hard on the rebound for actress Merle Oberon When he learned that she too only wanted him for his money and power, he gave up on love and became a truly prolific bachelor. *Author's collection.*

Joe Schenck, Merle Oberon, Norma Shearer, and Irving Thalberg on vacation. It appears that Oberon and Shearer are the ones having a moment. *Author's collection.*

In Midwood, Brooklyn, stood Vitagraph Studios, the first motion picture studio, and the place where Norma Talmadge made her first 250 pictures. Today, the studio site is occupied by a modern building, called The Vitagraph in commemoration, and all that is left of the original facility is the landmark smokestack. *Author photos.*

The Schencks' good friend Irving Berlin lived to be 101 years old. His son Irving, Jr. sadly died as an infant on Christmas Day. His grieving dad went on to write a very sad song called "White Christmas" that became the most popular song of all time. Father and son are buried side by side in Woodlawn Cemetery in the Bronx. *Author photos.*

For their work together during the 1920s, creating some of the greatest films ever made, Joe Schenck (6757 Hollywood Boulevard) and Buster Keaton (6619) received stars on the Hollywood Walk of Fame. *Author photos.*

Marcus Loew and Joe and Nick Schenck share Maimonides Cemetery in Cypress Hi Brooklyn, as their final resting place. In fact, their tombs are only about 120 feet Joe and Nick are eternal roomies. *Author photos.*

appreciated the situation. Joe and Buster were friends. They never stopped doing things together. Ballpark. Track. The fights.

BACK EAST, NICHOLAS M. SCHENCK'S HAPPY LIFE—RUNNING AN AMUSEMENT park up close and a show business empire from afar—was about to come to a crashing halt.

Everyone knew Marcus Loew was a sick man. He looked older than his years and increasingly feeble. Never robust but usually full of beans, now Loew tired quickly, and paid less and less attention to business matters, which raked in millions without his input. He, with Caroline and the boys, spent his later years in a marble palace known as Pembroke, built in 1916 by Captain Joseph R. De Lamar for his bride in Glen Cove, N.Y. It was designed in a French neoclassical style by architect C. P. H. Gilbert. The estate was on forty-six acres. It had a palm court, bowling alley, cave, seventy-foot belvedere water tower, and an elevator leading to a tea house—eighty-two rooms in all. There was an indoor tennis court that Loew never used, a massive pipe organ at the base of the main staircase that was never played, and stained-glass Tiffany windows. There was a long party room to entertain hundreds of guests, and a private boat landing on Long Island Sound.

Increasingly, Marcus gazed at the image of Captain De Lamar's bride in stained glass at his front entrance and seemed a little sad that his business carried on just fine without him.

Nick had taken to giving Marcus only the good news: "Eddie says the pictures are all good, the business flourishing, theaters are paying the rent, and the West Coast studios are all in perfect condition," Nick would say.

"Nicholas, you're a sweet man. I won't tell anybody, but you are. Now tell me, how are things really going?"

"Seriously, Marcus, everything is fine."

On September 4, 1927, Marcus Loew, fifty-seven years old, traveled by yacht, the *Caroline* (named after his wife), to Saratoga Springs where he visited Nick at Nick's vacation house. He seemed tired, but that was all the time now.

Following the meeting, Loew sailed back to the north shore of Long Island, arriving home late at night. At 6:30 a.m. the following morning, September 5, 1927, Marcus Loew had a heart attack and died in his sleep.

It was estimated that, in New York alone, eight thousand customers attended Loew's theaters on an average night. MGM's two biggest hits at the time of Loew's death were *Ben-Hur*—his biggest gamble—and King Vidor's *The Big Parade*, which each made $5 million at the box office. Loew's estate was estimated to be worth $35 million—a multibillionaire in today's dollars.

On the day of Marcus's funeral, September 8, all Loew's theaters went dark. Funeral services began at eleven a.m. and were officiated at Pembroke by the Rev. Dr. Aron Eisman of the Bronx. Outside was a long line of autos, Long Islanders who wanted to pay their respects. Good friends and complete strangers covered the considerable lawn with flowers. There was a quarter of a million dollars in flowers, someone said, counting the lawn and the bier display that enveloped the casket. A crowd of two thousand gathered just outside the gates, hoping to see someone famous.

Pallbearers included Nick, William Randolph Hearst, Lee Shubert, and Adolph Zukor. Honorary pallbearers included William Fox, Louis B. Mayer, and D. W. Griffith.

Marcus Loew was interred in Maimonides Cemetery in Cypress Hills, Brooklyn, on a perfect late summer day, temperature in the low seventies under clear skies with a fresh breeze. The hearse parked outside the cemetery gates at the curb of Jamaica Avenue, and the pallbearers, including Nick, carried the casket to the tomb on their shoulders. Joe and Nick and Joe owned a plot forty yards from Loew's, both plots purchased at the same time. It's hard to believe Nick didn't at least give his own plot the side-eye as he carried Marcus past.

Caroline Loew was well veiled and stayed on her feet in the cemetery, with one son at each elbow, David on the left, Arthur on the right. Her sobs became audible, and her knees buckled as the coffin entered the tomb, but she stayed up.

As mourners gathered at Maimonides in Brooklyn, the Sands Point Casino, a "yachting and bathing club" known well to Joe and Nick out on the North Shore of Long Island, burned to the ground. It would be the site of Nick's future home.

The next day, all shows at Loew's theaters began with the orchestras and organ playing "Lead, Kindly Light."

WHEN MARCUS LOEW DIED, HIS WIDOW INHERITED FOUR HUNDRED thousand shares of Loew's Inc., a controlling interest. William Fox, years before his studio would merge with Joe's, wanted those shares.

After Loew's funeral Mrs. Loew took Nick by the hand.

"Nicholas, I do not want outsiders taking control of Marcus's company. The boys aren't ready. I want you to take charge," she said through her veil.

"Thank you, Caroline."

"On one condition," she added.

"Anything," Nick said.

"Don't fire John Gilbert, he's my favorite."

"Deal," Nick said in a soft tone, and gave Caroline's hand a little squeeze.

And so, Caroline Loew sold her four hundred thousand shares of Loew's Inc. to Nick, giving him absolute control over Loew's empire. And the besotted John Gilbert signed a new contract.

One day soon thereafter, in Mayer's office in the presence of Eddie Mannix, Gilbert told Mayer that he planned to marry Greta Garbo.

Mayer shot back, "Why do you want to marry her? Why don't you just continue shtupping her and forget about the wedding?"

Gilbert said nothing and instead put his hands around Mayer's throat and squeezed. Mayer's eyes threatened to pop out, so Mannix stepped in, grabbed Gilbert, and tossed him against a wall.

Mayer gasped and screamed: "You're through! I'll destroy you!"

Gilbert laughed. "My contract is with Nick Schenck. Three pictures for a million bucks. Nothing you can do about it."

And there wasn't. Because of his deal with Caroline Loew, Nick was in charge of all things John Gilbert—and strangling Mayer was not a deal breaker.

"I'm going to have to give up the park," Nick thought sadly.

WITH NICK IN CHARGE OF THE LOEW'S EMPIRE, MAYER TOOK TO CALLing him (behind his back but within earshot of Eddie Mannix) Mr. Skunk. In exchange, Nick told Mayer if he didn't shape up, he was going to change the name of the company to Metro-Goldwyn-Schenck. They were off to a great start.

With Loew gone, both Schenck brothers, and Nick in particular, navigated a huge upheaval, swooshing in to fill the void left by their partner. Some things stayed the same. Mayer and Irving Thalberg remained MGM studio head and production chief respectively.

At first, the transition was smooth. Then, a month after Loew's death, *The Jazz Singer* opened, the first film featuring both a synchronized musical soundtrack and dialogue. Only portions of *The Jazz Singer* had sound, mostly Al Jolson's five songs and dialogue leading in and out of those numbers.

The Jazz Singer was a bad picture that has aged horribly. There are blackface scenes, the acting is stilted, and the timing of the entire picture seems off. It didn't matter, though. Jolson sang "My Mammy," the audience heard it, and went home *astounded*.

Joe and Norma went to see *The Jazz Singer* opening night. Norma later recalled that they held hands during the picture. She said, "By the end of the picture both my husband and I were speechless. 'What do you think of it?' I asked. He said, 'It's a fad! Talking pictures won't last once the novelty wears off. I'll give them a year.'"

The Vitaphone innovation meant another upheaval not just for studios, where soundstages needed to be built, but also for theaters where new projectors and speakers needed to be installed. While MGM wanted to start making sound pictures immediately, Nick—confronted both by future shock and the reality of theaters unprepared to show talkies—initially took an "anti-sound stance" like his brother. But *The Jazz Singer* was a hit, Nick saw the light, and MGM transformed efficiently into a company that sang and danced.

Joe hung on longer. Ever the gambler, he placed a bet that motion pictures wouldn't talk. Joe told a reporter, "We have so much of everything, we are always seeking novelties. But talking doesn't belong in pictures. Pictures are on a silent ground. Sound reproduction, however, is a great asset in pictures. The sound of a zeppelin would enhance a drama, and a knock on a window would build up a mystery play. But I don't think people will want talking pictures long." Joe added that his friend Irving Berlin didn't agree. Sound was solid gold to a songwriter. But he'd still bet against sound being around for long.

Joe, of course, lost that bet, but only for a month or two after which he quickly revamped UA for sound. A little more than a month after calling talkies "novelties," Joe sang a different tune: "I saw the sound tests for Miss Pickford and Miss [Lupe] Velez and they were sensational, their voices were perfect, just astounding for their naturalness. I may have been panning talking pictures in the past, but now I am going to make them!"

UA produced sixteen features in 1929, all silent. Howard Hughes's film *Hell's Angels*, a big-budget World War I epic featuring biplane dogfights in thrilling action sequences, was stopped midway and retooled for sound, not coming out until 1930, allowing audiences to first hear Jean Harlow's smart-alecky voice.

ON SEPTEMBER 15, NICK OFFICIALLY MOVED FROM VP TO PRESIDENT OF MGM, at least for the remainder of Marcus Loew's unfinished term.

At first he spent several days a week at his happy place, riding the roller coasters, and mingling with his people. Concessionaires would call out "Hello, Nick!"—and he would give them a cheerful wave. Palisades Park made him feel alive. It was an extension of him. "His soul," as Joe put it. And just as much as he wanted to always bathe in the bright lights atop the Jersey cliffs, he wanted to stay three thousand miles away from MGM. He had a complicated job involving many Hollywood people, but there were only a few he wanted to shake hands with.

"Hollywood people are like buildings on a set," Nick said. "All front and no depth."

Eventually he had no time for the park at all. A part of Nick's joie de vivre faded when he became a full-time Loew's man.

A new daily ritual for Nick was screening a picture a day in the State Theatre's private projection room. If it was an MGM picture, he could better choose where to book it. Nick became a picture guy through and through. Even though he worked in Times Square, he seldom attended the legitimate theater.

Nick became reclusive, rarely seen in public. Once a creator of publicity stunts, he now complained he hadn't expected his new role at Loew's Inc. to involve so much press. Constantly bugged by reporters, Nick allegedly said, "How long will this keep up and how often must it really be done?"

He was, however, patient enough to sit for a *New York Times* reporter during the spring of 1929. He said plans were for MGM to produce and distribute forty-four features that year in a variety of styles and subjects. Sometimes certain types of pictures shrank or grew in popularity. Popular at that moment, he said, were "flapper pictures" about the "Jazz Age," a phrase coined by F. Scott Fitzgerald. "Collegiate stories are also big now."

Nick said short subjects had a "cultural future" even more interesting than that of features. Long films were usually fictional subjects, whereas short subjects were malleable, and cheap enough to make to allow for experimentation. MGM was now making their own newsreels, Nick boasted, after years of using newsreels made by Hearst. "MGM pictures look better than ever from the use of incandescent bulbs for studio lighting." The bulbs, he added, enabled very large sets to be illuminated.

MGM, he said, was working to help *education*. MGM crews were filming surgical procedures. These films could then be shown to medical students. It was a lot easier than performing all surgeries in front of a gallery of students taking notes. Plus, the close-ups showed the procedures more clearly than could be seen when attending a surgery in person.

Nick concluded by discussing how his product was helping the whole world: "There is much more of a community of feeling between different countries than ever before. Pictures have proved themselves to be the great world medium. Location trips—frequently long and expensive, such as the five-month sojourn in the South Seas recently completed by a unit from our studio—are part of the order of the day, and I know it is the desire of most producers to obtain actual atmospheric shots whenever time and conditions permit. Louis B. Mayer informs me that we have crews filming right now in Canada, North Africa, and Europe, all obtaining special locale photography for the coming season's product."

Of course, making a film that the public would like was always a risk. "There is no such thing as an average picture, any more than an average man. If I could find a truly average man, I would pay him a million dollars to tell me which pictures would be financial successes, and which ones wouldn't."

WHILE THE INDUSTRY METAMORPHOSED, THERE WAS A SHAKEUP IN the personal lives of both Nick and Joe. One day Irving Berlin came to visit Joe and the two were talking about the old days.

"Remember that day you asked me to talk to Norma and find out if you had a chance with her?"

"Yes, I remember that day very well. I wish that day were back again."

"What's wrong, Joe? Aren't you and Norma getting along?"

Joe shrugged and looked away. He knew something was wrong. A few days later, at breakfast with Norma, he'd find out what it was.

"Lambie, I'm in love with another man," Norma said. She looked at him with a steady gaze that he failed to return.

"Who is it?"

"Gilbert Roland." Her co-star for her most recent pictures.

Both were quiet for a few minutes. Breakfast grew cold.

"I can't blame you," Joe eventually said. "I'm not handsome and he is. I am no longer young, and I've never been exactly romantic—while he is both."

Joe paused and looked at her for the first time. "Why, Child, you are the most priceless possession I have ever had, and it is my own fault that I have lost you."

"That's wonderful of you to say."

"No, it is just common sense. I'm trying to put myself in your place and see your side of it. I've neglected you in a hundred different ways. I have been so busy working for you that at times I've completely forgotten about you. I know how a woman appreciates the little things, the things that I insist upon in love scenes in my pictures. She wants to be told that she is loved, not just occasionally but constantly."

"That's right," Norma said.

"And when her husband is away, she wants to at least know that he is thinking of her. She wants phone calls and telegrams and flowers and letters. I've been so busy putting those things in pictures I have neglected them in life."

"Then you don't hate me?"

"Why should I? I created circumstances that made you no more able to help falling in love with another man than you could help getting hungry. What do you want me to do? Do you want a divorce?"

Norma burst into tears. "No! Let me put a face on it for a while and see if this other thing doesn't pass over."

"I'll do anything you want me to. I'll give you my name for as long as you want it, if it will be any protection to you."

Norma kissed Joe and ran tearfully from the room.

(This conversation is how both Joe and Norma portrayed the scene in interviews. However, during the marriage when Joe was out with the boys, some of his behavior was not quite so nice, and he frequently expressed the anger one might expect from a cuckold. Writer Barney Oldfield—not to be confused with auto-racing daredevil Barney Oldfield—said that Joe had known for years that Norma was cheating on him, that she tended to sleep with her leading men, and that he'd had investigators follow her and knew where she went. Oldfield claimed that Joe said he tried to make sure Norma was always paired with gay leading actors, and once when he caught her cheating asked Eddie Mannix to have some of his boys castrate the guy and present Norma with the severed genitals. It was just talk, apparently, but in sharp contrast to the civility of their re-created breakfast breakup.)

After that, she still put on a front of being Mrs. Joe Schenck, but moved out and into her own place. She showed up to events in public on Roland's arm. He was eleven years younger than Norma.

Norma and Roland might've been hot offset, but on-screen not so much. It was the era of hotsy-totsy flappers. Audiences—men, in particular—didn't find Norma sexy, and she didn't flap. New stars were sexually provocative (Greta Garbo) and assertive (Joan Crawford). Norma's little-girl-in-trouble act had seen its day. Each Norma picture now made less than the one before.

On August 2, 1928, Samuel Goldwyn's secretary, Valeria Belletti, wrote in a letter, "Did you know Norma Talmadge and her husband Joseph Schenck are no longer living together? I believe they are going to be divorced very shortly. Of course, Norma has been carrying on dreadfully with Roland Gilbert for the last year and she hasn't taken any pains to conceal it. And so it goes—all marriages seem to break amongst the Hollywood crowd."

The newspaper gossipers said poor, poor Joe. He lost his best friend, Buster Keaton, and now he was losing his wife to a young stud. Norma announced that she would be making a film with Roland in Europe. Reporters noted that Europe was very far from Hollywood Boulevard.

Hollywood sided with Joe. One famous hostess said in public, "I will never invite Norma Talmadge to another party."

When Joe heard about that he sought out the hostess and said to her, "Look here, if I hold no grudge against Norma, neither should you."

With all three Talmadge sisters between husbands, they took to hanging out at the Keaton home, where Buster wasn't. Actress Louise Brooks described the scene as three women who had money through marriage but little to do.

Constance was "naturally delightful," Natalie was a "comfortable lump," her kids coming and going as they pleased, and the women quietly waited for their husbands to die. So it was a bluesy scene in the Schenck/Talmadge camp, rich but bluesy, as Hollywood squinted at the grandeur of a new era: sound.

Nick Schenck's personal life was changing rapidly as well. Nick being Nick, the historical record is not packed with details, but here's what we know: On April 19, 1927, several New York papers published a small piece that said, in essence, "Mrs. Annie Schenck yesterday filed suit for divorce in the Supreme Court, Manhattan, against her husband, Nicholas M. Schenck, official of Loew Enterprises and brother of Joseph M. Schenck, husband of

Norma Talmadge. Justice Peters appointed H. Mott Brennan referee. The co-respondent was not named." Who? When were she and Nick married? How did they meet? We don't know. She never appeared in an extant public record and, although Nick's offspring knew Annie existed, they knew nothing about her. In 1924 Annie and Nick entertained "Elsie Rockefeller and her kids" (that's the great-niece of Standard Oil) at the Schencks' summer cottage on Ruffle Bar, an island in Jamaica Bay known for its clams and oysters before pollution turned it into a ghost island.

During the summer of 1927 Nick granted Annie her divorce. According to one report, she'd been the former wife of a Brooklyn police officer, although where that comes from we don't know. She is a phantom, visible only here, clearing out and disappearing again, making way for the woman who would be the true love of Nick's life. . . .

She was vaudeville dancer Pansy Wilcox, born December 13, 1898, and raised in Morgantown, West Virginia, daughter of James Wilcox, an optometrist who owned a drugstore. She graduated from the University of West Virginia.

Two of Pansy's five siblings became well-known. Her brother was director Fred MacLeod Wilcox (*Lassie Come Home* in 1943, and *Forbidden Planet* in 1956) and her sister was Ruth Selwyn, who was one of the first women producers on Broadway and became rich as an initial investor into Palm Springs, California. Her dad married six times, twice to the same woman. All six kids came from his first wife.

Pansy first made the newspapers in January 1921, age twenty-two, when she was the maid of honor at the West Virginia wedding of her friend Gayle Pauline Dick to W. Preston Burton. Her next public mention came in 1926 when she attended the wedding of her sister Ruth Wilcox to Broadway producer Edgar Selwyn in the municipal building in Manhattan. She was never big enough in vaudeville to receive name billing. The third time she made the papers, in 1927, was the charm: an announcement of her own wedding to Nick.

Nick and Pansy were married on August 1 in a ceremony held at Palisades Park. They honeymooned first in Saratoga Springs, taking in the waters and the ponies, then on to Europe. Nick told reporters that this was his "first time abroad." He'd previously been too busy. Being born abroad, and growing up there, apparently didn't count.

Returning stateside Nick and Pansy moved into an apartment that occupied the entire fifteenth floor of a new apartment building on East 58th Street, where Nick and Pansy successfully began to build a family. (A year later, Pansy gave birth to daughter Marti, who caught the showbiz bug from her parents and became a singer/actress, best known for her TV work in Hollywood from 1958 through '82, making appearances on *It Takes a Thief, The Love Boat, Hart to Hart, Kojak*, and *Mannix*. Nick's daughter on a TV show named *Mannix*. No one got the joke. Nick later said that being a dad was the favorite part of his life. On August 1, 1932, Nick and Pansy had their second daughter, Joanne, seven pounds, zero ounces, born on East 61st Street at the Alice Fuller LeRoy Sanitarium. In December 1933, Nick and Pansy completed their family with the birth of their third daughter, Nicola, known as Niki. Like older sister, Marti, Niki was born with the show biz bug and would go on to be a successful actress.) As his family grew, Nick moved it out of Manhattan to a mansion on Long Island's North Shore, at Great Neck.

The more Nick learned to love being home with his family, the less he wanted to deal with MGM. In 1929, finding Hollywood as distasteful as ever, he thought of folding his hand and leaving the table.

It began when William Fox met with Nick and proposed to buy out MGM, which would then merge with Fox. Nick stood to pick up a quick ten million, and lose the burden of running the MGM portion of Loew's Inc.

"I'll have more time to spend at the park," Nick thought.

The sale was made on February 24, 1929, and there was an immediate furor. MGM stockholders sued. Mayer had been blindsided and went to the government—he had pals in high places—and suggested the Justice Department nix the sale of MGM to William Fox on antitrust grounds.

And that was what happened. MGM reverted to Nick's control. Fox's failed attempt to acquire MGM began a string of bad luck. On July 17, Fox was on his way to play golf with Nick when he was seriously injured in a car accident in which his chauffeur was killed. That fall the stock market crashed, and Fox's fortune was wiped out. Nick never forgave Mayer for costing him that money, although the Great Depression probably rendered Nick's beef moot. Fox was destitute when three years later Joe Schenck saved him by merging Fox's company into his own.

NICK WAS IN LOVE, CREATING A FAMILY. JOE WAS HEARTBROKEN, STILL deeply committed to a woman who everyone said had been using him. And Joe's good friend, songwriter Irving Berlin, was in mourning.

On Christmas Day, 1928, Irving Berlin's three-week-old son died, so for the rest of his life Christmas Day, a holiday he did not celebrate because he was Jewish, became a day of sad reflection. Thirteen years later, three weeks after Pearl Harbor, Bing Crosby debuted Berlin's most famous song on the radio, a melancholy tune called "White Christmas," which went on to win an Academy Award and become the best-selling song ever—but for Berlin it surely meant something different than it did to the rest of the world.

BY APRIL 1929, THE CONVERSION FROM SILENT TO SOUND WAS WELL underway. Nick closed theaters in shifts to be reequipped. Loew's was first to convert all its theaters. Talkies were being made all over Hollywood. Tinseltown buzzed with excitement and dread. Art directors learned to hide microphones. For a clunky period, microphones and actors had to remain stationary. Later, the boom mic was invented. Singers and dancers rejoiced. Stage performers looked west. Old-time screen stars silently fretted.

An entertainment reporter for the *L.A. Times* opined that talkies might change the world's perception of *beauty itself.* Among the people he asked about the coming of sound and its possible effects on Hollywood's future was Joe, who said, "The voice has altered everything. It will open the way for a throng of new people. Regarding the physical attractiveness of its players, it will overthrow the limitations by which we were handicapped in the past when we had to find a girl who would justify her character's mesmerizing effect by her personal allurements alone. In the future a heroine will not have to be as beautiful as this. Provided she is attractive and has a good speaking voice, she will be able to create the illusion of beauty. She will be able to do this especially through her voice, because in the new medium you are not fascinated by appearance alone but will be interested in mental powers to a much larger degree." Pictures, in that sense, Joe said, would become more like the stage, a world where Sarah Bernhardt could play young parts even when she was sixty.

He added that a lot of nervousness around town was unfounded. He predicted that the great majority of silent picture stars would make the transition just fine and continue being stars in the talkies.

But there were many who didn't make the switch. Caroline Loew's favorite, John Gilbert, was one of the first adversely affected. Gilbert's first talkie—an experiment on MGM's part, dipping their toe into the murky waters of synchronized sound—was a feature called *The Hollywood Revue.* When it was shown by Thalberg to test audiences, it resulted in roars of laughter from audiences who hadn't expected Gilbert's voice ("I love you, I love you, *I love you*") to be high and, some thought, less than masculine. In the film, Gilbert and Norma Shearer chewed scenery in a burlesque of the *Romeo and Juliet* balcony scene. Thalberg wanted to cut the scene, but Nick overruled him, saying the picture needed the "star power."

In retaliation, Mayer cast Gilbert in stinkers, and in smaller and smaller parts until in his last film he played a small part as a riveter.

Gilbert was released as soon as his contract was up in 1933 and this time Nick did not come to his rescue. The actor dedicated his remaining days to drinking and died in 1936, his liver in ruins.

Characters based on Gilbert continue to pop up in pictures about Hollywood's party-hearty early days. Most recently, he was the basis for Brad Pitt's character "Jack Conrad" in director Damien Chazelle's 2022 ode to Hollywood excesses, *Babylon*.

Another career that stumbled during the sound conversion was the Schencks' old friend Lillian Gish. When her contract with MGM expired, the industry was in flux, and she began to send ideas to Joe Schenck for possible future projects. Joe couldn't make it happen—writing things like "*The Happy Hypocrite* is not worthwhile for production and will not do you much good," and "I tried very hard to get Irving Thalberg to give or trade me *Anna Christie* but he said he must have it for Greta Garbo"—and "after discussing the matter with Nicholas," Joe suggested she might be better off seeking featured parts rather than starring roles.

Lillian did okay, though. She returned East and worked on the stage exclusively for a while, then alternated between films and the live stage for the rest of her career, which stretched into TV roles (*The Love Boat*) during the 1970s. Joe found a vehicle for her in 1930, with *One Romantic Night*—one of only two pictures she made during the 1930s. As difficult as it was, her transition to sound went more smoothly than most. She picked up an Oscar nomination for *Duel in the Sun* in 1946. Her final screen appearance was her widely celebrated role in *The Whales of August* (1987).

JOE WAS FREQUENTLY REMINDED OF HIS PREDICTION THAT TALKIES were a fad. He always laughed. "Only a fool won't admit it when he's wrong, and boy I sure was," he said. Later he recalled how, once the decision was made to "go sound," the transformation of UA studios and theaters got underway posthaste. All UA actors agreed to make sound pictures—well, except for Chaplin.

Over at MGM, Nick's only holdout was Lon Chaney, known as "The Man of a Thousand Faces," who told brass he would "never make a talkie." He changed his mind, making a sound remake of his silent classic *The Unholy Three*, but died, unable to talk, in 1930 of throat cancer.

Joe might've predicted most silent stars would transition just fine, but he was worried about Norma. In 1928, Norma was among the screen stars appearing in a live radio broadcast that was also piped into theaters. It was here that Norma first realized that her world was changing, and not necessarily for the better. Her voice brought catcalls in a Detroit theater. She seemed tongue-tied in a straight-out-of-Brooklyn way, with a husky middle-aged voice, many miles from her girl-in-trouble image. America laughed.

The public did not get another opportunity to hear Norma's voice until January 1930. The "event" was announced by a large ellipsis-happy ad run in the *Los Angeles Evening Express*. At the top left was a drawing of Norma in profile. It read: "An announcement you have waited one year to read. Like a meteor whirling in its orbit . . . a new . . . a greater . . . a golden voiced . . . NORMA TALMADGE is headed for the living screen . . . a Norma you have never met . . . speaking to you for the first time with the voice millions have waited to hear . . . enacting a role that raises her to the pinnacle of dramatic art with the sheer inspiration of unfaltering genius . . . never have you seen or heard this Norma Talmadge . . . with the beauty . . . the temperament . . . the fire . . . the humor . . . the heart stirring appeal . . . she brings to you in . . . 'NEW YORK NIGHTS.' Her first all-talking picture for United Artists. Displaying an artistry matched only by the beautiful settings . . . gorgeous costumes . . . enchanting music by Al Jolson . . . and the superb cast of stage and screen players. The perfect star, the perfect voice, the perfect picture. A Joseph M. Schenck Presentation."

The ad failed to mention that, in preparation for her sound debut, Norma endured a solid year of vocal coaching—rain on the plain, Moses supposes, that kind of thing—to lose her Brooklynese. Critics called it her "Vitagraph accent."

In *New York Nights*, Norma played a chorus girl with marital woes who is pursued by a gangster. At the premiere, the feature was preceded by a comedy short called *In and Out*, and a Fox newsreel. When the picture hit the eyes and ears of her audience, Norma's inexperience at vocal acting was apparent. She spoke clearly and had kicked some of her accent—but her voice was stiff, heavy, and much deeper than expected. She suddenly seemed too mature for her role, woefully miscast, in fact.

Norma did not have to worry about money. Joe would always take care of her, plus mother Peg had set up trust funds for her daughters leaving them financially secure. According to some sources, it was a telegram from sister Constance, who never made a talkie, that convinced Norma to retire as an actor.

"Quit pressing your luck," the telegram read. The message referred to Norma's age. She was pushing forty.

The obituary on Norma's career ran in 1932 when the New York *Daily News* ran a full-page Florabel Muir feature about Hollywood. The article began with a nostalgic memory only ten years old: Norma Talmadge swooping down a corridor ghostly in white stage makeup. In the hallway she encounters handsome star Douglas Fairbanks, dressed as a Spanish don.

"Hello, Doug."

"How are you, Norma? How about a malted milk?"

"Just where I was headed. Come on! We'll go to the Dirty Spoon."

"To the Dirty Spoon!" Douglas Fairbanks exclaimed in his best swashbuckling voice.

Only ten years had passed since that day, but that was a "hundred years in Hollywood time," Muir wrote. Careers came and went—yet Norma was still in Hollywood, less bloom in her cheeks but otherwise similar in appearance to the olden days. The Dirty Spoon, across the street from D. W. Griffith's Fine Arts studio on Sunset Boulevard, was long gone now, but in its day served more stars per day than L.A.'s finest restaurants. Back in those days a girl could have three, four malted milks a day and never put on a pound. The stars ate candy by the handful. Mabel Normand was known to pound down salted peanuts day and night. The 1932 version of Norma was older, wiser, and sadder—and eloquent about her ennui: "There was a time when everything thrilled me. I was swept off my feet by anything that I liked. It might be a role in a picture, it might be seeing a new stage play in New York. I can remember not sleeping one night because I was going to Coney Island the next day. In the old days at the Dirty Spoon, we laughed over anything and everything. We didn't care about how we appeared in public. Today none of us can be like that even if we want to. No longer can I go downtown to a store shopping and lose myself in the throng. And you'll never know what it means to be deprived of a pleasure like that. The public forgets that stars are people. They criticize us too readily for what we do and how we appear on the screen. They forget that our lives are so utterly different."

Norma was not giving stock answers. This was the real stuff. She went deeper, from philosophical to confessional: "Why, even the romance of the screen is bound to shape our actions. The portrayal of emotion becomes part of our lives. We need it and the companionship that goes with it. Love is therefore a different thing to us. Perhaps that is why the romantic side of our lives is misunderstood. My feeling for Joseph Schenck has often been misinterpreted. Joe and I have a deep understanding between us. He is and always will be the most wonderful of men. He does things constantly for others. Nobody can know it better than I, how big his heart is. Let this fact be stated once and for all: I married Mr. Schenck because I loved him. People have inferred that it was because the marriage was a good match, but this was not the case. Joe and I grew up together financially. When we filmed *Panthea,* it was an even chance to win or lose. There is no obligation in that sense—financially. And he would be the last person in the world to hold such a thought."

Muir asked Peg about her daughter's love for Joe Schenck.

"Norma as a child had a tremendous admiration for Napoleon," Peg Talmadge said. "My daughters and I have always allowed Joe to advise us on financial matters and supervise our investments."

Joe, Peg liked to point out, started out with nothing. Joe's career was as remarkable in its way as the meteoric rise of her daughters.

"Joe has escaped the pompousness, the self-complacency, and intolerance of the average self-made man. Success does not change real simplicity of soul and since it may not be becoming language for a grandmother to use, I quote my daughter Constance when I say that Joe has always remained just a regular feller."

Blabbermouth Peg got into Norma's business deals with Joe. At her peak with UA, Norma made $200,000 per film. When she started, pictures were so infantile that, for many, Norma Talmadge was the first screen actress that they knew. *A Daughter of Two Worlds* and *The Sign on the Door* were among the first flickers that there were. During the 1920s she made $5 million. Joe handled Norma's money, but he was honest and wise. Norma owned large parcels of real estate, including the Talmadge Apartments. She owned and sometimes lived in the mansion in Queens. She had two houses in Hollywood. She had a stock and bonds portfolio that could choke a thoroughbred. Total value? Peg didn't want to say.

Not that it mattered. The Talmadges were fixed for life. As far as stage moms go, Peg was a hall-of-famer. Even Mary Pickford, silent Hollywood's alpha actress, wasn't *richer* than Norma.

By the time sound came into pictures, Peg Talmadge and whichever of her daughters were unattached lived on Ocean Front Avenue in Santa Monica, a road now known as Palisades Beach Road. (The house later was home to Cary Grant and Randolph Scott, and in the 1960s to director Roman Polansky and wife Sharon Tate.)

Muir's article was kind to Joe and Norma. Gossip columnists were blunter.

They wrote things like "hollowed-shell of a marriage." For Norma, words like "cashing in."

On February 16, 1932, Norma first acknowledged her troubles at home. She told a New York reporter that she was planning to obtain a "Paris divorce" from Joe. She said Joe had agreed to it. They'd each spent so much time on business that they didn't have time for each other. But Norma lied about Joe saying it was okay. He didn't, and the Paris divorce didn't happen.

One two-inch newspaper account of her divorce announcement referred to her as a "once famous screen star." That must've stung. The United Press dispatch quoted Norma as saying that her life after pictures was "quiet and obscure."

Norma then got on a train and headed west. Getting off in Pasadena she addressed reporters: "My divorce against Joseph M. Schenck has been canceled—for the time being, at least. And if I do file proceedings, Reno will be the place and not Paris. I must take care of some business here. Then I plan to return to New York and travel abroad before I do anything else. Of course, I am a woman, so I reserve the right to change my mind."

That got a laugh.

"What business are you in town for?"

"It's all in connection with my property," she said matter-of-factly. "I want to rent my house and attend to some other important matters before leaving. For that reason, I cannot say how long I will stay, but it will not be for many weeks, I am sure."

"Is this property you own with Joe?"

"No, all of our property matters with Joe have been settled."

"How about marrying again?"

"Oh no, not that. I'll cross my heart to that."

"Norma, do you . . ."

"That's all, gentlemen. Thank you."

She daintily stepped back from the scribes and left with Peg, Natalie, Constance, and Roland Gilbert.

WHILE SOUND CONVERSION CREATED CASUALTIES, THE DEATH OF Marcus Loew had a few as well. Like vaudeville, for example. Under Marcus Loew's direction, his theaters always presented a combination of filmed and live entertainment. When Marcus passed, it was the day vaudeville died. With Nick in charge, Loew's theaters presented fewer and fewer live acts until eventually there were motion pictures only. Some vaudeville acts survived in Hollywood, making films, and some had radio careers, but most packed it in.

In the meantime, Nick moved into Marcus's penthouse office. He planned to run Loew's Inc. the same way Marcus had: build, build, build. He was blissfully unaware that the world was only months away from an economic malaise that would make Marcus Loew's slogan seem foolishly extravagant.

CHAPTER NINE

WONDER THEATERS AND BREAD LINES

WHEN THE STOCK MARKET CRASHED, NEWS OF THE FINANCIAL disaster spread more quickly than any news story ever had before. In New York, great men of finance jumped to their deaths from high windows. Some were less panicky. Three thousand miles from Wall Street, Joe Schenck got word while sitting naked with a towel draped across his lap in Douglas Fairbanks's steam room on the UA lot. Beside him sat close friends.

"I'm cleaned out," Irving Berlin said.

"Me too," Douglas Fairbanks added.

"Don't worry, boys," Joe said. "We'll make it all back. Who's up for a game of golf?"

WHEN MARCUS LOEW DIED, NICK'S FIRST BOLD PLAN WAS TO CONstruct in Greater New York City the Wonders of the Theater World, massive and ornate structures that would uplift their communities and allow all New Yorkers an experience of luxury at a price they could afford. Those six palaces opened in 1929–30, each featuring identical "Wonder Morton" theater organs manufactured by the Robert Morton Organ Company, each organ with a four-manual console and twenty-three ranks of pipes.

Loew's Inc. competed with the other theater chains for the most awesome organ, a contest that Nick won when he instructed some of the Wonder organs' tubes to be placed inside the walls so the theater would vibrate when it was played. Not every engineer liked the idea, but Nick got his way.

The first of the Wonders to be completed was the Loew's Valencia on January 12, 1929, with a seating capacity of 3,500, at Jamaica Avenue and Merrick Road in Jamaica, Queens. The interior of the theater was in Spanish Colonial and pre-Columbian styles, with a façade made of brick and terra-cotta. The interior walls featured many statues, towers, and parapets that meant just maybe you weren't in Queens anymore. The opening program featured *White Shadows in the South Seas* starring Monte Blue and Raquel Torres, plus live acts, a Mort Harris revue called "Mantilla," and Don Albert's orchestra.

On September 7, 1929, two Wonder Theaters opened simultaneously. One was just south of Fordham Road in the Bronx. At first it was called "Loew's Paradise on the Grand Concourse," but soon shortened to the Paradise. It was designed by John Eberson and held four thousand seats. It had an Italian Baroque-inspired façade, and the interior gave the illusion of a Mediterranean outdoor villa under a night sky. From the incredible lobby, patrons looked up at three domes with ceiling murals. The opening-night show featured the Huberts, Al Norman, the Chester Hale Girls, Dave Schooler and his Paradise Serenaders, and Wesley Eddy and His Kings of Syncopation. Then at last the picture: *Our Modern Maidens* with Joan Crawford.

The other Wonder to open that day was the Kings Theatre on Flatbush Avenue in Brooklyn, designed by Harold Rambusch to resemble Versailles and the Paris opera house. There were 3,676 seats. The opening program featured the film *Evangeline*. Following the screening, the picture's star Dolores del Rio made a live appearance. There were also vaudeville acts, a performance by the pit orchestra, and a set by the organist.

Three weeks after the double opening, the lights went on at the Loew's Jersey, seating capacity 3,021 on Journal Square in Jersey City, N.J. It was designed by the architectural firm of Rapp and Rapp in a Baroque-Rococo style. The first tickets were torn at eleven o'clock on a Saturday morning, and the first picture shown was *Madame X,* starring Ruth Chatterton and directed by Lionel Barrymore.

On November 23, the Loew's Pitkin opened at the corner of Pitkin and Saratoga avenues in Brownsville, Brooklyn. Seating capacity: 2,817. Upon entrance, one saw a Moorish foyer with majolica plaques and embroidered hangings. The auditorium was multitiered and featured Greek statuary along the side walls and the proscenium. The first picture was *So This Is College*, tagline: "The perfect all talking, singing, dancing, and musical comedy." The first stage show: *Café de Paree*. The women's lounge was Persian, the men's decorated with African tribal weapons. Architect: Thomas Lamb.

The Loew's 175th Street Theatre, seating capacity 3,400, opened February 22, 1930, taking up an entire Manhattan block. Also designed by Lamb, interiors by Harold Rambusch, the theater was called a "kitchen-sink masterpiece" because it combined Byzantine, Roman, Hindu, Chinese, Moorish, Persian, Rococo, and Art Deco design elements. The first program featured MGM's *Their Own Desire* starring Norma Shearer, and a musical stage revue called *Pearls*.

By this time, it was starting to sink in that the previous fall's stock market crash was resulting in prolonged economic strife, and the reception for the new 175th Street Theatre was accordingly muted. As the doors opened for *The Virginian* with Gary Cooper, and vaudeville acts the Watson Sisters and the Venetian Carnival, public perception had changed regarding the Wonders. People were hungry. Couldn't at least *some* of this money have been spent on *food*? It was the peak for the cinema. Accommodations for watching pictures would become steadily cheaper and shabbier for the century's remaining seventy years.

Loew always told Nick that the thing to remember was no matter how large a studio they might control, they sold tickets to theaters, not to pictures. It was a motto that now slowly grew obsolete.

When the Great Depression came, MGM was less affected than other studios. Although Loew's theaters were all magnificent, there was never more than 150 of them, all downtown palaces. Paramount had a thousand, Warner and Fox each had more than five hundred—more mortgages to pay once the downturn came.

WHILE NICK WAS GETTING HIS FINAL WONDER THEATER READY FOR its grand opening, brother Joe wrote a long New Year's piece for the *L.A. Times* with the official-sounding title MILLIONS IN CELLULOID: AN INDUSTRIAL SURVEY OF MOTION PICTURES. It began, "In the excitement and confusion which has been brought about in the past two years by the arrival and development of talking pictures, a question frequently asked is: 'Has not the advent of sound made the film industry unstable?'"

Joe said no. True, the first days of sound caused some inevitable uncertainty. What industry had ever been called upon to completely retool overnight like that? But Hollywood was filled with many smart people, and the retooling was done, and the uncertainty ceased. With that emotional stability came financial stability.

Joe wrote that Hollywood employed thirty thousand persons, an all-time high. True, in the old days, there had been twice as many studios, but only half the current number of pictures were being made. The industry's total payroll was approximately $82 million, and that number was going to go up in the coming year. Production budgets totaled $165 million. The properties owned by the studios were worth $58 million, and he only expected California real estate values to "skyrocket." The value of public stock in the motion picture industry was rising. Buyers were eager to invest. Hollywood was "a sound and established investment." Joe remembered his concern that sound would alienate the audience so used to pantomime performances, but their acceptance had been immediate and enthusiastic. Talkies even brought more critical acclaim than silents had.

Competition between the majors, Joe said, was the type that only increased the quality of the product. In the old days the battle was for theaters. Now it was for writers, stars, and material. "Never has there been such an assortment of playwrights, novelists, musicians, and experts of the theater in Hollywood as there is today."

But it wasn't all competition. The sound engineers, the few on earth who truly understood and excelled at recording sound for motion pictures, were passed around between the major studios, a cooperative situation that helped everyone get their best product on the screen.

Another point Joe felt strongly about: The writers and makers of silent films had not been fired to make way for the new wave of talent. They were kept on and retrained.

Playwrights and songwriters benefitted most from talkies. New writers and composers were hired every day. "Every studio now employs a large orchestra and a staff of dancers for chorus. These, moreover, are not transient employees, as were the extra players of the old days."

Joe concluded, "The development of talking pictures is the greatest boon to the industry since the invention of the camera. The event is hardly less important to the world at large."

UA PICTURES DURING 1930–32 WERE MOSTLY COSTUME DRAMAS AND light comedies, all designed to get people's minds off the Depression. Joe, in typical "glass half full" fashion, saw the downturn as a business opportunity, and he bought acres and acres of California real estate cheap.

Always interested in the "next new thing," the next thing to get in on the ground floor of, Joe accompanied Douglas Fairbanks and Mary Pickford to San Francisco to look at a new device called "television." The purpose of the machine, Joe explained, was to "broadcast talking motion pictures into the home." The technology being developed was still in its infancy, but Joe predicted it was coming, just as talkies had come.

On February 18, 1930, again with Pickford and Fairbanks, Joe hosted the president of the United States and his wife, Mr. and Mrs. Calvin Coolidge, at a luncheon held on the UA lot, specifically the drawing room of Pickford's "bungalow."

AS ECONOMIC DOLDRUMS CONTINUED, NICK SYSTEMICALLY REWARDED Loews Inc. employees, in particular theater managers and their families, with free days at Palisades Park. Others were invited up to Saratoga Springs to drink the waters and watch the horses run. By the autumn they had a new slogan for MGM: "More Stars Than There Are in Heaven."

In December, Nick felt the Christmas spirit. On December 22, 23, and 24, after-school matinees at Loew's theaters were "at the disposal" of ten thousand underprivileged kids. The show began with an *Our Gang* short, followed by three features. Afterward, a Christmas party. Columnists proclaimed the truth could no longer be hidden: Nick Schenck was the real Santa Claus.

That same holiday season, Joe was in New York on business. Irving Berlin was in town as well, and the two had dinner, Joe picking up the tab as the songwriter was still hurting from the stock market crash. And, as we know, Christmas was not Berlin's favorite time of year.

"I hear you're still broke, Irv," Joe said, chewing on a piece of mutton.

"Sure, but how can I write a hit song when I'm upset?" Berlin asked.

"You're upset because of money worries, that's all. Your talent is as good as ever," Joe said.

Berlin agreed that was probably true.

"I have a building here in town that I picked up cheap. It nets me a thousand a week on a lease. You take over the thousand a week for a year and get down to work."

Berlin's eyes welled up with tears. "Joe, you've shown me what guts really are—and what friendship is. I'll get down to work without the money from that house."

And sure enough, Berlin's writer's block was over. He went home, sat at the piano, and began to write. "Heaven. I'm in heaven," Berlin sang. It was the beginning of "Cheek to Cheek," soon to be a Fred Astaire/Ginger Rogers classic.

CHAPTER TEN

NEW WORLD OF IRIDESCENT SPLENDOR

THE TALKIES BROUGHT NEW STARS, JUST AS BEAUTIFUL AS THOSE before, and with the gift of gab as well. On March 3, 1932, Nick paid Howard Hughes $30,000 for sexpot Jean Harlow's contract. The call from MGM dragged Harlow from the arms of Newark, N.J., bootlegger Longie Zwillman. Harlow became MGM's latest superstar, the "project" of MGM exec Paul Bern. MGM paid Harlow $1,250 per week, compared to $150 she'd been getting from Hughes.

For Nick, there was a perk hiring Harlow. She would be box-office dynamite, of course, but he also knew that Mayer couldn't stand her. "She's a slut," Mayer said. Anything that made Mayer froth was a perk. Soon thereafter, milquetoast producer Paul Bern married Harlow, befuddling the entire industry, which collectively envisioned a sexual mismatch. It was tough to picture them, you know, but . . . whatever. Love is a funny thing.

Two months later Bern was found dead with a gunshot wound to his head, officially a suicide. There was a note that implied that sexual inadequacy—"only a comedy"—was behind his despair. But who knows the truth? As usual when ghastly things occurred, Eddie Mannix got to the death scene before police. (Later, the suicide note was looked upon with skepticism. "I got a little dick, too, but I ain't killing myself over it," was the joke.)

Mayer visited Harlow after learning of Bern's death and found her in hysterics.

"I must get to Paul, he needs me!" she cried, and threatened to leap from her balcony.

Mayer, man of action, plucked her from the edge, yanked her to safety, slapped her a few times to snap her out of it, and threw her into the bedroom where a doctor injected her with a sedative. Mayer later told MGM execs that it was a good thing that Bern killed himself, as he was "a homo and impotent for women." Unexpectedly, the execs, including Thalberg, defended Bern, calling him straight as an arrow, which infuriated Mayer. Harlow was in no condition to finish *Red Dust*, so Mayer called Nick for instructions.

"Hire Tallulah Bankhead to play the role," Nick said.

That didn't work. Bankhead wanted too much money and Mayer ended up tossing her out of his office. It was a long toss as Mayer had the world's largest office—an idea he stole from Lewis Selznick—a quarter-mile long, with a desk the size of a heliport built on a platform. Those who visited him had to walk the length of the room and then look up at him.

After a few days, Harlow miraculously recovered from her grief and was able to complete the picture herself.

(Harlow herself did not have long to live. On June 7, 1937, at age twenty-six, she died of cerebral edema, brain swelling. But the overall cause was uremic poisoning, kidney failure. By the time her longtime illness was correctly diagnosed, it was too late for doctors to do anything. It would be eight years before the first kidney dialysis machine. In Hollywood, one grieving fan was Norma Jeane Baker, an eleven-year-old resident of the Los Angeles Orphans' Home.)

IT WAS AN UGLY TIME AT MGM, SO IT WAS PERHAPS FITTING THAT, simultaneous to Paul Bern's death, *Dracula* director Tod Browning was on the lot making a horror picture called *Freaks*, an ugly film trying to make a beautiful point, with a cast of real-life human oddities from the carnival. When the cast came into the commissary to eat, they were seen as so repulsive that people walked out. Allegedly, some vomited. When *Freaks* came out, audiences did the same.

CONSPIRACY THEORISTS—AND WHENEVER JEWISH POWER IS CONCERNED, there will be conspiracy theorists—pointed to a secret society known as the Mayfair Club, as proof that there was insidious communist propaganda sublimated into Hollywood pictures. In reality, the Mayfair Club, exclusive and limited to Hollywood's most beautiful and powerful people, was superficial but not insidious. The group, sometimes known as the Hollywood Four Hundred, met nine times a year in the Biltmore Hotel ballroom, and celebrated glamour, the glow of powerful men and the brightest stars in the Tinseltown firmament.

The powers behind the balls were Joe Schenck, Adolph Zukor, and Jesse Lasky—three originals from the Bowery. About the Mayfair balls, Jewish songster Eddie Cantor once said, "I marveled at this new world of iridescent splendor representing many millions, many romances, many miracles and it had all come into being through the imagination and the business brains of a former furrier (Zukor), a former druggist (Schenck), and a former cornet player (Lasky)."

The balls glittered but weren't much fun. Everybody was there to look at each other. The day after, the papers would merely print a list of who was there. Some thought that was all the Mayfair Club really was—a list. Still, everyone wanted to be on it.

NICK'S TIGHT SHIP TURNED A PROFIT DESPITE THE BLEAK TIMES. MGM was the only studio to remain in the black. Nick, by this time, was at the peak of his power. Nick's empire employed twelve thousand people, most of them on the other coast. Nick kept MGM afloat by cranking out series, comedies and dramas, using the same casts and sets, to make episodic features, as in a TV series. Three of MGM's most popular were the Andy Hardy pictures starring Mickey Rooney and Judy Garland, *The Thin Man* series with William Powell and Myrna Loy, and the Dr. Kildare pictures, with Lew Ayres and Lionel Barrymore. For every prestige picture the studio heads insisted upon, Nick made sure that he had a steady flow of income from pictures with the lowest overhead. He also padded out programs with newsreels, travelogues, and short subjects.

Thalberg still argued that artful pictures helped MGM through prestige, even if no one went to see them. But, during the hard times, his view was increasingly isolated.

"MGM does not make art pictures," Nick liked to say. "MGM makes popular pictures."

Some said that discussing artistic matters at MGM was like "talking about love in a whorehouse." Beside the point.

FOR THE SCHENCK BROTHERS, 1932 WAS ANOTHER WHIRLWIND YEAR of maneuvering, budgeting, and celebrating. On April 2, the Joe Schenck/

UA picture *Scarface* opened in New Orleans. Some were concerned that it glorified a life of crime. Joe argued that it was a constructive influence against organized crime. *Scarface* was a hit, and the controversy went away. The same day as *Scarface*'s premiere, Roscoe Arbuckle, of all people, opened a stage act at Eugene Stark's Bohemian Café on Santa Monica Boulevard. He did shtick with a singing chorus of leggy dancing girls. Went over like a lead balloon.

On June 15, Walt Disney joined UA. Headlines read, MICKEY MOUSE A PRODUCER. Mickey would be sitting behind "a mahogany desk with all of the dignity of Joseph M. Schenck, Louis B. Mayer, Jesse Lasky, or any of the big names of the motion picture industry." The move meant that Mickey Mouse cartoons would be added to shows at UA theaters, and the opening credits would refer to each cartoon as "Joseph M. Schenck presents Walt Disney's Mickey Mouse."

On July 15, Nick announced that all Loews Inc. employees who made $1,500 or more a week were having their salaries slashed by thirty-five percent. Those making less were unaffected. Times were tough, Nick said. Nick dealt with the press. He left Mayer to tell the MGM talent.

On July 26, Joe was among a slew of Hollywood celebs who took a train to the Shriner Convention in San Francisco and rode on a float in the parade. The party train had Joe enjoying himself with Buster Keaton, Wallace Beery, Edward G. Robinson, Hedda Hopper, Joan Blondell, Frankenstein monster Boris Karloff, and Victor McLaglen (the only man to fight a heavyweight boxing champion and win an Oscar). By all accounts a splendid time was had by all.

EVEN THOUGH IT TOOK FIVE DAYS TO TRAVEL CROSS-COUNTRY VIA train, Eddie Mannix made the trip (and back) once every two months to meet with Nick in person so they could discuss subjects that couldn't be securely discussed by phone. The system, of course, drove Mayer nuts. It was during Mannix's September trip westward that Eddie met future wife, twenty-six-year-old Toni Lanier.

She was a New York girl, born Camille Bernice Froomess, her dad a French immigrant who decorated department store windows in Rochester, N.Y., her mother a Catholic. Toni had seven brothers and three sisters. Changing her name to Toni Lanier, she became a Ziegfeld girl, and her most noteworthy screen appearance was in MGM's *The Great Ziegfeld* (1936). Toni became Mannix's mistress for many years. The pair didn't get married until 1951, the same year that she began her affair with TV's Superman, George Reeves.

Also on Mannix's train were Joe and Nick, who were met in Pasadena at the station by Mayer and Thalberg. The press tried to figure out what was up, so much power on one train platform, but none of the men had much to say. Joe said, "Business is up. We see a further speeding up in the near future."

Soon thereafter, Thalberg threatened to quit unless he got a big raise. He played the press, denying that he was thinking of quitting MGM so often that he received offers from the other studios. Nick headed west. At Culver City, Thalberg told Nick that it was he and not Mayer who was responsible for MGM's success and he wanted to be compensated for it. In an example of the Schencks working together, Joe stepped in and bribed Thalberg with one hundred thousand shares of Loew's Inc. stock, "selling" the shares to Thalberg at well below market price. Thalberg would stay on at MGM, but the meeting with Nick drove a wedge between Mayer and Thalberg that never healed.

If Mayer was feeling squeezed by a suddenly power-hungry Irving Thalberg, his anxieties were eased some by Thalberg's health, which continued to deteriorate. At the 1932 MGM Christmas party, Thalberg danced, drank, went home, and had a heart attack. It didn't kill him but kept him out of work for months. His wife, Norma Shearer, nursed him, and the pair went on a long cruise from San Pedro to New York through the Panama Canal, and then to Europe. According to Thalberg, he had another heart attack in Berlin, sort of an aftershock. While he was hospitalized, Thalberg had his tonsils out. (Doctors thought his sore throat and faulty heart were somehow connected.) In the meantime, Mayer took deep breaths again, but felt the void left by Thalberg's extended vacation. To fill the gap, Nick hired Mayer's son-in-law David O. Selznick, who was running RKO at the time, to come to MGM and operate an independent production unit.

One day in January 1933, Nick received his daily phone calls from Mannix and Mayer, both of whom mentioned Thalberg's cadaverous appearance. He was back from his get-well trip and he didn't look that well. Nick sensed an opportunity to "rein in" Thalberg. Nick relieved Thalberg's duties as a centralized producer, "for Thalberg's health," believing that there were plenty of producers at MGM who'd worked under Thalberg long enough to learn his tricks. He'd hire a few name producers to fill any void, and Thalberg, when and if he regained his mojo, could concentrate on "prestige pictures."

Despite the friction at the top, the MGM machine remained well oiled and, not surprisingly, well suited to deal with crisis. At 5:54 p.m. on March 10, 1933, the Newport-Inglewood fault slipped, and a magnitude 6.4 earthquake rocked Southern California, epicenter at Long Beach, where 120 people died. The fault ran under Culver City, where crews, used to the pace, went to work through the aftershocks repairing the damage. Production went on with surprisingly little delay.

JOE AND NORMA WERE STILL TECHNICALLY MARRIED, BUT SEPARATED—and Joe's life as a bachelor got off to a rollicking start. We get a fleeting glimpse of Joe's new lifestyle when the famous aviator Colonel Roscoe Turner completed the first one-day airplane flight from Mexico City to Los Angeles, 1,700 miles, in a Gilmore Lion monoplane, and with him on the plane was Joe Schenck, who had conferenced with Mexican president Rodriguez about producing a film down there, and fun-time actress Lili Damita. When exiting the cabin at the Burbank airstrip, Miss Damita was reportedly tipsy and photographed sporting the sombrero Joe bought her as a souvenir. The implication was that a couple of aviation firsts were involved here, one for the pilot, and one for his passengers who became charter members of the "mile-high club."

IN 1934 AUTHOR UPTON SINCLAIR, WHOSE "TAX-THE-RICH" POLICY caused a rocky relationship with the moguls, ran for governor of California. Although the bosses never publicly admitted it, they got together and created propaganda that would turn the public against Sinclair. They shot faked newsreels that featured "real citizens" talking in truly misleading terms about why they wouldn't vote for Sinclair.

Joe even addressed the subject with a reporter: "I'll move the studios to Florida if Sinclair is elected."

He was asked if the studios were getting together to defeat Sinclair, and Joe denied it. He did add, however, that Hollywood players who voted for Sinclair were cutting "their own throats." The campaign worked and Sinclair was defeated that November in a landslide.

California taxes and a possible move to Florida came up again two and a half years later when there was a Depression-inspired proposal in California to place a thirty-five percent income tax on state industries. Seemingly in response, Florida ratified an amendment exempting the film industry from taxes for fifteen years.

Joe, representing UA (and MGM on Nick's behalf), considered plans to move those studios to Florida to save money. Joe flew to Miami. He told reporters he was going to set up a studio in Miami. Nick told Joe to see if he could get Florida to, in addition to the tax exemption, build $10 million worth of studios which they could rent to Hollywood companies for $250,000 per year.

About the plan, Joe said, "When the public has invested its money in studios, we then have a very definite guarantee that to protect their own interests they will not permit detrimental legislation. Civic-minded contributors are most desired. We want to move to Florida if we are guaranteed security. Florida will benefit tremendously. The Hollywood companies spend a hundred and fifty million dollars a year."

The downside to moving was a) Florida was hotter and much more humid in the summer than was California, and b) pancake-flat Florida was visually less appealing, particularly when filming Westerns. Unless you were making a picture about swamps, beaches, or fruit groves, you had to travel to shoot on location or you needed to build a set.

Asked about the geography, Joe said, "Transportation is a major asset and Florida has that. And, if we must have mountains, it isn't far to the Carolinas."

When the bill to tax California industries didn't pass, all urges to move to Florida again passed—for the time being.

JEWS IN AMERICA WERE USED TO BEING EXCLUDED. SO IT HAD BEEN exciting for the moguls back during the summer of 1928, when the Agua Caliente resort opened just outside Tijuana, Mexico. The complex featured a casino, a five-hundred-room hotel, an Olympic-size pool, a health spa, a golf course, and racing tracks for thoroughbred horses and greyhounds. Best of all, everyone was welcomed. Joe loved the place, and it became his home away from home. Even before track construction was completed, Joe had invested $50,000 in the new facility. "This new track is going to be a huge success," Joe said. "I wanted to get in on the ground floor."

Once Joe Schenck got involved with Agua Caliente, pouring money into the facility and leasing land from Mexican president Abelardo Rodríguez Luján, it blossomed into a monument to gambling and fun. It was a six-hour drive from Hollywood to Agua Caliente, so it became a weekend destination.

The party never stopped, the huge bar six deep with the bold and beautiful. On Sundays, everyone sat hungover in their luxury convertibles, sun glaring off the new-fangled chrome, in the seemingly endless line to get back across the border.

Joe's increasingly deep investments in Agua Caliente served a couple of purposes. It guaranteed the resort would remain inclusive, so Jewish men could play there, and it was an effective reaction to the deep debt Joe and his friends were in because of gambling losses south of the border. It got to a point where it was cheaper just to buy the place. "Now we are losing to each other, not to outsiders," Joe said with a laugh.

Joe eventually became president of the Agua Caliente Jockey Club, and gave the place a pink adobe casino, upgrades of the tennis courts, new golf course, hot baths, and thinly disguised brothels. Joe had built an exclusive club on the clubhouse roof, and a private clubhouse dining room for meals and evening dancing. All roads leading to the track were rebuilt, a new electronic starting gate was employed, mutuel machines were in place to keep track of bets, and the stables along the backstretch wore banners and pennants bearing each stable's colors. Newspaper ads in L.A. read, "A Dreamland of Old Mexico eighteen miles below San Diego."

The grand opening of the "New" Agua Caliente was Christmas Day, 1932, offering an eighty-day meet of thoroughbred racehorses. The Christmas Day opener featured seven stakes races.

Joe took a crack at thoroughbred breeding, although without much success. He talked the other moguls into breeding as well, another way for them to gamble with one another at a high level. F. Scott Fitzgerald theorized that the moguls bought horses because of Russian history. Mounted Cossacks had abused pedestrian Jews. Owning horses made the rich men feel safe. Harry Warner had horses. So did Harry "Columbia Pictures" Cohn. Mayer was a latecomer to the breeding game but had the greatest success. Mayer would eventually get so thoroughly into his thoroughbreds that boss Nick would worry it was cutting into his MGM time. Mayer spent so much money purchasing and breeding the superior animals that his horses almost always won. They went off as prohibitive favorites. Crowds booed when they heard Mayer's name, not because he made bad pictures, but because he was a racetrack bully. When Jewish leaders went to Mayer's office in Culver City and asked him to quit the horse game, he gave them the heave-ho.

Joe's partners in the Mexican resort included Jacob Paley, the uncle of William S. Paley who founded the Columbia Broadcasting System. Another was a Mexican drug lord, name not spoken aloud. Dealing with the underworld was nothing new for Joe, who'd survived the Bowery and counted among his business acquaintances hoodlum "Handsome" Johnny Roselli. To run the meets, Joe brought in William Koch, the former New York betting commissioner. Joe promoted the track by staging vaudeville shows there—his old job, after all.

"We're putting on a show that will make Flo Ziegfeld turn green with envy!" Joe boasted.

ON APRIL 10, 1933, NICK AND JOE, HARRY WARNER, CARL LAEMMLE SR. (Universal), and Harry Cohn (Columbia), met in Hollywood and discussed surviving the Depression. They agreed that everyone must tighten their belts, budgets needed to be slashed.

Twelve days later, Nick played golf with Mayer at Hillcrest Country Club. Mayer had complained about not feeling well earlier in the day and collapsed while addressing his ball on the third tee. They carted Mayer off for a rest. Nick finished the round without him.

While "The General"—as Nick was now called—was in town, he inspected the troops, with Mayer, Thalberg, and Mannix in tow. In brief visits, Nick enjoyed Culver City, always impressed by the MGM machine: twenty highly prized directors, seventy-four writers, and 253 actors and actresses. Mayer and Thalberg had created an efficient assembly-line studio that was also a comfortable "familial" nest where creativity could flourish. Nick didn't like those people, but he liked what they did.

Nick was sure to be out west on the first Sunday in June each year, for the MGM golf tournament, where everyone from actors to crew to technicians to costumers, etc., hit the links and played for the coveted Lon Chaney Trophy.

ON JUNE 29, 1933, ROSCOE ARBUCKLE, ELEVEN YEARS AFTER THE SCANdal, suffered a heart attack at the Park Central Hotel in New York and died at age forty-six. Few hotels are as known for the people who died there as the Park Central. Along with Arbuckle, gangsters Albert Anastasia, whacked in the barber shop off the lobby, and Arnold Rothstein, shot upstairs while playing poker, died there.

At the time of his death, Arbuckle had a new wife and had been making a bit of a comeback, appearing in short talkies for Warner Brothers made in Midwood, Brooklyn.

About Arbuckle's passing, Joe wrote in an exceedingly generous statement for the press, "All who have ever known the real Roscoe Arbuckle will always treasure the memory of the great, generous heart of the man—a heart big enough to embrace in its warmth everyone who came to him for help, stranger and friend alike. And to the end he held no malice."

ON SEPTEMBER 29, 1933, PEG TALMADGE DIED IN HER SANTA MONICA home at age sixty-eight. She'd caught the flu, it developed into pneumonia, and after ten days in bed she was gone. Her daughters were there when she passed, although they may have started an epidemic or two getting there. Norma flew through a horrible storm to get to Peg's bedside. Constance was in Chicago and flew west, despite a bad case of the whooping cough. Natalie was already in L.A. but was also bedridden with the flu, so they put her in an adjoining room in Hollywood Hospital.

Peg was entombed in the Hollywood Forever cemetery. Neither Joe Schenck nor Buster Keaton showed up to say goodbye to their former mother-in-law. Gilbert Roland was a pallbearer.

One obituary noted that Peg was not easy to make laugh, which is why Charlie Chaplin enjoyed bouncing routines off her. If he could make Peg laugh, he was certain everyone else would, too.

Following Peg's death, the Talmadge girls kept an apartment in the Beverly Wilshire Hotel. Constance lived there until her death in 1973.

THE DEPRESSION BROUGHT DESPAIR AND DEATH, BUT NEVER DISCOURaged Joe Schenck from making gambles, both at the card table and in the motion picture biz. Joe Schenck always kept tabs on the talent at the other studios. He knew who worked where and when their contracts were up. So, he'd had his eye on a fellow named Darryl Francis Zanuck, who was a picture-making machine at Warner Brothers: gangsters, fedora-wearing desperados who bumped off banks with machine guns, pictures like *Little Caesar* with Edward G. Robinson and *The Public Enemy* with James Cagney. Joe and Zanuck knew each other socially but had never conducted business together.

"I didn't think we'd ever partner up," Joe recalled. "He seemed to be so much a part of Warner Brothers."

But that changed in 1933 when Zanuck had a dispute at WB and walked out in a huff. Every studio wanted him.

Zanuck later said he considered Joe Schenck to be the smartest man in Hollywood. "I didn't want to make a move until I'd consulted Joe."

The pair got together for a meeting in Joe's office in the Talmadge Apartments on Wilshire. Joe had one question: "Darryl, do have confidence in yourself?"

"Unlimited," Zanuck replied.

"In that case, let's form a new company on our own, make pictures, and release them through UA. You will be in complete charge of production, without any interference whatsoever."

The men shook hands. It was Joe's biggest gamble.

What followed that handshake looked and sounded like a Marx Brothers sketch—*party of the first part, party of the second part, everybody knows there ain't no sanity clause*—as the men decided to write up the contracts themselves without lawyers. Joe pulled out old contracts he had lying around and they plagiarized when they could. After a while they tired of writing things down and got out a pair of scissors to cut and paste pieces of contracts together until they had something that seemed to say what they wanted it to. Ragged with paper clips and Scotch tape, it was a storyboard of a contract. They were very proud of themselves when they turned the resulting mess over to a lawyer, who had the document retyped.

"They only had to change a few commas," Zanuck later bragged.

The result was Twentieth Century Pictures.

In defiance of the Sherman Antitrust Act, Nick helped finance the newly formed company. On December 1, 1933, Nick and Louis B. Mayer put up $750,000 apiece. Mayer's son-in-law William Goetz became a major partner. Joe resigned from UA, and then he and Sam Goldwyn bought all properties and assets of United Artists Corporation Limited on behalf of Twentieth Century Pictures.

Goetz had worked his way up through Consolidated Films to Fox Films to RKO to joining Joe and Darryl Zanuck at Twentieth Century. (Goetz would later become vice president of studio operations for Twentieth Century-Fox. He resigned in 1943 to form International Pictures, which soon thereafter merged with Universal to form Universal-International where Goetz oversaw production.)

Pictures had their own individual producers, but Zanuck served as supervising producer for all of them, and all major decisions needed to be run past him. He made casting decisions, watched the dailies, supervised editing, sent detailed memos to writers including strict instructions regarding character and plot. It was a dream come true for Zanuck.

Joe wanted the first Twentieth Century picture to be special, something that would be symbolic of his own life's journey. That picture turned out to be *The Bowery*, starring Wallace Beery, George Raft, Fay Wray, and Jackie Cooper, and directed by Raoul Walsh. The film depicted a gritty and realistic look at New York's Lower East Side, and immediately established Twentieth Century as a major player—not that anyone had any doubts.

The House of Rothschild followed, another hit, best remembered for being a black-and-white picture with the final sequence in Technicolor. Again, the topic was significant, depicting wealthy Jewish bankers enduring violent anti-Semitic attacks. The parallel to current events in Europe couldn't be ignored. This was the first Hollywood picture to be blatantly anti-Hitler. *Time* magazine said it out loud in their review. The picture was "shrewdly timed to touch obliquely on current Jew-baiting in Germany." (Six years later, scenes from *HOR* were included, obviously without permission, in an anti-Semitic propaganda picture out of Nazi Germany called *The Eternal Jew.*)

The House of Rothschild was Oscar-nominated for Best Picture but lost to Columbia's feel-good romp *It Happened One Night*.

Twentieth Century Pictures was thriving, but Joe was a gambler, and it would be less than two years before the company name picked up a hyphen—and all over an actress less than four feet tall.

In 1932, a composer-agent named Jay Gorney went to the picture show at the Fox Ritz on Wilshire and on his way out saw an adorable little girl dancing a jig in the lobby.

"What's your name, little girl?" Gorney asked.

"I'm four and a half and my mom taught me," she replied.

Just then, Mom stepped up. The little girl was Shirley Temple. Gorney made a phone call. Next stop, Fox studios. Shirley sang and danced for Fox exec Winnie Sheehan, and was signed on the spot.

William Fox, wiped out by the car crash and the stock market crash, had further damaged himself by reneging first on a gambling debt and then a pledged charitable contribution, rendering him persona non grata with anyone powerful enough to want to help him. When Joe bought Fox Studios out, William Fox had nothing—nothing, that is, except Shirley Temple. But when Joe met with the tiny Temple, showbiz dynamite, he instantly knew she was enough.

"Box office gold for years," Joe said with a broad grin. "Twentieth Century and Fox must merge immediately."

And Shirley Temple became the 1930s' number-one Hollywood moneymaker. Nick Schenck spent Loew's money, and some of his own, to help pay off Fox Studios's debts when the final merger took place, thus putting Fox's theaters and distribution system back in business, and Joe's studio was renamed Twentieth Century-Fox. It was a mouthful. Around town, it was just Fox.

Joe was always nice to his tiniest star, of course, but some thought he overindulged her, giving her lavish gifts and insisting she call him Uncle Joe. Once, when Shirley was feeling tired, Uncle Joe perked her up by buying her a pony. Uncle Joe also protected her from inappropriate attention—not always the case at other studios—and she grew up just fine.

BEFORE THE MERGER, ZANUCK HAD BEEN ARTISTICALLY FULFILLED BY his job at Twentieth Century, budgeting $4.5 million for twelve pictures a year, but he knew from the card games and the yacht outings that his business deal was not as lucrative as others—even though his pictures made Twentieth Century millions of dollars a year. Twentieth Century was dependent on UA for distribution, dependent on Sam Goldwyn for a studio lot, and dependent on MGM for loaned-out talent. Zanuck was making about ten percent of the net profits from each of his pictures.

After the merger, Joe sweetened Zanuck's deal. Nick jumped in to pay off William Fox's debts. Zanuck fired almost all Fox employees—except Shirley Temple. He also retained Sol Wurtzel, master at churning out B-Westerns at the Sunset-Western studio annex, a ninety-six-acre Western set on Pico Boulevard in Beverly Hills, the lot that was originally a ranch owned by silent cowboy star Tom Mix and would become the home of Twentieth Century-Fox.

It was a sad end of an era in 1934, when Nick and Joe sold their interest in Palisades Amusement Park, where they had been absentee owners for years anyway. Under new management (Jack and Irving Rosenthal, former Coney

Island concessionaires and builders of the Concy Island Cyclone, who purchased the park for $450,000), Palisades Park became a top venue for popular music concerts, during both the big band and rock and roll eras.

IN HOLLYWOOD, WITH ZANUCK RUNNING THE SHOW, JOE HAD DOWNtime, time to go fishing, play golf, and play poker, no limits. His career with starlets was apparently underway, but he still missed Norma, still technically his wife. He knew she'd never come back, nor was he sure he wanted her to.

Joe was asked if he and Norma would ever get back together, and he said, "When a marriage breaks up for any reason, it's usually done for, and it is foolish to try to patch it up if the tear is very big. A patched-up marriage is just like a patched-up automobile tire. It just isn't the same as it was originally. I don't recommend hasty divorces, but a trip to Reno is better than a lifetime of misery."

Norma had moved on from Gilbert Roland and was now involved in a full-fledged scandal in which she was accused of giving her new boyfriend, comedian George Jessel, $100,000 to divorce his wife in Reno. She denied giving Jessel the money. Jessel's ex-wife sued Norma for a million dollars claiming "alienation of affection."

Norma told an *L.A. Times* reporter, "There has been no million-dollar alienation suit and with Mr. Jessel's ability to earn ten thousand dollars a week it seems ridiculous that anyone should be asked to guarantee a paltry one-hundred-thousand-dollar property settlement. I have no intention of marrying Mr. Jessel. I am still married to Joseph M. Schenck, and I have no intention of getting a divorce. I am getting quite bored by this whole business. It is probably because Mr. Jessel and I have been so much together on the stage."

Jessel added, "Miss Talmadge's name was dragged into my divorce suit only because she was my partner in a joint vaudeville contract and I had to put the contract up as security." Jessel added that the lawyers were getting all the money anyway, and Mrs. Jessel's lawyer said, "As a gentleman, I cannot call Miss Talmadge a liar."

In April 1934, minutes after Jessel's divorce became final, Norma told Joe she needed to divorce. Joe said okay, and they got a quickie divorce in Juarez, and nine days later, Norma married Jessel. Norma had built a fantastic estate just off Benedict Canyon on Angelo Drive. The Jessels lived there until the end of their five-year marriage, at which time Norma sold it to actor Cornel Wilde. She was between husbands in 1941 when a reporter asked her about Joe Schenck.

"Joe has been my whole life. I'll always love him," she said.

Joe took the blame. "I'm through with women, emotionally anyway," he told Irving Berlin. "From now on, nothing but fun."

But the lesson didn't take, and it wasn't long before he fell into the tender trap all over again.

CHAPTER ELEVEN

MERLE OBERON

After Juarez, Joe sought a change of scenery. During the summer of 1934 he told Douglas Fairbanks that he "needed to get away, needed to forget." Fairbanks himself had recently broken up with Mary Pickford, and understood the feeling.

"Let's do London," Fairbanks said with wild eyes. "We can stay at my townhouse, Old Sock."

"I don't know . . ."

"You must come! Darryl [Zanuck] and his wife will be there. I have plenty of room. We'll have a ball!"

Joe accepted the invitation, sailed eastward, and soon learned that at bachelor Doug's London, the fog never lifted and the party never stopped. Joe, who usually didn't drink much, was having wine.

At some point a beautiful British actress named Merle Oberon arrived at Fairbanks's townhouse.

"Joe, you know Merle," Fairbanks said. "She was in *The Private Life of Henry VIII*, she played Anne Boleyn."

"I enjoyed your work," Joe said, locking eyes with this woman of extraordinary beauty. There was a *ping* in his heart. She came to the party and never left. Also ringing the doorbell, then falling in at Fairbanks's side was Sylvia Ashley, who through a former marriage had gained the title Lady Ashley. (Fairbanks and Ashley later wed.) Oberon, it seemed, was Joe's date.

One morning, at about two a.m., Doug's eyes lit up. He pointed a finger at the ceiling.

"Eureka! We should move this party to the French Riviera!"

Two travel days later, Fairbanks and Ashley, Joe and Oberon, and the Zanucks were in Cannes soaking up the sun. The paparazzi spotted Joe and the actress cozying up under a beachside umbrella and clicked their cameras. What a story. The recently divorced mogul and the exotic starlet!

Fairbanks, feeling mischievous, said, "You two should tell them you're engaged."

"But we are not in love," Oberon said.

"What difference does that make?" Fairbanks asked, the sun gleaming off his teeth. "It would be an engagement in name only."

"What do you think about it, Mr. Schenck?" Oberon said. She flapped incredible eyelashes.

"I think it's a good idea!" Joe said with his widest grin of the year. His arm slipped around Oberon's slender waist.

Joe looked up and down until he spotted a New York entertainment runner he recognized. The guy—a kid, really—was sort of hovering. Joe waved him over.

"What's your name, son? What paper you with?"

"I'm Richard Esher, Mr. Schenck. *Herald-Tribune*. Well, freelance. They pay me by the item."

"I have an item for you. Tell them it is worth two items and to pay you twice. Miss Oberon and I are engaged. No date for the wedding has been set."

"Congratulations."

"Now, we are formally requesting privacy. You and your photographer friends over there beat it, okay?"

"Yes, sir."

The whole let's-pretend-we're-engaged idea was immature, something out of a Constance Talmadge picture. It grew worse when, by the time the bird dog got the item to the *Herald-Tribune* entertainment editor, which went on the wire, which was miscopied by a boy at the *L.A. Times*, it said that Joe and Oberon were married.

But Joe didn't find out about that until the next day—and there was a whole night of pretending in between. As it turned out, the playacting was an excellent icebreaker, and things warmed quickly.

By the next morning, Joe had forgotten—a little bit, anyway—that none of this was real. He was being a swinging jet-setter and was careless in a myriad of ways.

The next morning, the Zanucks teased Joe and Oberon. When's the wedding? Tee-hee-hee.

Joe tugged Oberon to a private spot and held her close. "What's wrong with becoming really engaged?" he asked.

"Nothing at all," she purred. "I'd love to."

Joe had tiny red hearts flying off his eyeballs and giddily gave Oberon an eighteen-karat ring—and a United Artists contract. She played an innocent starlet act for Joe's sake, but in reality, Oberon had a ponce-like manager who introduced her to powerful men in hopes of easing her road to success. Of these men, Joe was the latest. Somehow the manager had gotten to Fairbanks and had him set it up. Joe's friends hoped he wasn't making another mistake. It would be one thing if Joe was just having fun, but he went sappy around women he liked, lost his mind. His love for Merle Oberon was so, so real.

But as it turned out not much about Merle Oberon was real. Like Hollywood itself, she was an illusion. Playing Joe Schenck's fiancée was just like playing in *Wuthering Heights*. Same skill set. She was Estelle Merle O'Brien Thompson, born 1911 in Mumbai. When she was born her grandmother Charlotte Selby was twenty-six years old. (Merle was raised thinking her grandmother was her mother and that her actual mother, Constance, twelve at the time of Merle's birth, was her older sister.) She lived in India until she was seventeen. She attended La Martiniere College, where she studied French, Latin, and Hindustani, and appeared in amateur theatricals. Though her mother was from India and Dad was part Sri Lankan, she denied having Asian blood.

"I am French-Irish," she always said.

In her late teens, Merle—known by the nickname "Queenie"—worked rich men at Indian society parties. She scored young Englishmen, hoping one might be her ticket out. At nineteen she arrived in London and took a job as a hostess at the Café de Paris. While she was performing her duties one day, the British film director Alexander Korda and his portly wife came in. Mrs. Korda pointed at Queenie.

"She has the most striking face I've ever seen," she said.

Alexander agreed, gave her a contract for some extra work, and changed her name from Queenie Thompson to Merle Oberon. Soon thereafter, Korda became an independent film producer and cast Oberon as Anne Boleyn.

Oberon's career was greatly boosted during her time as Joe Schenck's whatever, as she became for the first time a star in the U.S. and was nominated in 1936 for a Best Actress Oscar for her role as Kitty Vane in *The Dark Angel*.

On October 20, 1934, Joe arrived in England aboard the liner *Majestic*. Reporters meeting him at the dock asked if he were there to marry Oberon, who was filming *The Scarlet Pimpernel*.

"There's no hurry. We're both young," the fifty-seven-year-old Joe said cheerfully.

But then it was over. Oberon moved on. Joe, confused, tried to get in touch for an explanation, but Oberon ignored him. For the remainder of 1934, Oberon feigned annoyance as she fielded press questions about her and Joe. She seemed downright exasperated as she told them she'd rather discuss her work as an actress.

But then she talked about Joe: "I broke with Joe because I felt marriage would interfere with my career," she said. Joe was left looking foolish. And as far as we know Joe never again had a romantic relationship. He had a lot of fun, but he kept his wits about him. "Just fun," he said to Irving Berlin again. This time he kept his word.

Oberon coolly returned to Alexander Korda. They married in 1939 and, when he was knighted, she became Lady Korda. From love child to titled. Three years later, Oberon's exotic beauty was marred, mildly, by an automobile accident that left her with scars. She subsequently had an allergic reaction to cosmetics that further marked her skin. Although her film career continued, a special camera called "The Obie" had to be used when filming her.

Oberon was no longer talking to him, but Joe remained on good terms with his ex-wife. Joe bought Norma the Villa Riviera Hotel, located on a beachfront bluff in Long Beach, for her to manage. Give her something to do. It was a twenty-story Gothic-revival/Chateauesque high-rise. Completed in 1929, the Villa Riviera's design won awards. It was the second-tallest building in Southern California, second only to L.A. City Hall. Managing it was a complicated task, and far beyond Norma's capabilities. She forgot to pay the bills and controlled the hotel for less than a year.

JOE'S ROMANTIC WOES SADDENED NICK, WHO HAD FOUND DOMESTIC bliss. When it came to work, the sympathy went in the other direction. At MGM, Nick continued to experience nothing but aggravation. Nick would've loved to clean house and replace the top brass in Culver City, but they were too damn good at what they did. What they needed was a shaking up, so during the summer of 1934, Nick summoned Louis B. Mayer to come east for a meeting. The grim topic was Irving Thalberg's future with the company—or lack thereof. Nick had talked to Thalberg's doctors and knew how fragile he was. The only person who didn't seem to know was Thalberg himself, burning the candle at both ends, approaching his job like a dictator. For Nick, Thalberg's primary fault was his insistence on making art rather than money. *Would it kill him if I fired him?* Nick asked himself. While he was wondering, he pictured LB's face if he thought he was about to have the rug pulled out from under him. So, Nick gave Mayer an intimidating come hither and Mayer came.

Mayer traveled with his lawyer Edwin Loeb and fixer Howard Strickling. They stayed at Nick's house during the visit, a rare invasion of Hollywood people in the private Nick Schenck nest. The visit didn't go well. While Mayer and Nick plotted to replace Thalberg, Mayer got wind that Nick was plotting to replace him with David O. Selznick. There was a heated argument at the meeting. Neither Mayer nor Thalberg were axed, but Mayer returned to Culver City grinding his teeth. Selznick, who had married Irene Mayer and was his son-in-law, did not take Mayer's job, but continued on as a successful MGM producer. Nick established himself as still firmly in charge.

The following summer Selznick wrote Nick a letter in which he asked Nick to accept his resignation from MGM. "I must have my fling or regret it all my life," Selznick wrote. He went on about what a difficult decision it was, as Nick had given him more money and freedom than he could find in any other opportunity. He told Nick that he would finish the two pictures he was in the middle of, *Anna Karenina* and *A Tale of Two Cities*.

Nick wrote back, clearly irritated, reminding Selznick of all MGM had done for him: "Estimate your position in the film business today," Nick wrote. "You are a very well-known producer, highly considered, and doubtlessly high paid and sought after. When you came with MGM you were not so well known, and a doubtful quantity with sufficient promise to make us take a gamble. We consented to contract clauses with you which were designed solely to increase your prestige. We not only lived up to those contracts, but the spirit of the publicity department and your associate executives was such that you got far more than you bargained for."

Selznick did go on to become an independent producer, making *A Star Is Born* in 1937. But in the long run he saved his best for MGM in 1939 with *Gone with the Wind*. Nick still thought of him as the smart kid who told his "Pop" that getting in Nick's way was bad business.

IN SEPTEMBER 1936, IRVING THALBERG'S HEALTH, PRECARIOUS AT BEST, went suddenly south. The prince was still at his desk—but off his game. He passed on *Gone with the Wind* saying, "people don't like Civil War pictures." Then he missed the MGM picnic suffering from pneumonia, took to his bed, slipped into a coma, and died.

Strickling issued a press release, which contained nary a word of truth. Thalberg, the release said, died surrounded by friends, reciting the Lord's Prayer (a Christian prayer!), while bravely telling Norma Shearer, "Don't let the kids forget me!"

His funeral was at the Wilshire Boulevard Temple and thousands of starstruck fans clogged the street out front, hoping to get a glimpse of shiny mourners.

Nick traveled cross-country to be there. On his way out of the temple, Nick talked to a reporter: "I came to California to pay my respects to his memory and to give my sympathy. This has been done and I am leaving for New York."

"What's the future for MGM, Nick?" the scribe queried.

"MGM is an organization managed by and composed of those who honored and respected Irving Thalberg, and his unfinished work will be left for completion in those capable and willing hands," Nick replied.

Nick decided not to replace Thalberg, leaving Mayer with complete artistic control over MGM. Nick still held the purse strings, of course, but Hollywood's biggest studio would now reflect Mayer's personality alone. Bring on the dancing girls and small-town hijinks. Lose the powdered wigs.

When the ceremony was over, Joe and Norma, together one last time, and Mayer accompanied Thalberg's coffin to Forest Lawn to observe the burial.

CHAPTER TWELVE

HOT TODDY AND OTHER TRAGEDIES

JOE SCHENCK MET ROLAND WEST BACK IN VAUDEVILLE, A TEEN-ager who acted in bits and went on to write and direct them. Joe booked him on the Loew's circuit. He and Joe made the move to flickers at the same time, and West, now a filmmaker, became one of Joe's first California friends.

West pretty much invented the haunted-house picture, and many of the tropes we associate with the genre—paintings with moving eyes, haunted suits of armor, secret passageways, etc.—come from West's silents. Rather than focus on his work, the press became obsessed with West's refusal to wear a necktie. Men *always* wore a tie. They wore a tie to breakfast. West's open collar made it into the lead of every story about him, as if it were a sign of a faulty character.

Joe's business relationship with West dated to the dawn of Joe's life in pictures. . . .

"Tell me, Roland, do you believe that moving pictures have a future?" Joe asked.

"I do, Joe. Pictures will keep getting better, finding new ways to entertain."

Joe liked that answer. "Would you be willing to direct a picture for me?"

"Sure," West said with a bit of a shrug. How hard could it be?

"All right. I read a story in a magazine. I have rented space in a studio on Forty-Eighth Street. I'll work on the story with you after I buy it, and I figure we should be able to make the whole picture for twenty thousand dollars."

"Who are we going to put in the picture?"

"I've got a big name: Josie Collins." She was a well-known stage actress. "She's willing to make it."

Less than two weeks later the picture was done. It was called *Lost Souls*, a fifty-minute melodrama about a beautiful Italian immigrant forced into white slavery. The subject matter was such that finding a distributor was an issue, with William Fox coming to the picture's rescue with a distribution offer in 1916, but only after the title was changed to *A Woman's Honor*. (This favor may be the reason Joe was willing to save Fox decades later when Fox was down and out—well, that and Shirley Temple.) West's first picture was one of the first to be promoted primarily on its star rather than its story.

The next year, when Joe set up the production company for Norma Talmadge pictures, West became its general manager. He directed one Norma Talmadge picture, *De Luxe Annie* (1918) in which Norma played sort of a Jekyll/Hyde type character. West's films were atmospheric, spooky, all shadows and contrast, using lighting techniques that future directors would evolve into post-WWII noir. Among West's best remembered pictures were *The Monster* (1925) with Lon Chaney, *The Bat* (1926), and *The Bat Whispers* (1930). His 1929 drama, *Alibi*, received an Academy Best Picture nomination. *The Bat Whispers* was the first-ever horror talkie—a remake of his own silent classic, now utilizing the sounds of creaky doors, relentless thunderstorms, and screams in the night. The cinematographers built a system of steel cables and tracks enabling the camera to move in a first-person POV from room to room. A dolly was built which allowed an eighteen-foot zoom in a fraction of a second. Replicas of famous paintings were made to decorate the haunted house set. The film was shot both in the standard 35mm format and in 65mm, an early widescreen format called Magnifilm. To test the new process, a thirty-eight-foot screen was built on a UA lot, and the results were positive.

Joe, of course, footed the bill, telling a reporter, "Wide-film shown on giant screens is the answer to a public demand for progress in motion picture entertainment."

West added, "The new process enhances the stereoscopic effect so there is less distortion for those sitting at the extreme sides of the theater."

It all made for great talk, but theater owners didn't want to reequip their theaters again. They just got set up for sound and were not in the mood for any more innovations, thank you. The 65mm version of *The Bat Whispers* went unwatched until 1988 when there were screenings at UCLA and back east at MOMA in New York. The 35mm version was popular, but *The Bat Whispers* had been so expensive to make that it barely recouped its costs.

West's career was on the downslide after that, but he and Joe remained close friends and confidants. When Joe moved money around in hopes of getting around annoying tax laws, West was his accomplice.

In 1935, West met comedienne and actress Thelma Todd—a beautiful strawberry-blond former schoolteacher and model from Lawrence, Massachusetts—on a yacht heading for Catalina. Instant crush for the married man. Todd had appeared in about 120 pictures since 1926, originally for Hal Roach where she was teamed with Zasu Pitts, Patsy Kelly, and Laurel and Hardy. West divorced to make room in his life for the actress nicknamed "Hot Toddy."

West and Todd became lovers and business partners, going in together on a nightclub restaurant on Pacific Coast Highway (a.k.a. Ocean Highway, a.k.a. Roosevelt Highway) in the Pacific Palisades. The building was a three-tiered California Mediterranean, Spanish Colonial Revival with Moorish influences. The restaurant was in West's old house and was called Thelma Todd's Sidewalk Café. She lived in an ocean-view apartment on the top floor, on the same level as an exclusive Hollywood club called Joya.

On December 16, 1935, Todd was found dead—battered, bruised, and asphyxiated from carbon monoxide—in her car in a garage belonging to Roland West's ex-wife Jewel Carmen, who lived nearby. Her death scene was just outside her café.

She wasn't just the mistress of one of Joe Schenck's earliest friends in Hollywood, but also of *capo dei capi* Charles "Lucky" Luciano—so, there were all kinds of reasons to suspect foul play. Studio fixers—probably including Eddie Mannix moonlighting for his boss's brother—swarmed the scene, and prepared it like art directors for an audience of keen police investigators. In some cases, evidence couldn't be removed and needed to be confused.

A grand jury investigated Todd's death and, predictably, discovered conflicting evidence. Spots of blood were found inside the car and on Todd's mouth. It appeared she'd been knocked out and then put inside the car. Her blood alcohol level was .13, which meant she was "stupefied."

The theory that she'd entered the car other than under her own power was supported by the fact that there was no dirt on her high-heeled shoes, as there would have been if she'd walked to the garage and gotten into the car herself. An unidentified and smudged handprint was found on the driver's side door of the death car.

Witnesses heard by the grand jury said that Todd had been depressed and spoke of ending it all. She had tax troubles and was heading toward bankruptcy, witnesses testified. The grand jury ruled suicide.

Regarding those statements under oath that Todd was depressed, friends said poppycock. Her career was going great. She'd just wrapped one picture and was eager to start another. When her contract with Hal Roach was up, she would be signed by Joe Schenck at Fox. She was busy supervising renovations on her café's top-floor lounge.

Then she was dead.

Then came the whispers.

Had the death been ruled homicide, West would have been a prime suspect, the love interest. Years later, when it came out that he was working with Joe Schenck to dupe Uncle Sam when Todd died, West's reputation took another hit.

The most popular rumor regarding West was that he killed Todd on his yacht, the *Joyita*, and planted her body in the car. There was no evidence to support this, but the suggestion was enough to end West's career, which was moribund anyway.

West and his wife divorced, and he went into seclusion. In 1950 he suffered a stroke and a nervous breakdown. According to his friend Chester Morris, West, while delirious on his deathbed in 1952, confessed to killing Todd. But no one believed him. Todd's biographer Andy Edmonds writes that whoever killed "Hot Toddy" was also able to arrange a complex cover-up, way beyond West's capabilities.

IN MAY 1937, THERE OCCURRED HOLLYWOOD'S ALL-TIME MOST REVOLTing scandal, one the fixers could contain but never conceal. It is astounding to a civilized mind that it could have happened, that these men who ran large companies providing wholesome entertainment for the masses could be so naïve and indifferent and sexist.

Louis B. Mayer, a stickler for squeaky clean pictures, held a convention of company salesmen in Culver City. A slew of showgirls, like a hallucinatory Busby Berkeley number, greeted the boozed-up salesmen at Union Station in L.A., with Louis B. himself there with a toothy grin and a statement that would come back to haunt him.

Referring to the showgirls in their scanty costumes, Mayer proclaimed,

"That's to show you how we feel about you, and the kind of good time that is ahead of you. . . . Anything you want."

The "convention" was scheduled to last for five days. And things remained fairly civilized for the first four. On the fifth, Hal Roach invited the men to come to a "stag party" at his ranch.

"It'll be a party where men are men!" Roach added.

Awaiting the three hundred partying men at the ranch were five hundred cases of Scotch and champagne. The 120 women invited to the party were not informed of Roach's comments. In fact, they were told it was a "casting call." The surprised starlets arrived ready to audition and ended up spending their time fleeing wolves. Not all were quick enough.

One witness, presumably a waiter, later told a grand jury that this was "the worst, the wildest, and the rottenest I have ever seen."

Among those who didn't run fast enough was a twenty-year-old named Patricia Douglas, referred to as "Girl 27" on the call sheet for the event. She was under contract with MGM, but up until that time had appeared only as a chorus girl in musical numbers.

A salesman from Chicago named David Ross, a pudgy thirty-six-year-old "Catholic bachelor," and a friend grabbed Douglas, pinched her nose to force her mouth open, and poured Scotch into her.

Ross raped Douglas in the back seat of a car. According to later testimony from a parking lot attendant who observed the scene, Ross slapped Douglas when she lost consciousness, saying, "Cooperate! I want you awake!"

After a time, Ross fled, and Douglas fell to the parking lot with her eyes swollen shut. She was taken to Culver City Community Hospital, basically MGM General, where she was douched and released. Hal Roach Studios sent her a check for $7.50 for her day's work.

Douglas was supposed to keep her mouth shut but instead took her story to the L.A. district attorney's office. She had no luck there as they served at the pleasure of Louis B. Mayer. She had better luck with the Hearst newspapers, which broke the "studio orgy" story, but still the article didn't mention MGM by name but printed Douglas's name, picture, and home address.

When Douglas insisted on a prosecution, Mayer's personal lawyer took over the defense. Witnesses were paid off (including several party girls and the parking-lot attendant who recanted his story and was in return given a job for life).

Douglas tried a civil suit, claiming that Hal Roach, Eddie Mannix, and others had "conspired to defile, debauch, and seduce me for the immoral and sensual gratification of male guests."

When the suit was dismissed by a judge, Douglas took her case to a federal court, claiming that the men who conspired to rape her had violated her civil rights. None of it worked. Hollywood was too powerful.

A campaign commenced to ruin Douglas's reputation. An effort was made to get a physician to testify that he'd treated Douglas for a venereal disease. Eventually Douglas's lawyer stopped showing up in court, apparently also paid off.

Douglas disappeared from public view, and—although Eddie Mannix once claimed that he'd had her killed, his idea of a joke—she lived until 2003, but the crimes against her went unpunished.

Interviewed shortly before her death by a documentary filmmaker, Douglas said she's been a virgin when she was raped and was never able to enjoy sex.

(Patricia Douglas's futile attempt at justice became the subject of a documentary film by David Stenn in 2007 entitled *Girl 27.*)

This was the trashy behavior that made Nick Schenck so happy he was on the opposite coast.

IN 1937, EDDIE MANNIX'S WIFE BERNICE DIED IN A CAR CRASH. MANNIX was violent with women. He once broke Bernice's neck. A mistress, a Ziegfeld Girl named Mary Nolan, endured fifteen abdominal surgeries after Mannix beat her up. Now Bernice was dead, and cops found a second set of tire tracks at the scene indicating her car had been violently sideswiped, but there was no follow-up investigation. Bernice's death freed up Mannix to spend more time with Ziegfeld Girl Toni Lanier, the so-called "Girl with the Million Dollar Legs." Toni would become the second Mrs. Mannix, but only after wasting her best years as his sideline gal.

CHAPTER THIRTEEN

HOLLYWOOD VS. NAZIS

DURING THE EARLY 1930S, THE MOGULS WERE AWARE OF THE NAZI menace in Europe, but hesitant to react. There was money to be made in Germany, and they didn't want to turn off that cash faucet until necessary. (Nick wouldn't react to the war until June 1940 when he shut down production of a film shooting in Denham, England, in anticipation of a Nazi invasion of Great Britain, one that thankfully never came. And, of course, Pearl Harbor changed everything, and Hollywood's wartime films couldn't have portrayed Nazis as more evil, or the Allies as more glorious and courageous.)

BY 1937, MUSSOLINI HAD EXERCISED SEVERE SANCTIONS ON ALL AMERican pictures. To address the situation, Nick summoned his brother Joe, Louis B. Mayer, and Howard Strickling to come east for a sit-down. Mayer spent a week in Great Neck, staying with Nick and Pansy, before he boarded the *Rex*, and sailed the stormy Atlantic, a legendarily rough crossing. He sailed to Naples, and then trained to Rome where he met with Vittorio Mussolini, son of the dictator, who explained that the sanctions on U.S. pictures were there not so much to hurt Hollywood, but to promote Italy's own filmmaking industry. The fascists had also put a cap on how much money they could spend annually on film rental from the Hollywood studios. Mayer's visit was ineffective, but the cause raged on, eventually solved when the U.S. State Department stepped in. In exchange for the elimination of sanctions and a currency limit, MGM would release five Italian films.

On the other side of the coin, Hitler wanted nothing more in America than to control Hollywood, the world's number-one propaganda machine. Hollywood control, Hitler figured, could lead to global control. And it was run by Jews, so Hitler considered it a soft target. He would need allies in the region, and he knew where to look: L.A.'s old money, the oil millionaires who were there before the first picture makers came west. L.A.'s oil wells clustered most dramatically in two spots: just south of downtown and around La Brea and Wilshire. People with modest homes drilled for oil in their backyards. If you lived in L.A. during the 1930s, there were constant reminders of this, oil fields with dozens of genuflecting derricks pumped new money to put on top of the old for the lucky landowners. That oil money was purely gentile.

The Hollywood set—disproportionately young and beautiful, with their sunglasses and hangovers—lived in Beaux Arts mansions off Wilshire Boulevard, only a few closeted fascists among them. They made left-leaning pictures, explored themselves, coupled and tripled regardless of gender, drank, and took drugs. And those were just the ones who were successful. Vulgar wannabes were everywhere, gorgeous and vacant, pouring into L.A. at a rate of three thousand per year.

The oil millionaires weren't the only Angelinos who didn't think Hitler was so bad. The Ku Klux Klan and organized crime were active and powerful. They had among their ranks top cops from both LAPD and L.A. County Sheriff's Department.

There was the vein for Hitler to tap into, so he sent scouts. Soon after their arrival, a Jewish attorney named Leon Lawrence Lewis put together a squad of spies to combat the California Nazi menace. Lewis was in touch with the foreign press and knew that Hitler was encouraging Germans in America to form "active cells." Lewis's spies learned that the Nazis were thinking big. They'd had secret meetings in which they discussed lynching twenty top Hollywood stars and moguls—an all-Jewish roster including Joe Schenck, Sam Goldwyn, Louis B. Mayer, Al Jolson, Eddie Cantor, and Charlie Chaplin—and leaving the bodies hanging in public places to maximize the terror. (Chaplin, though widely perceived to be, was not actually Jewish. He never denied being Jewish, however, as he felt it would play "into the hands of anti-Semitism.")

As Hitler eyed L.A. hungrily, he couldn't conceive of just how new and *without tradition* the city was. When the Nazis arrived, fully half of L.A.'s residents had been in the city for less than five years. There was no "German neighborhood" as in other cities. Recruiting would require publishing. Pamphlets were printed, recruiting meetings held.

Lewis tried telling the LAPD about the plotted espionage and didn't get the response he'd hoped for. The policemen said that Lewis was only interested because he was Jewish and that Jews had made it hard for Germans to compete economically, that the actions of Germany seemed like they were all for the good. They were sure that the Nazis in America would only do good as well.

Lewis left the LAPD encounter horrified. Desperate to find the good guys, he tried the U.S. government. Surely, it would be interested in what amounted to a plot to overthrow it. He met with Joseph Dunn, then the Southern California chief of the Justice Department's Secret Service. Dunn didn't criticize Jews the way the L.A. cops had, but he didn't help, either.

Lewis realized that to save L.A. from the Nazi threat, he would have to do it himself. Still, he'd need backing. He took his case to Tinseltown, where he knew he'd find a few sympathetic ears and perhaps a deep pocket or two.

He held a secret meeting at the kosher dining room of the Hillcrest Country Club on Pico Boulevard—also the golf course where the Three Stooges had filmed *Three Little Beers* in 1935. Hollywood bigs like Joe Schenck, Sam Goldwyn, Louis B. Mayer, Al Jolson, and the Marx Brothers were Hillcrest members. Still, to have studio moguls there all at once brought attention. Nobody'd seen this many limos since the last big premiere at the Chinese.

Joe sat at the table with Louis B. Mayer, Ernst Lubitsch, Jack Warner, entertainment attorney Mendel Silberberg, and a still-alive Irving Thalberg. Lewis started talking Nazis, and the men paid attention. Lewis told them he wanted to "create a war chest" for his already-trained-and-in-place spies within the California Nazi scene. Thalberg volunteered to help with the fundraising. He'd been squeezing money out of people for years and supposed he could do it to fight Nazis.

"I had a fucking heart attack in Bad Nauheim last year," Thalberg told the others. "I have witnessed the Nazi repression." Then he volunteered to be the liaison between Lewis and the studio heads.

Louis B. Mayer said he was willing to organize "money and intelligent direction" to the anti-Nazi cause.

"Me too," Joe said.

Warner and RKO were in.

They formed a committee that battled L.A. Nazis and transformed over time into the Community Relations Committee, representing the interests of rich L.A. Jews in the political arena.

The studios kicked over with money—MGM, Paramount, Warner Brothers, Universal, RKO, Twentieth Century-Fox, UA, and Columbia. They acted in secret at first but, after the Nazis closed down Hollywood distributing offices inside Germany, the moguls no longer had a reason to play nice. The movement to stomp Hitler's agents went full bore. In exchange for the money, Lewis's clandestine army helped keep Nazi spies out of Hollywood.

The plan that led to the eventual Nazi defeat was a strike at what Lewis perceived to be the Nazis' weakest point, the fact that the three leaders in L.A. all seemed to be self-centered egoists who saw each other as competition rather than as allies. Now, in addition to gathering intelligence, Lewis's spies were to carefully spread disinformation, gossipy items that would sew trouble into the Nazi hierarchy. Lewis's crew, many of them women, went "behind enemy lines," sparked dissension among the Nazi leaders, and then poured gasoline on it. As trust in leadership rusted away, operations broke down in the planning stage and infiltration of Hollywood never happened. Even after Pearl Harbor, Lewis's efforts came in handy. When the U.S. government was looking to keep Nazi sympathizers out of defense jobs, Lewis had a list that made the job easy.

In 1936, the moguls formed an organization called the Hollywood Anti-Nazi League. It was easy to pick out the anti-Semites in power because they condemned the HANL, calling it a "communist" organization. In 1937, acclaimed Nazi filmmaker Leni Riefenstahl came to Hollywood and received the iciest of all shoulders.

In 1938, Australian actress Mary Maguire, just finished with a brief and tepid run at Warner Brothers, jumped into Joe Schenck's lap. She told him she was the daughter of a man who, after playing Australian football and boxing, struck it rich breeding thoroughbreds.

Joe made a couple of statements to the effect of "I believe in Miss Maguire's career," which indicated carnality, but once Joe decided he didn't want her at Fox, after one picture, she moved on. We mention this interlude here because, at the time of the assumed affair with Joe, Mary was engaged to a Nazi. Was she a spy trying to get inside the Hollywood machine from the top? If so, it didn't work.

"My fiancé and I never talk politics," Maguire said. "How could I work in Hollywood if I were a Nazi?" she asked.

Moot point. Hollywood never hired her again.

IN 1939, NICK AND LOEW'S INC. MADE A FULL-FLEDGED ANTI-NAZI picture. They purchased the rights to Ethel Vance's novel *Escape*. Vance was the *nom de plume* of Grace Zaring Stone, incognito because her daughter was in Germany. The film told the story of a young man searching for his mother, who'd been taken away by the Nazis. Nick had trouble finding Jewish cast and crew as they were fearful of Nazi reprisals. *Escape* came out in 1940, starring Robert Taylor and Norma Shearer, directed by Mervyn LeRoy, with a screenplay by Arch Oboler and Marguerite Roberts.

The first Hollywood product to directly lampoon Hitler was *You Nazty Spy!*, a Columbia short starring the Three Stooges, with Moe Howard playing the fuehrer. A few months later, Chaplin's Hitler spoof in *The Great Dictator* (a UA picture) drew more attention, but Moe's was better.

At Fox, as war approached, Darryl Zanuck wanted to make a picture about religious intolerance called *Brigham Young*. Joe didn't like the idea, saying, "The European war is going from bad to worse. By the time your picture is done, the intolerance of Brigham Young's day will seem pleasant compared to Nazi brutality."

The picture was made, but Joe had been right. It wasn't the big hit that Zanuck thought it would be. When telling the story Zanuck always added that Joe never said, "I told you so." He wasn't that kind of guy.

NOT EVERYONE IN HOLLYWOOD WAS ANTI-NAZI. THERE WERE A FEW "isolationists." In 1940, Hitler sent Charles, Duke of Saxe-Coburg-Gotha, who was both an SS general and a cousin of the Duke of Windsor, to L.A. to assess how much Hollywood juice Hitler had. On April 5, 1940, German consul to the U.S. Georg Gyssling held a secret party for the duke in a bungalow of the Beverly Hills Hotel. We only know about it because the guest list was seized by U.S. Army Intelligence. Notable attendees were Walt Disney, L.A. County Sheriff Eugene W. Biscailuz, Gary Cooper, Marion Davies, Mr. and Mrs. William Randolph Hearst (which meant Hearst was there with both his wife and his mistress), Will Hays, and USC president Dr. Rufus von Kleinsmid. Details of the meeting are unknown. It was held without a press leak. Scary stuff, but a movement eventually silenced by the attack on Pearl Harbor, at which point all Hollywood studios went gung-ho for the U.S. war effort. Those who'd previously leaned Nazi now kept their mouths shut.

And so, MGM and Fox (and the other non-Schenck studios) became all about patriotism and morale, the brave boys over there and the stalwart women back home.

CHAPTER FOURTEEN

MGM'S GREATEST YEAR AND LEGAL WOES

In 1939, MGM produced what are arguably its two greatest achievements, *Gone with the Wind* and *The Wizard of Oz*, both credited as directed by Victor Fleming (although multiple directors worked on both). These productions, groundbreaking both in subject matter and in technological achievement, had problems making it to the screen, and there were several tough decisions for Nick to make along the way.

Oz overcame a range of production difficulties, including a delay-inducing use of a three-strip Technicolor process. Buddy Ebsen, the original Tin Man, had an allergic reaction to his silver makeup. Wicked Witch Margaret Hamilton was severely burned by a special effect gone wrong as she tried to magically disappear from Munchkinland. She needed three months to heal before she could continue. Various attempts were made to make Judy Garland appear younger, blond wig (rejected), heavy makeup (rejected), flattened breasts (kept). Garland popped pills to battle fatigue. One scene that took forever to shoot was the Cowardly Lion's entrance, which caused Garland to Benzedrine giggle. Director Fleming reportedly slapped her to get her to stop ruining takes, which worked, but left the set on edge. Later he told the crew he was ashamed of himself and invited Garland to slap him back. She kissed him instead and the show went on. *Oz* premiered on August 25, 1939.

Gone with the Wind had spent a frustrating two years in pre-production. Producer David O. Selznick was determined that Clark Gable play the lead, and there were delays waiting for him to become available. The search for the female lead was the stuff of legend, with 1,400 actresses auditioning. George Cukor was the original director but was fired a few weeks into shooting—he disagreed with Selznick on both the script and the pace of shooting—and replaced with Fleming, who himself failed to finish the picture due to "exhaustion," though some called it a nervous breakdown. The picture was finished by director Sam Wood. In reality, it was Selznick's baby.

For the wonderful readers who weren't around in the 1930s, a bit about Selznick. Long before powerhouse producers such as Steven Spielberg or James Cameron were thrilling audiences with spectacles such as *Jaws* and *Avatar*, Selznick wrote the playbook on hands-on film production. He was directly involved with every aspect of *Gone with the Wind* and the day it premiered was a statewide holiday in Georgia. Decades before people would see *Tim Burton's A Nightmare Before Christmas*, even though it was directed by Henry Selick, *GWTW* was very much and will always be *David O. Selznick's Gone with the Wind*.

Despite the fact that Nick and Mayer agreed most of the time, they rubbed each other wrong and saw each other as very different people. One difference, apparently, was the size of their bladders. Within days of the completion of principal photography, *GWTW* was screened for Nick and Pansy, who watched it straight through. Afterward, Nick proclaimed it "the greatest picture ever made." Out west, Mayer needed multiple breaks during his screening to visit the rest room and complained about the length. The final version was three hours and forty-two minutes long but did come with an intermission.

GWTW was released on December 15, 1939. It won eight Oscars—but not for its male lead, Clark Gable.

Whereas *Oz* has remained a children's favorite, *GWTW*, though still awesome in many ways, hasn't aged as well. To some it registers as sinister today with its mythical view of the plantation South and the Civil War. Even the slaves are happy! Only the white cast members were invited to the premiere. It cannot be televised today without a disclaimer for offensive content. Despite controversies, the picture as of 2023 had globally grossed, adjusted for inflation, $3.44 *billion*.

MGM's biggest year resulted in an almost unthinkable boost in Nick's net worth. A list came out in 1940, the top ten richest men in America. Nick was number eight, the only Jew on the list. He winced when he saw it. Now, he knew, he had a target on his back. Sure enough, the U.S. Treasury Department saw the list, and went to work. Eventually, they narrowed their investigation on Joe rather than Nick. While Nick hid behind clever accountants, Joe's failure to pay his taxes was more blatant.

AS MGM PEAKED, FOX CRANKED OUT MORE THAN FIFTY FEATURES IN 1939, most modestly budgeted, including multiple low-budget entries in popular series such as Charlie Chan, Mr. Moto, and Cisco Kid. Two Shirley Temple pictures made the most money. The year's prestige picture at Fox was *Young Mr. Lincoln* with young Henry Fonda.

Joe spent much of the year investing in real-estate development. His biggest project was the construction of a luxury two-hundred-room hotel north of San Bernardino. It was called the Arrowhead Springs Hotel. The hotel was built on the site of a major fire that had destroyed the Village Inn and the Arrowhead Lodge. Joe was part of a purchasing syndicate that also included Zanuck and Constance Bennett. It came with a dozen luxury bungalows, tennis courts, and a riding stable. (In 1949, the hotel and its environs were purchased by Conrad Hilton for $2 million.)

Labor issues occupied Joe that summer. As chairman of a film producers negotiating committee, Joe announced a tentative agreement had been reached with the International Association of Theatrical Stage Employees for a five-year closed-shop contract covering all crafts under IATSE jurisdiction. (This union was different from the rest, as we'll learn.)

JOE HAD BEEN INVOLVED IN SERIOUS CHARITY WORK FOR YEARS. IN 1937 and '38, Joe headed the motion picture branch of the Los Angeles Community Chest. He raised $396,000 in 1937, and $365,000 in 1938, breaking the previous record by more than $100,000. This got the attention of First Lady Eleanor Roosevelt, who told FDR that Joe was a "party fellow" and knew how to raise money. That got Joe the job of planning FDR's birthday balls, the proceeds for which went to the National Foundation for Infantile Paralysis. One day the president summoned Joe to Warm Springs, Georgia, where FDR believed the baths were good for his polio. Arriving, Joe led by telling the president that he'd won $25,000 betting on the election. FDR laughed.

"I have an idea," FDR said. The idea was the March of Dimes and they discussed it mostly in FDR's personal car, which he drove without his legs using a jerry-rigged contraption. The men drove country roads looking at the Georgia red clay, with another vehicle filled with Secret Service agents, looking for all the world like Keystone Kops, determined to keep the president from losing them with evasive maneuvers, which happened sometimes. FDR did try to ditch the agents, driving faster and faster until he had the car up to seventy-five miles per hour, fast enough to make Joe hold on for dear life.

"Chief," Joe said with white knuckles, "don't you think if the people of the United States knew how fast you were driving that they would be worried?"

FDR laughed, his chin pointing upward. "Tell the truth, Joe," he said, "who are you really worried about?"

After the meeting, Joe became the first California State Chairman for the March of Dimes, the anti-polio charity that would use theaters across the country to raise money one dime at a time. Joe took the idea first to Eddie Cantor. Cantor recruited Shirley Temple. Joe called the other moguls and asked for help. And so it went. Hollywood stars from all studios filmed fund-raising pitches to run before and after feature films.

Later that year, FDR again invited Joe to visit, this time to his Hyde Park home. As the men discussed the future of the March of Dimes, unbeknownst to either, agents of the U.S. Treasury Department were crawling all over Fox's offices, seizing accounting books and looking for improprieties. It was the beginning of Joe's legal troubles.

ON JUNE 3, 1940, JOE WAS INDICTED BY A FEDERAL GRAND JURY ON twenty-four counts of income tax fraud. He heard the news while dining at Dave Chasen's Hollywood restaurant. Joe was eating a pompano that Chasen had had flown in from Florida, when he was called to the phone. Chasen watched the blood drain from Joe's face.

Hours later Joe formulated a damage-control strategy and spoke to the *L.A. Times*: "Income tax problems are always complex and subject to dispute. The charges against me are grossly unfair. I will come east whenever they ask me to."

He and his private secretary, Joseph H. Moskowitz, were charged with colluding to evade $412,045 in taxes from 1934 to 1936. Moskowitz, known in Hollywood as "Carnation Charlie" because of his omnipresent boutonnière, was indicted because he was the man who filled out Joe's tax returns during the key years. Taxes had brought down Al Capone, and now it was threatening to bring down Joe, who had never used the word "tax" without adding "bullshit" in his life, and now it was catching up with him.

Joe's trial was to be held in New York, but Joe was free and allowed to tend to business in California until the trial began later that winter. As his lawyers worked to develop his case, Joe technically resigned from Fox so as not to "distract from business." But he never stopped being in charge.

JOE'S SPECIFIC PROBLEMS WITH THE LAW WERE CONCURRENT TO WHAT became known as the "Paramount case," in which the federal government decided that studios owning their own theaters—which was all the majors except Universal and Columbia—constituted a monopoly. The July 1938 Justice Department antitrust suit listed eight Hollywood studios, which it divided into the "Big Five" and the "Little Three." The bigs were Paramount, MGM, Warner Bros., Twentieth Century-Fox, and RKO. Universal, Columbia, and UA were the littles.

Individuals from each studio were listed by name in the complaint. It might have saved paper if they'd listed just the Hollywood execs who weren't indicted. The theater operators whose complaints spawned the Paramount case were particularly upset by a practice known as "block booking," which meant that a studio would rent their hit picture, but only if the theater also booked other less popular studio products. The government eventually backed down from its demand that the studios cut themselves loose from their theater chains, but they did limit the size of block booking (no more than five films to a package, one A- and four B-pictures). The studios agreed to the compromise and the Paramount case was settled. Independent producers were livid, as they could still make pictures but couldn't find a theater to show them. Also unhappy were the theater operators who had hoped that block booking would have been abolished completely.

ACCORDING TO NICK AND JOE'S GREAT-NEPHEW, TV PRODUCER GEORGE W. Schenck, "Nick lived very well. He came to work by yacht every day from his large estate at Great Neck. His chauffeur would pick him up in a limo at the pier in Manhattan and drive him to his office, and then take him back to his boat at the end of the day."

Nick, by choice, didn't get his name in the papers much anymore. He wanted his Loew's Inc. power to be invisible—like God's power. And though he was not a partier or a social butterfly or a ladies' man, he did enjoy the trappings of being one of the top-ten richest men in America. Nick's commute was comparatively modest in terms of distance, but more than anything else in his life, more than his Gatsby-like home, his beautiful wife and daughters who wanted for nothing, his Loew's State Theatre penthouse office—best place to be on New Year's Eve when the ball came down—and his ability to affect thousands of lives with a single phone call, his watery commute aboard his thirty-eight-foot $18,000 sailing yacht *Martha* made Nick feel like a rich man.

To do the actual sailing, Nick hired a man named Captain Charles Burd. Nick often "took the wheel" but launching and docking were Burd's job. Brother Joe had sailed through the Panama Canal but he also brought a "pilot" along. Nick's pilot was more like his chauffeur, and each morning they would sail, mainsail pulling full-speed ahead or tacking laboriously, simultaneously battling and becoming one with Long Island Sound.

And the commute, as adventurous and invigorating as it was, almost always went off without a hitch. Out there on the waters there were no traffic jams. But on the morning of October 3, 1940, Nick had sailed successfully through the westernmost sound and into the East River when there was a thud and a lurch that caused immediate alarm.

"We hit something," Burd said. Hanging over the edge, he screamed, "Driftwood! Punched a hole in the hull. We are taking on water."

Nick looked all around. The nearest land was the 139th Street pier. He got on the radio and called the Port Authority. He was told a New York City garbage tug was nearby and would come to the rescue. The *Martha* had taken on four feet of water and was listing badly by the time a tugboat arrived. The tug, the *Mathilda 11*, pulled the yacht alongside the 139th Street pier, and Nick was wet but only about an hour late for work, which didn't matter because he was the boss. Captain Burd left the *Martha* beached in Uptown Manhattan. Nick arranged for it to be picked up, repaired, and sailed back to Great Neck.

IN SEPTEMBER 1941, LESS THAN THREE MONTHS BEFORE JAPANESE DIVE bombers rendered the matter moot at Pearl Harbor, the right wing of the U.S. Congress was worried that communist Hollywood was siding with Joseph Stalin, urging America to enter the war, a war that many thought was "none of our business." The moguls heard the undeniable tone of anti-Semitism. In their rhetoric "Jew" and "communist" were synonyms.

Spokesman for the anti-Hollywood movement was Senator Bennett

Champ Clark (D- MO). He said, "Dozens of pictures are used to infect the minds of their audiences with hatred to inflame them, to arouse their emotions, and make them clamor for war. And not one word of the argument against war is heard. This is because the men, the small handful of men, who run Hollywood are themselves dominated by these hatreds." Clark added that control over "what eighty million people can see in theaters each week is too dangerous a power for any democracy to permit, concentrated in the hands of a few men."

The U.S. Senate Interstate Commerce Committee held public hearings on the matter and Nick Schenck was the first mogul to testify regarding Hollywood's anti-Nazi bent. Committee members called Nick the "czar of the motion picture business."

Nick took the oath to tell the whole truth on September 22, looking distinguished in a powder-blue suit, matching shirt and tie, with a deep tan and gray hair.

"You are the top man at Loew's Inc., isn't that correct? You are it, in charge, correct?" asked one senator.

Nick answered the question in the third person: "Mr. Schenck and the board of directors are responsible for it all, there is no doubt about that."

"And you and the other top men in Hollywood represent a dynasty, do you not? Isn't it true that Hollywood's top executives are all members of families connected by blood or marriage?"

Nick paused and thought. He understood the question, correctly saw its subliminal anti-Semitism, and answered, "When you live in a society, after all, with a small group of people, it is a natural thing for boys to be thrown with girls, and for girls to be thrown with boys, and they will get married."

It was a surprisingly charming answer and there were chuckles and even a couple of warm sighs from the gallery.

Nick testified that he certainly did not see MGM pictures as propaganda. "We present accurate portrayals of the plight of Great Britain and the menace of Nazi Germany," Nick said. "Pictures do not mold the public. The public molds us. I would not produce pictures that would make one race of people hate another. But I would produce pictures of this sort when something is happening on the other side, in the balance of the world that is occupied by Nazis. You can correctly charge me with being anti-Nazi, but no one can charge me with being anti-American."

One senator thought it suspicious that Hollywood functioned outside the American investment mainstream. How had Nick managed to get so rich and powerful without involving Wall Street?

Nick didn't answer right away. He lit a Pall Mall as he thought. Wall Street understood only money but running Loews Inc.—in particular MGM—involved things that couldn't be measured monetarily, he said.

"As I understand it," Nick finally testified, "a few years ago the bankers came to Hollywood and went through the business and said we were all crazy—that they would do this and that. But those suggestions were made because they did not understand us. After all, it is just a business where you deal with brains and imagination and creative ability, and you cannot buy that from us."

In its way, it was the greatest compliment he ever paid Mayer. MGM was a mystery, a creator of miracles. MGM was magic, and Mayer the head magician. You couldn't measure it in money. Bankers didn't get it.

At one point, Nick's taxes came up. Nick's voice firmed and he didn't want anyone to think he wasn't paying his fair share. "The last two years I have had to borrow money to pay my taxes," he exclaimed.

Senator Charles Tobey (R-NH) wanted to demonstrate how powerful Nick was by having him list the corporations he controlled, but Nick said there was no way he could remember details like that.

"Such details are unimportant," Nick said. "Loew's theaters are held individually or in small groups through separate locally financed corporations. That way we can adjust for rentals and interest rates on mortgages according to local conditions. There is no need to remember the names. I would be glad to get the records. What interest is it to me in solving a problem to know what company owns, say, the State Theatre in New York, when I knew we do own it? I've trained myself to discard such things from my mind. How could I do my job if I locked up my thoughts with things not worth remembering."

Senator Tobey disagreed: "If you are Exhibit A of the average corporation director of this country, God help America. God save your stockholders! Do you read documents before you sign them?"

"They bring me papers and I sign them—if I see my lawyer's name on it first."

"Do you sign checks the same way?"

"Oh, I don't sign checks."

The flabbergasted Tobey began to fire questions without giving Nick time to respond.

"May I answer?" Nick said with a patient but chilly smile. "We have been very successful."

"You'd be more successful before the country if you came here to give testimony and could say what corporations you are director of."

"I don't think you should put me through this kind of workout when I am trying to answer your questions," Nick said.

To Tobey's chagrin, the gallery erupted into cheers. From then on, every time Tobey interrupted Nick's testimony, the gallery hissed at him.

The hearings broke for lunch, but Nick was back in the hot seat for the afternoon session, this time quizzed by Senator Clark, who asserted that all domestic motion pictures were supervised by a small group of men.

Nick explained that executives of the major film companies never "got together" to prevent independents from producing or marketing pictures. Such action would be "the worst kind of a crime." What Clark saw as collusion was actually just good business. "Independents have trouble borrowing stars from the major companies because the majors want to protect the stars' box-office appeal. For that reason, independents who prove themselves wind up eventually with the major companies."

Clark changed the subject: "You have an interest in the Gaumont-British chain of theaters, the largest such chain in England?"

"We do have an interest, a three-point-five-million-dollar investment, but not a controlling interest. Three English brothers control the company under a stock agreement."

"Are all of the Gaumont-British theaters in the U.K.?" Clark asked.

"No, there are three in Canada, seven in Australia, and one hundred and twenty-nine here in the U.S."

That got Senator Tobey freshly steamed: "The witness has a great memory now for details, but he will not remember the names of companies that he is the director of."

Tobey switched the subject to specifics, hoping his luck would improve.

"Loews Inc. supervised the making of a picture called *Escape*, isn't that right, an anti-Nazi picture?"

"That's right."

"Were you personally involved in the acquisition of rights to make that film, Mr. Schenck?"

"Well, I read the book on a train and urged the studio to produce it."

"And why did you find that particular subject so appealing?"

"Well, Hitler has been in the news a lot. I figured the public would be interested."

A Senator Downey seemed to put an end to the anti-Semitic fun when he read a statement saying that he'd made a review of Hollywood films distributed over the past couple of years and had found no "insidious propaganda for war as has been alleged."

Nick endured a full day of questioning and did it without a break in composure or the slightest mist of sweat. Among the other Hollywood figures called to testify was Charlie Chaplin—who was quizzed about his motives in making the film *The Great Dictator*, in which he portrayed Hitler tossing an inflatable globe around like a play object.

At MGM, the hearing caused a brief pause in the production of anti-Nazi films, then it was full speed ahead.

CHAPTER FIFTEEN

THE SILVER SCREEN SKIM

DURING THE EARLY 1930S, HOLLYWOOD GREW A LARGE AND UGLY underbelly. Frank Nitti, the Chicago mobster, had his evil eye on Hollywood, with its drug addicts and homosexuals and rampant promiscuity, and he saw the potential for all kinds of extortion.

"The goose is in the oven just waiting to be cooked," Nitti said.

The first worms in, the ones laying parasitic eggs in show business's bowels, were a pair of seemingly mismatched hoods: a dapper racketeer named George E. Browne, and a roly-poly ex-pimp and Al Capone bagman named Willie Bioff, who had the lascivious grin of a cartoon wolf. Bioff's name was pronounced BEE-off, but after he gained notoriety, some took to calling him BUY-off.

Browne was a quiet, reserved alcoholic, most often seen earlier in the day and in a finely tailored dark suit. Bioff was chattier, a close talker with a smarmy manner. They got their start bootlegging and pandering but the repeal of Prohibition killed the first vocation and the Great Depression slowed down the second. So, they had to improvise.

Browne and Bioff (B&B) started out extorting Fulton Street butcher shops, and other mom-and-pop stores, selling protection. Browne worked the gentiles, Bioff the Jews. They progressed to theaters. *Pay me and nothing bad will happen.* The threat didn't need to be specific—Browne could be frightening, Bioff terrifying—although if a theater owner seemed slow on the uptake the menacing messenger might mention the "beatings" and "bombings" that had been going on.

Despite being a thug, Browne was a canny businessman. Why shake down theaters one at a time when you can score big with a whole chain of them at once?

THEIR FIRST ATTEMPT AT A BIG-TIME THEATER SHAKEDOWN WENT smoothly. It was early 1933, and they targeted a chain of Chicago theaters owned by Barney Balaban, who later ran Paramount, and Sam Katz, who later became part owner of MGM. Like the Schencks, Balaban and Katz were into pictures as well as theaters, starting in nickelodeons and producing flickers. B&B extorted the chain for $25,000, under the official guise of collecting money for a local soup kitchen. A donation could prevent problems, Bioff explained.

The pair of thugs were filled with optimism at their easy success, convinced that the owners would repeatedly pay to avoid violence on their property. To celebrate, B&B took their loot to an illegal Chicago casino called Club 100, where they drank heavily, flapped their gums, and played roulette. They were noticed by the casino owner, a surly hood named Nick Circella, who worked for syndicate lieutenant Frankie Rio. In fact, Rio and Circella were in the corner in the back, sipping espresso at the owner's table, watching B&B as if they were exhibits in a zoo. They'd known these guys for years, especially Bioff, and knew his scams to be strictly door-to-door.

"Where do a couple of losers like them get that kind of cash?" Circella asked.

Circella reported the incident to Mr. Nitti, the man in charge of Chicago with Capone doing time. Nitti snapped his fingers, and the next day, B&B were escorted by Rio to Nitti's twenty-room mansion. Browne and Bioff were sweating through their stiff collars, convinced they were about to be whacked.

"Gentlemen, I have one question," Nitti said. "Where did you get all the money?"

Browne explained that they'd collected protection money from a chain of theaters using a fake soup-kitchen charity.

Nitti hadn't risen to the top of the underworld on ruthlessness alone, he was well educated and intelligent, and Browne's expansive thinking gave Nitti an idea that made him smile.

The frightened visitors slowly realized that they were not about to die. No one was going to blowtorch their armpits.

Nitti told B&B that they worked for him now. Mr. Capone, before his tragic downfall, had said the Outfit should grab a piece of Hollywood. This was the way to do it. Nitti knew Hollywood would be easy to extort. Bad things there tended to be swept under the rug. That meant money was exchanging hands.

It didn't hurt that L.A. was corrupt through and through, the government and law barely more sophisticated than that of the Old West that Hollywood so loved. Nitti informed B&B that they were going to take theater protection to the next level, global rather than local.

"We are going to make millions, not thousands," he said.

Nitti laid it out for them. It had to be done *carefully*. Nothing messy like bombs or guns. Better to have it *appear* that *no crime* was being committed. Do it through the unions. Control the unions and you could bring the business to its knees by threatening a strike. Nitti had made the scheme work in other industries. Control the unions and you controlled everything.

The plan had another perk. Nitti had been working on forming an allegiance with organized crime in other parts of the nation. This could solidify Nitti's coast-to-coast influence. Nitti met with key mobsters in New York and Los Angeles, and formed a national syndicate, with one of its primary goals being a silver-screen skim.

Nitti installed Browne as president of the International Alliance of Theatrical Stage Employees union, commonly referred to as the stagehand union. IATSE was formed in 1893 to protect vaudeville workers. With Al Jolson and *The Jazz Singer*, IATSE was decimated, adapting slowly to the new sound era. Sound technicians organized elsewhere, IATSE fell out of favor and dwindled at one point to 175 Hollywood members. Installing Browne as head of IATSE was, for Nitti, the path of least resistance. Browne's election was easily accomplished. One memo: "Mr. Nitti wants you should vote for Mr. Browne."

As head of IATSE, Browne was able to execute a coup d'état at the projectionists' union, and that turned out to be all the leverage they needed. The shakedown of the big studios commenced. Bioff was appointed Browne's "first assistant special vice president" and, just in case, his "international representative." Bioff was the kind of guy who would pick his teeth with *your* fork, a perfect choice as the operative sent to "organize Hollywood."

As the operation commenced, everyone saw less and less of George E. Browne, who retreated behind his closed office door and reportedly quaffed a case of lager a day. It was Bioff—now in charge of Locals 37, 883, and 695—who did the legwork.

B&B increased union dues by $5, then pocketed every dime of it. They threatened a strike by the New York City projectionists. And that meant threatening Nick Schenck. Bioff had no qualms about visiting Nick at his office overlooking Times Square.

According to Nick's testimony years later, Bioff began by bragging about himself, about his power.

"Now look, Mr. Schenck, I'll tell you why I'm here. I want you to know I elected Browne president, and I am his boss. He is to do whatever I tell him to do. Now, your industry is a prosperous industry, and I must get two million dollars out of it," Bioff said.

Nick sputtered with indignation. "Impossible," Nick said. "I cannot do it. I can never do it. There is no reason in the world for it. You are crazy. How could that much money be taken out of the companies and why should the industry pay to continue in business?"

"Stop this nonsense," Bioff said. "You know what is going to happen. You know you will have to pay me sooner or later. We'll close every theater in the country which has producers in Hollywood. Within twenty-four hours we can close every theater in the United States. All we do is pull the projectionists. You're shut down. You think it over. I'll see you later."

"I'm telling you, it is impossible," Nick said.

After a few days Bioff returned.

"I've been thinking it over," Bioff said. "How about one million?"

Nick's eyes twinkled. Bioff had admitted a willingness to negotiate.

"Still impossible. It is simply too much money in one lump."

On April 18, 1936, Bioff came back with his final demand.

"Maybe you can't get up a million dollars at one time," Bioff said. "I want fifty thousand dollars a year from Warners, Paramount, Loew's, and Fox. I want twenty-five thousand dollars a year from the rest, and that's final."

"Give me a sec. I got to make a phone call," Nick said.

He called Joe, and they discussed whether to give in to the extortion. Joe suggested that paying the bribe could have tax benefits if they arranged it correctly. They were not novices at this sort of thing, they agreed, recalling some of the things they'd had Eddie Mannix do back in the Palisades Park days.

"Okay," Nick said, and Bioff grinned.

They arranged for the first payment. Nick made the initial payment himself, carrying a little bundle with $50,000 in it to a suite in the Waldorf-Astoria Hotel. Nick entered and dropped the bundle on the bed. He looked out the window and saw Sidney R. Kent, representing Fox, entering the building with a bundle under his arm. When both moguls were in the room, Bioff opened the packages and counted the money.

On his way out the door, Nick said, "Willie, I'm a guy who likes to get his money's worth. No raises."

Bioff flashed Nick an evil smile. "I'm certain you will find labor cooperative with management's way of thinking during these difficult times," he replied.

A year later Nick received a call from Bioff, and the drop-off was repeated. By this time the tables had largely turned. The Schencks proved to be the superior businessman, masters at making lemonade out of the sourest lemon. They wrote off the payments to unions as business expenses to avoid paying tax on that money. To further discourage revenuers, Nick said the second payment was not going to be in cash. Instead, he would arrange for a friend of Bioff's to sell film to the studio, and Bioff's pay would come in "excess commissions." They even upped their payments to the mobsters with the agreement that some of that money would be kicked back to them.

The Schencks quickly understood that a corrupt union was cheaper than a legit one. These guys took their cut, sure, but they weren't filled with silly notions regarding fair worker compensation. Some have estimated that during the B&B era, the Schencks, between them, saved as much as $15 million in wages they didn't pay. As Bioff later realized, he'd been turned into Joe Schenck's bagman.

Nick, ever the real-estate expert, bought Bioff a big Southern California house with mahogany paneling and rare Chinese vases. Bioff had a library filled with rare first editions, even though he could barely read. Nick cleverly hid his payments in the Loew's Inc. books.

When the studios had actual problems with the unions, they used mob muscle to squash it. The national syndicate was getting its bite of the Hollywood apple and yet everyone was happy!

Everyone, that is, except for the unionized workers. Hundreds of thousands of dollars were changing hands between the moguls and the projectionists' union, but not a single dollar made it into the pocket of a projectionist.

Plus, while the squeezing of the moguls had provided a steady flow of income, the squeezing of the workers never stopped. All unions under mob control had to charge their members a two percent "union war fund" to "pay bills in case of a strike," except there was no war fund and that money went straight to Chicago.

Nitti's plan was to eventually rule every union in Hollywood. They were about a fifth of the way home when B&B encountered their worst nightmare: a fearless man with genuine scruples.

"I HAD HOLLYWOOD DANCING TO MY TUNE," BIOFF LATER RECALLED. But only until he took on the Screen Actors Guild (SAG) and, to his surprise, tough-guy tactics didn't work. SAG's president was another tough guy, actor Robert Montgomery, who throughout his career played some rugged characters, including the hard-boiled detective Philip Marlowe in *Lady in the Lake*. But none of his on-screen personae compared with the courage he showed in real life when he stood up to Bioff, saying, "Not here you don't."

The beginning of the end for Bioff came on May 9, 1937, at a meeting held at Louis B. Mayer's beach house. At that time IATSE and the Federation of Motion Picture Crafts were battling over which would serve as the umbrella group for Hollywood's craft unions. The meeting was held to determine which of those unions would become affiliated with SAG. Joe Schenck was there representing Fox. Mayer repped MGM. Robert Montgomery and Franchot Tone repped SAG. Bioff represented IATSE. Montgomery and Tone laid out their demands. Bioff and Mayer then left the room for a private caucus and when they returned announced that the studios would recognize SAG, and SAG announced they would team up with IATSE. Montgomery was troubled by the Mayer-Bioff caucus. Why would a hood like Bioff be involved in making a studio decision? Montgomery was curious enough to hire a private detective, who quickly reported back with details of the mogul-mobster conspiracy. Montgomery told both the press and the Treasury Department about the unwholesome relationship, and an investigation ensued.

Joe fell first. He was called in to testify unaware that the feds already knew about the union kickback scheme. He immediately perjured himself.

WITH HIS BROTHER IN TROUBLE, NICK CALLED THE ENTERTAINMENT editor at the *Hollywood Spectator* to divert attention and hopefully accomplish a measure of damage control. Because Nick was so reclusive, he knew that he'd make it into print no matter what he said. Nick told the columnist that the Hollywood phenomenon was global. Everyone wanted to get into pictures. Just the other day he'd received a visit at his Time Square office from three of Joseph Stalin's commissars, just in from Russia. They wanted to buy, not rent, *buy* three MGM pictures.

"That's going to cost you," Nick said. "How much money do you have?"

"Oh, we *haff* no money," the commissars puffed. "What we *haff* is world's greatest caviar, and *lots* of it."

Nick said he had to think about it and told the Russians to come back in two weeks. Which they did. Nick was stuck in a meeting, so he instructed they be taken to a screening room and shown a picture. Perhaps one they might want to purchase, Nick said distractedly. He didn't give a rat's ass *which* picture and didn't specify. That was the last he heard about the Russians. Only later did he learn they'd been shown the Greta Garbo film *Ninotchka*, which made relentless fun of the way Stalin ruled Russia.

The funny item in the papers might have boosted the Schencks' popularity, but it did nothing to deter the Treasury Department's ongoing investigation. Joe's legal troubles grew.

If any of this troubled Nick, he didn't show it. According to future TV star, then columnist Ed Sullivan, Nick was thinking about one thing as the month of October began, the subway World Series between the Yankees and the Dodgers. Tickets were hard to come by, especially the games at Ebbets Field where seating capacity was about half of that of Yankee Stadium. Nick called the girls at the ticket counter in the lobby of the Hotel Astor. He was told that none of the ticket brokers in town had them, that they'd been bought up by scalpers and were being sold for fifty bucks a piece—then an outrageous price.

SOON THEREAFTER, A FEDERAL GRAND JURY INDICTED B&B. NICK WAS granted immunity from prosecution in exchange for his testimony against B&B. Within weeks, B&B were on trial, Judge John C. Knox presiding. U.S. Attorney Mathias Correa headed the prosecution (as he would at Joe's subsequent tax evasion trial, see next chapter). Defense attorney Martin Conboy defended Bioff. Jury selection took only two and a half hours.

Simultaneous to jury selection, in Seattle, Washington, the American

Federation of Labor (AFL) Executive Council announced moves to oust George Browne as head of IATSE. An AFL rep said, "We are cleaning house, and he must go."

Back in the courtroom, Correa told the all-male jury that the defendants had "baldly demanded" $2 million on threats to drive Hollywood studios out of business. Correa promised that Nick Schenck would be a key witness.

And he was. In court, Nick looked dapper, standing tall, bald except for a rim of gray, and tortoiseshell glasses. He took the oath, identified himself by name and as the president of Loews Inc. Jurors were surprised to hear his Russian accent. He verified that he knew Bioff, boss of IATSE, and yes, Bioff had extorted money from Hollywood moguls, a fact that he knew firsthand.

"You personally were extorted by Mr. Bioff?"

"I was."

Bioff's lawyer leapt to his feet. "Objection, the witness is not an expert in the law."

"Sustained. Rephrase your question."

"Did Mr. Bioff speak to you about you needing to give him money?"

"He did. He said I had to pay, or bad things would happen."

"Did he explain what he meant by bad things?"

"He meant that if the heads of the studios didn't pay up there was going to be labor problems."

"How much did Mr. Bioff want in exchange for peaceful labor relations?"

"His first request was for two million dollars."

Nick described the April 24, 1936, Waldorf-Astoria payoff.

"What did you say to Mr. Bioff when you arrived?"

"I skipped a greeting and got down to business. 'Here it is,' I said, and I threw a roll of bills on the bed. 'Count it,' I said."

"Did he count it?"

"He did, very slowly, putting bills of different denominations in neat stacks across the white counterpane. Thousands in one pile, five-hundreds in another, hundreds in another."

Nick described how the second payment to Bioff, a year later, was camouflaged as commissions following the purchase of film by the studios from a friend of Bioff's.

"We kicked back seven percent of the commission to agents of Browne and Bioff," Nick testified.

"No further questions," said Correa.

Bioff's lawyer stood to cross-examine Nick. "Your general manager is Charles Moskowitz, is that correct?"

"Yes, sir."

"He is the brother of Joseph Moskowitz, who is general manager for your brother Joseph Schenck, is that correct?"

"Yes."

"Did Mr. Moskowitz ever contact Mr. Browne in connection with a threatened strike?"

"Yes, sir. In 1935, Browne threatened a strike of projectionists. Moskowitz told me that Browne agreed the strike could be settled, at a cost of one hundred thousand dollars. That time we hired a man from Chicago, one Mort Singer, and paid him by check, so it would appear regular on our books."

There followed a lengthy stretch in which the defense attorney Martin Conboy tried to get Nick to tell the jury how much money he made. Nick didn't want to do it.

"You don't know your annual income?"

"I'm not sure."

"Do you receive a salary from Loew's Inc."

"Yes."

"And how much is that?"

"I don't know. Two hundred fifty, three hundred thousand, something like that. Maybe."

"If you knew you were being, quote, extorted, unquote, why didn't you tell the authorities?" Conboy asked.

"I didn't complain to anyone because I was afraid of what would happen to our business. I was afraid that it might be destroyed by strikes and other things," Nick said.

"Isn't it true that the payments to Browne and Bioff constituted wage increases for union employees."

Nick laughed. "That's silly," he said.

"Isn't it true that you weren't even at that April eighteenth meeting at the Waldorf?"

"That is too silly for me to talk about," Nick replied.

As cross-examination continued, Nick began to show signs of fatigue.

Judge Knox said, "Mr. Conboy, is there any way we can wrap this up. The witness appears to be near collapse."

"I'm going as fast as I can," Conboy said. "Mr. Schenck, isn't it true that simultaneous to this alleged 'extortion,' the IATSE was demanding increase in wages for its members?"

"All unions demand raises. The Browne-Bioff organization cannot be singled out from the rest."

Eventually Conboy gave up trying to get blood from a stone, and Nick's time on the witness stand came to an end. It had been grueling, but he'd done what he agreed to do. He'd given the prosecution all they needed to put B&B behind bars.

Later in the trial, Bioff took the stand in his own defense.

"Did there come a time when you had lunch with Nicholas Schenck?" his lawyer asked.

"He don't eat no lunch. He eats an apple," Bioff replied. "I had an apple with him."

Bioff went full bore after his accusers. He said the Schencks were the only ones making any dough off the scheme. He testified that he "did it all for Joe and Nick," that he gathered up money and repeatedly crossed the country delivering payoffs to Joe in L.A. and Nick in New York. When asked why the Schencks were accepting payments from the stagehands' union, Bioff grew vague and testified that it had to do with the Schencks being sandbagged by legislation. That was all he knew.

"I ain't no lawyer," Bioff said.

Asked about his background, Bioff revealed that he and the Schencks had some things in common. Bioff too had been born in Russia and came over on the boat when he was five. He'd been on his own since his mom died when he was fourteen. He eventually got a job with the Teamsters driving, organizing, and making collections, paid $30 or $40 a week.

Bioff remembered Nick telling him about the condition of the business. "He said that I could be very useful to him, that they have to transfer cash moneys to the West Coast to his brother Joe, and that would I mind doing him a favor when I'm in New York or Chicago, that I might call on people that he will tell me who they will be and make these pickups and deliver them to his brother."

Ever since the government started getting ridiculous with the taxes, Bioff said, the Schencks had to do more business off the books. In 1938, Bioff said, Joe told him that the feds were looking at studio books searching for Bioff's name, so maybe he best make himself scarce for a while.

Bioff was sentenced to ten years behind bars, Browne eight. Each was fined $20,000. The feds did not stop there. By 1943, six of the players in Nitti's plan to skim Hollywood were indicted, an unprecedented number of mobsters under indictment simultaneously. They were Nitti's number-two man Paul "The Waiter" Ricca, Louis "Little New York" Campagna, Phil "The Squire" D'Andrea, Charlie "Cherry Nose" Gioe, and Frank "Frankie Diamond" Maritote, and their trial began on March 18, 1943.

The following day, March 19, Nitti went home to the Riverside section of Chicago, got drunk, and, enveloped by a complex gloom that only he understood, wandered hopelessly across an open field, to the Illinois Central Railroad tracks. He pulled a .45 from his belt and, after firing wildly at a nearby group of people, put the gun to his own head and squeezed the trigger.

In May, Nick and his nephew Marvin H. Schenck testified at the trial. With all of those defendants, the defense table was long enough for a banquet. Security was tight. Nick told the jury that he'd been in on the agreement made with that union back in 1926, and said the alleged extortion involved the terms of that deal. Nick testified that Bioff had threatened Louis B. Mayer, as well as himself, that Bioff's threat followed a California State legislative committee in 1937 beginning an investigation of labor conditions in West Coast film studios. Nick said that there came a time, when he was negotiating with Bioff regarding the extortion payments, when a bomb was found in a Loew's theater.

"Bioff was angry with Mr. Mayer," Nick testified. "'There is no room for both of us in this world,' Bioff said. 'And I will be the one who is here.'"

Defense counsel James Murray seemed taken aback by this testimony.

"Do you mean that Mr. Bioff threatened to kill Mr. Mayer?" Murray asked.

"What do you think?" Nick replied. "He said there wasn't room for both of them in this world. Mr. Mayer was terribly scared."

"Where was the threat made?"

"In the home of my brother, Joseph Schenck."

"Who was there?" Murray asked, skepticism in his voice. He was hoping beyond hope that the jury wouldn't find Nick credible, but it only took a quick glance to reveal that the panel was eating this up.

"Myself, my brother, Bioff and Browne, and Mayer."

"You were convinced that by a gesture, Bioff and Browne could destroy the film industry?"

"Yes."

"Did it ever occur to you that you owed a duty to your state and your government not to yield and make these payments?"

"I did not. I simply was faced with a situation where I had to yield."

"Didn't you consider that if the world knew about Browne and Bioff's demands, that it would be the end of Browne and Bioff?"

"I didn't think anyone would believe it."

"Why did you not report the extortion to the authorities?"

"I could not afford to do so."

"Did it ever occur to you that the police could have marked the money that you gave to Browne and Bioff?"

"No."

The six Nitti thugs went up the river, but the story ends on an unsettling note. In 1945, not long after he took office, President Harry Truman arranged for early release for the mobsters jailed over the Hollywood scandal. The Kefauver Committee, investigating organized crime, later called Truman's move "an awesome display of the syndicate power and ability to wield political influence."

Reportedly, Truman's attorney general, Tom Clark, was in the hip pocket of top Outfit guy Murray Humphreys, so the mobsters were released. If Nitti had been able to see the future, he perhaps would have been less hasty about committing suicide. Not only were the prison sentences short but, other than nominal fines set down by the judge, the hoods were allowed to keep their money.

Two final footnotes to this gangster business:

In July 1942, Nick and Pansy and the girls moved from Great Neck to a new mansion at Sands Point, one bay further east on Long Island's North Shore—and more exclusive. The family had been there for five months when a body washed up on shore just outside their new home. Nick's first thought was "What the hell is this?" He was relieved to learn it had nothing to do with mobsters or unions or power, it was just a sixty-year-old man who'd gotten sick and fell off a dock at Port Washington.

After prison, George Browne successfully disappeared. Willie Bioff tried to disappear but wasn't as successful. He got himself a gig in the Witness Protection Program, changed his name to William Nelson, and became an accepted member of Phoenix society where he attended and hosted la-di-da parties. One morning in 1955 he started his car, put his foot on the accelerator, and was blown to smithereens by a bomb, victim of an industrious hitman settling an ancient score.

CHAPTER SIXTEEN

THE TRIAL OF JOSEPH SCHENCK

JOE WELCOMED 1941 PLEASANTLY, BY HOSTING WITH BOB HOPE the March of Dimes New Year's celebration. Joe was happy being the leader of Hollywood's battle against America's number-one scourge. Whenever near a microphone, he talked infantile paralysis. Money was needed more now than ever. More kids were getting sick.

But all the time, the specter of legal troubles tempered his happiness. For one year, he'd deducted eighty-three percent of his gross income as business expenses, a figure that made even his staunchest defenders raise an eyebrow.

Joe was originally scheduled to go on trial in 1940, but his defense attorney, New York criminal lawyer Max Steuer, died. The next scheduled start date was March 3, 1941, but Judge Grover M. Moskowitz granted prosecutor Mathias F. Correa a brief delay to allow West Coast witnesses time to get to New York to testify.

In every daily newspaper, stories of Joe's tax nightmare ran alongside grim war news out of Europe. If convicted, the press noted, Joe could be fined $40,000, sent to prison for seventeen years, and assessed other penalties up to $620,000. Joe needed to change the subject, so the evening before his trial he called a New York press conference.

"I am considering purchasing the New York Yankees baseball club," he said. "I believe I can swing the deal on a million-dollar-down basis. The entire transaction would involve somewhere between four and six million. Let me note that my mentioning of these figures should not be construed as an offer."

The Yankees' previous owner, brewer Jacob Ruppert, died in 1939 and the family was looking to unload the club.

A reporter started to ask a trial question. Joe held up his palm. "Baseball questions only, please."

"Why the Yankees?"

"I've always been keen on baseball. About eighteen or twenty years ago I had a substantial interest in a club at Vernon, California, and we had some mighty fine ballplayers in those days. I have done no negotiating, as yet, with the Yankee representatives, but, when this trial is finished, I would like to confer with the attorney who represents the Ruppert estate."

The next morning Joe went to federal court in Manhattan, sat silently next to co-defendant Joseph Moskowitz, and their defense attorney, forty-year-old Harold Corbin, best known as the attorney who helped excavate Harry Daugherty from the Teapot Dome scandal. The jury listened as Corbin discussed how careful his client was with money, how detail oriented. We know from Joe's records that he spent $53 for a mattress for his sister-in-law, $209 to insure a young woman's automobile, and $130 to transport Joe's masseuse across the country by airplane. He watched his grocery bills so closely that his secretary was instructed to count the number of times he had lunch outside his home. Corbin told the jury that, although it was true that Joe once sold 67,707 shares of stock in the Agua Caliente hotel and gambling casino, for which he paid $403,000, to Hollywood restauranteur Roland West for $50,000, "it was a perfectly decent, understandable transaction between friends." Joe, according to Corbin, told West at the time, "If the stock turns out to be worth something, you may make the profit, but I'm not going to stand for your losing anything on it." Did that mean Joe had reformed from his gambling ways? No way. Corbin said Joe was "a born gambler, and always will be one." Corbin quoted Joe, who was always saying, "I spend three hundred thousand dollars a year, but I don't eat it. Mostly it goes to other people." The defense planned to show that Joe not only didn't owe the government any taxes, but that he had overpaid by $165,000 and was only indicted after he sought a refund. "The government would have you believe that Schenck made fake stock sales to friends to establish a tax loss. Well, if those sales were invalid then Schenck ought to get $165,000 back from the government, because those stocks are worthless. He ought to get a refund of $40,000 for 1935 and 1936 and $125,000 for 1937. Instead of hearing him, the government indicted him. The government is trying to hang him."

Correa gave his opening statement as well on March 5. He told the jury that the numbers were going to speak for themselves. In 1933, Joe Schenck, one of the most powerful men in the country, paid no tax at all. He reported no taxable income. His deductions plus losses on a sale of securities outweighed his gross income—he claimed. The next year, Joe listed his net earnings as $1,601,932 instead of the correct number, $2,016,007. Joe "concealed big gambling winnings." He made a mint betting on the 1936 presidential election and demanded cash in payment, refusing traceable checks. In addition to the masseuse flying cross-country, his sister-in-law's mattress, and automobile insurance for a young woman, Correa said, Joe deducted $40,000 in yacht expenses, claiming he used the *Invader* for business purposes. "Joe Schenck threw wild parties on his yacht, and the most remarkable people would make up the crew, Lady Ashley, Constance Bennett, Irving Berlin and his wife. Business? I don't think so." Joe had also claimed fake stock losses, Correa charged. "In our case, gentlemen of the jury, you will hear extensive details of Joseph M. Schenck's private life, including the cost of weekend parties that he listed as tax deductions. We will produce the evidence that these parties consisted of entertainment by Schenck of gambling companions, women friends, and in general people to whom his relationship was a purely personal one."

Following the opening statements, the prosecution called its first witness, John B. Codd, Twentieth Century-Fox controller, who also handled some of Joe's personal accounting. Codd said he didn't receive extra compensation for keeping Joe's books, but that Joe always gave him a nice suit of clothes for Christmas.

Codd testified that—on June 23, 1937, on Joe's orders—he did the following things: drew a check for $5,000 signed by Joe and payable to Arthur W. Stebbins, his nephew; drew up a note for $95,000 endorsed by Joe and signed by Stebbins, which was deposited in the Bank of America, Los Angeles branch; executed a note for $100,000, payable to Stebbins and signed by Willie Bioff; and drew a check for $100,000 payable to Bioff and signed by Stebbins.

"You did all of that in one day, Mr. Codd?"

"Yes, sir."

"What did Joseph Schenck do the next day?"

Codd said that Joe "paid out to the Bank of America one hundred thousand dollars in currency."

"And what did that currency represent?"

"It represented a return on a loan negotiated by Joseph Schenck on June sixteenth and seventeenth."

Correa asked, "Did your records show from where the money came?"

"No, sir," Codd replied.

"Did the money come from any of Schenck's bank accounts?"

"No, sir."

"Did the money come from any of Schenck's reported investments?"

"No, sir."

Codd testified that Joe never even looked at accounts of his personal disbursements. To his knowledge, Joe never once saw the ledgers, the receipts, vouchers, and financial reports on which his three-year $2 million income was calculated. More than fifty ledgers and files were introduced into evidence. They indicated, both sides agreed, that Joe entertained in a lavish style. The prosecution called it social activities, the defense said they were business expenses.

"Mr. Codd, I show you seven vouchers and ask if you recognize them," Corbin said.

"I do, these vouchers represent a payment of $30,905, Mr. Schenck's gambling losses for a single day."

"Do you know what Mr. Schenck's gambling losses were in total for 1937?"

"Yes, $63,894," Codd said, putting on a pair of glasses and referring to notes. "And fifteen cents."

Darryl F. Zanuck was mentioned as one of the winners who took Joe's money, accounting for $2,400 of that annual loss.

THE TRIAL GOT ITS FIRST SHOT OF STAR APPEAL THAT MONDAY WHEN Chico of the Marx Brothers took the stand and testified that he once lost $7,000 while gambling and was unable to pay the debt. "I was three thousand dollars short," Marx said, without a hint of an Italian accent.

"So, what did you do?"

"I went to see Mr. Schenck at his home near Palm Springs, California. I was reticent about asking him for the money. He asked me what I was worried about and I told him I'd lost money and couldn't pay it all. He wanted to know how much I needed and I said three thousand dollars. 'Go to bed and stop worrying,' he said. The next morning Schenck gave me the money."

"You are the business manager for the Marx Brothers, is that correct?"

"Yes, sir."

"At the time Mr. Schenck gave you the three thousand dollars, had you ever discussed with him the possibility of entering a contract for the Marx Brothers with Twentieth Century-Fox?"

At first, Marx said he had not, but on his second day on the witness stand, after considering the damage this answer caused Joe's case, Marx said he "might have" discussed a contract.

"But isn't it true that the Marx Brothers already had a contract with MGM?"

"Yes, sir." He recalled that the MGM contract was signed on October 6, 1934. "Irving C. Thalberg signed the contract on behalf of MGM."

Corbin said, "Was there a provision in the contract that gave the Marx Brothers the right to cancel it in the event Thalberg became incapacitated or otherwise unable to supervise the Marx Brothers' work under the contract?"

"Yes, soon after Thalberg's death, I availed myself of that provision and wrote a letter to an MGM official and said that the contract was terminated."

Correa asked Marx, "On Friday, after you left the witness stand, did you speak with Mr. Schenck?"

"Yes, I did."

"Did he remind you of those contract discussions?"

"No, he did not. I just said hello."

"Did you speak with Mr. Schenck over the weekend?"

"I did. I spoke to both Joe and his brother Nick last night—and, no, we didn't discuss the case."

Chico was replaced on the stand by his brother Harpo, whose film character was mute. The press always played ball. There were no published quotes from Harpo's testimony, leaving readers to wonder if he answered questions by merely squeezing a horn.

CHAPTER SEVENTEEN

LIKE DEER TO A SALT LICK

THE TRIAL WAS ON THE DRY SIDE, MOSTLY NUMBERS, UNTIL MARCH 12 when the prosecution gave the press what seemed at the time like it might be the story of the year. (That bragging right eventually went to the bombing of Pearl Harbor in December.)

On that day, the prosecution paraded before the jury a delectable assemblage of starlets who'd been the recipient, during the key years, of theoretically tax-deductible gifts from Joe. The prosecution wanted the jury to know that, for a mogul like Joe who was divorced and "eligible," finding playmates in Hollywood was easy.

Outside court that day, reporters and photographers feasted as the gals, thirsty for fame, did whatever the photogs wanted—"a little more ankle, Miss Poggi"—as they entered and exited the courthouse.

First on the stand was Grace Poggi, whose entrance silenced the gallery. She was gorgeous, feline, and graceful. Her face was all business, but her hips made their way to the witness stand rhythmically. She took the oath with black-gloved hands, left on the Bible, the right raised. She swung her philoprogenitive derriere into the witness box, sat with a settling wiggle, and poetically flapped dark eyelashes at the jury.

The prosecutor started his questioning with biographical questions. She'd been born and raised in California.

Correa cleared his throat: "What do you do for a living, Miss Poggi?"

"I am a professional dancer," she said. She pronounced it "doncer."

"Your specialty is the rumba, correct?"

"Yessss," she hissed.

Correa brought out that the witness had married a theatrical producer named Ivar Denavrogkty in May 1940 and was currently working in one of his shows, as a "doncer" in Miami, Florida. Yes, she knew Joe Schenck. They met while she was working with Eddie Cantor on a picture called *The Kid from Spain* for Sam Goldwyn.

"What year was that?"

Poggi flashed panic. The answer was 1932, nine years earlier, but the witness wanted to seem brand new. She eventually answered, "Some years ago." Correa let it go.

"How did you meet?"

"I was working on location at Santa Barbara, a beach scene. I was in a bathing suit. Mr. Schenck anchored his yacht just offshore and sent word that I could use his yacht as a dressing room if I liked."

"Did you take him up on his offer?"

"I did."

"Do you now or have you ever worked for Twentieth Century-Fox?"

"No."

"Do you now or have you ever worked for a concern managed all or in part by Joseph Schenck?"

"No. Um, I don't think so. Mr. Schenck has his finger in many pies."

A titter of laughter was followed by an embarrassed silence.

Background established to his liking, Correa got down to the crux: "During the spring of 1935, did you stay at the Savoy Hotel in London at the same time as Joseph Schenck?"

"Yes."

"Did Mr. Schenck pay your expenses during your stay?"

"I don't remember."

"Let me see if I can refresh your memory," Correa said. He produced a letter from the Savoy thanking Joe for paying Miss Poggi's $700 bill. "When Joseph Schenck was out of town, did he allow you full use of his home?"

"He did."

"Did Joseph Schenck once buy you an automobile?"

"Yes."

"Do you remember when?"

"It was 1934, soon after his divorce with Norma Talmadge was finalized."

That got a laugh. The judge banged his gavel, but even he seemed a little amused.

"You were married to a man named Lewis Arnold, is that correct?"

"Yes, sir. We were divorced in 1936." Of course, that was two years after Joe bought her a car.

"Did you live in Hollywood after your divorce?"

"I did."

"And isn't it true that your apartment was paid for and furnished by Joseph Schenck?"

"Yes."

"Did Joseph Schenck once pay for you to travel across the country and stay at the Hotel Ambassador in New York?"

"He did."

"And was Joseph Schenck staying at the Hotel Ambassador at the same time?"

"Umm, I don't recall."

"Oh, come on, Miss Poggi. You know very well that Joseph Schenck was occupying an apartment in the hotel."

"Objection, not a question," Corbin said.

"Overruled. Let her respond," Judge Moskowitz said softly.

Poggi lowered her eyelashes to a half mast of feigned shame, and even that move was a little bit slinky. "Yes," she said softly, then she shook it off and returned her gaze to the prosecutor. "I remember."

"Could you please tell us what sort of fur you are wearing, Miss Poggi?"

Her chin rose. "It is mink," she said, with a touch of defiance.

"And where did you get the mink?"

Dramatic pause. "Joseph Schenck gave it to me."

"No further questions."

The prosecution didn't even ask about the nature of Miss Poggi's personal relationship with Joe. What did you do to earn that mink, young woman? There was none of that. It didn't matter. Mr. Schenck and Miss Poggi did not have a business relationship—for him, anyway—and therefore those expenses were not tax-deductible. That was enough to make the case. The jury understood what Joe and the *doncer* were doing in those hotel rooms.

After a brief break, Judge Grover Moskowitz looked to Corbin. "Cross-examination?"

"Yes, Your Honor," Corbin said, rising to his feet behind the defense table. "Miss Poggi, Joseph Schenck was always decent and generous toward you, wasn't he?"

"Yes, he—"

"Objection. Relevance," Correa said.

"Sustained, strike the question and the answer," Judge Moskowitz said.

"No further questions," Corbin said, and sat down.

Grace Poggi gave Joe a pouty "sorry" expression and he smiled to let her know it was okay. Joe, eyes glazed with memories, turned to watch Poggi's exit.

Whatever ambitions Poggi might have had when she offered the court her purring testimony, it seems to have worked, to a degree. She hadn't made a picture in seven years when she testified. After, she was in seven pictures in the next few years, often playing a character known as "Specialty Dancer."

NEXT UP WAS AUDREY SUTHERLAND, A PLATINUM BLONDE ALSO WEARing mink. Unlike Poggi, who was all darkness and mystery, Sutherland was peaches and cream and girl-next-door. She was also about to come undone at the seams with nerves, so taut that you could hear her hum. She had proud, high breasts that led the way, and a tiny Betty Boop voice, shaky with stage fright. Judge Moskowitz had to repeatedly tell her to speak "nice and loud" so the jury could hear. "Play to the back row," he said, encouragingly.

"Yes, Your Honor," she replied loudly. Then her voice went back to a whisper. It was like she didn't want to hear her own words.

"Were you a single woman in 1936, Miss Sutherland?" Correa asked.

"Yes, sir. That is, I was divorced."

"Your ex-husband was a Hollywood director?"

"Yes."

She described the hotel rooms she had stayed in with Joe Schenck, mostly in L.A. There was one weekend in particular Correa wanted to know about, during the spring of 1936, in a luxurious suite in a Palm Springs desert resort. Yes, she'd been there. Yes, Mr. Schenck paid the bill. She assumed so. She didn't pay, that was for sure. She failed to suppress a quick laugh, then jerked in her seat to compose her face. Yes, the mink was a present from Joe.

On cross-examination, Corbin asked, "During the weekend at the Hilton, did you and Mr. Schenck conduct business?"

"Oh yes, in fact the next week I signed a contract with Twentieth Century-Fox."

"No further questions," Corbin said.

Correa leaped to his feet, "One question on re-direct, Your Honor."

"Proceed," Judge Moskowitz said. He was having a good time.

"What were the terms of the contract with the studio?" Correa asked.

"I got twenty-five dollars a week, whether I was in a picture or not," she replied.

"And did you get into a picture?" Correa asked.

"No," she said, and pushed a dainty hankie over her nose and mouth. Neither lawyer wanted to ask her any more questions, and she exited almost in a trot.

Following a fifteen-minute break, court resumed, with yet another beautiful young woman in the spotlight, Janice Dawson Pierse. Her biggest show-biz credit was the two weeks during April 1934 that she'd spent in the chorus of a show called *Broadway Interlude*.

"That was before I was Janice Dawson. I was Ruth Hoyt back then," she explained. All her names were equally unknown.

Correa steered the actress through her meeting Joe Schenck at a party and beginning a friendship in which he paid the bills, and she stayed in hotels. Again, sex was never mentioned.

"I bring to your attention one weekend during the spring of 1936, in a suite in a Palm Springs desert resort. Do you recall?"

"I do."

Alert spectators recognized that time and place from the testimony of the previous witness.

"You stayed in the suite with Joseph Schenck. Was there anyone else there?"

"Yes, sir, another actress by the name of Audrey Sutherland."

There was a series of gasps from the gallery as the implication sunk in.

"You and Miss Sutherland were with Mr. Schenck at the same time?"

"Yes, sir. He said he was interested in us working as a team."

A woman in the back row swooned and needed smelling salts. Several reporters ran for the door, digging in their pockets for a pay-phone nickel.

Correa got around to the witness's fur. "What type of fur are you wearing?"

"It is silver fox," she replied.

"Not mink?"

"I told Joe I preferred fox, so he bought me six of them," she said with a shiny smile.

Joe had been unflappable listening to the day's testimony, but now looked around a bit sheepishly.

There was visible and audible disappointment in the gallery when the last witness of the day was Fox studio manager Fred Metzler. Metzler identified receipts for flowers ordered by Joe, and for rentals of his yacht to studio executives, among them Darryl Zanuck, for "relaxation."

When court was through for the afternoon, Joe was scrummed by reporters asking about that very special date with two very special women.

Joe waved the question off. "Believe it or not, boys, I don't keep any women," he said.

Next day, Al Wertheimer took the stand. He was a self-proclaimed professional gambler. Wertheimer, it was said, had once run with the "Purple Gang," a.k.a. the Jewish Mob. He wasn't asked about his possible gangster background, but rather how it was that he came to California.

"Joe Schenck invited me," he said. "He offered me a job as an executive for Twentieth Century-Fox. MGM matched the offer."

Those in the know sensed that this was collusion disguised as a bidding war. Joe and Nick playing a game to create an illusion.

"How much experience in show business did you have when the studios suddenly wanted to hire you?"

"None."

Wertheimer went to work for Joe and was paid $500 per week. His accomplishments as a film executive were not explored during the questioning. The prosecution was more interested in Wertheimer's role in converting Joe's home into a gambling casino.

Wertheimer testified that in June and July 1935, he used Joe Schenck's Sunset Boulevard home as a gambling casino while Joe wasn't there. In case jurors were envisioning a few roulette wheels, a portable poker table, and a felt table covering for craps, the prosecution demonstrated that the conversion was far more involved than that. Wertheimer admitted that he'd had to "tear down walls" in the home to "set up a roulette layout." Joe didn't know about it and when he found out that his home was being used in that way, he "gave me the devil on the phone."

"How did he find out that his house was being used for gambling?"

"Well, the L.A. County D.A. had the place raided," Wertheimer said.

"To your knowledge, was Mr. Schenck paid for the use of his home as a gambling joint?"

"I don't believe so."

Of course, none of this made sense, but again the jury figured it out. Joe was allowing his home to be renovated into a gambling casino, which was not only illegal but income upon which he paid no tax.

Wertheimer, it was revealed, had a brother named Louis who'd been for some time receiving a $500 per week check from Joseph Schenck, although it was unclear what Louis did to earn the money.

Wertheimer testified that he and his brother Louis had a history in building gambling establishments, as they had since 1935 operated the Clover Club on Sunset Boulevard, which catered to the Hollywood community, actors and executives alike.

"Did Joseph Schenck go to the Clover Club?"

"He did."

"And do you recall him winning or losing any large amounts?"

"No, I don't recall. We had a limit of twenty-five dollars to a number on the wheels, two hundred dollars on a throw of dice, but no limit on chemin-de-fer." The latter, the witness explained, was a form of the card game baccarat.

"Did you ever witness Joseph Schenck playing gin rummy with David O. Selznick?"

"Yes, sir."

"Did Schenck win, and if so, how much do you recall him winning?"

"He did and he won one hundred and three thousand dollars."

"On one game of gin rummy?"

"Yes, sir." That sounded like a whitewash at a thousand bucks a point.

Once Joe's house became a character in the trial, the prosecution showed the jury photos so they could envision it, dozens of rooms, tennis courts, a swimming pool which Correa called "teeming with writers, directors, producers, and actors."

On cross-examination, Corbin asked if "anybody who was anybody in Hollywood considered Joe Schenck's place a second home." The prosecution objected to the question, claiming it too general, and Judge Moskowitz sustained.

"Getting back to the Clover Club, would you say that he was a partner?"

"Certainly not. He just played."

The subject returned to Joe's house, now minus a few walls. "During the time you used the Schenck mansion as a gambling casino, how big of a crowd did you attract?"

"Oh, never very big. Just small private parties came there to gamble. We used a living room on the first floor, toward the back of the house—we kept the front of the house so dark that it wouldn't attract much attention."

"Did you conduct gambling at the Dunes in Palm Springs?"

"Yes."

"Publicly?"

"Yes. That is, persons who were properly introduced could gamble."

Wertheimer explained that the Dunes was a convenient place for Joe to gamble because he rented a house in Palm Springs.

"He rented the house from my wife, Thelma," Wertheimer said. "Paid five thousand dollars a year for the place."

"And did Joseph Schenck entertain at his Palm Springs house?"

"He did." Among the guests, Wertheimer said, "were Basil Rathbone, Irving Berlin, Constance Bennett, Darryl F. Zanuck, Louis B. Mayer, and Myrna Loy."

Wertheimer glanced over to the defense table and was surprised to see that Joe had dozed off.

IN RESPONSE TO JOE'S TRIAL, BEN HECHT WROTE A COLUMN IN *BOXOFfice Magazine* entitled "Joe Schenck in Hollywood" in which he marveled at Hollywood's relentless irony, at how "in this wedding of Jabberwock and the Muses called Hollywood" material could be created that was "full of beauty, wit, and high purpose." But none of Hollywood's best could match the exquisite irony of the Joe Schenck trial. The government, Hecht lamented, wanted us to believe Joe was a criminal and should be sent to jail. He was a scapegoat, and a juicy one to boot. Hecht knew Joe Schenck, and he was the "last man" who belonged behind bars. It was worse casting, Hecht quipped, than when Joe decided Tyrone Power should play Zorro. Joe was Hollywood's "most humane and gallant gentleman." Hecht had been paying attention to the testimony and all he heard were examples of Joe "squandering dollars in secret charities." Joe made a lot, and he spent a lot, much of it on "broken down hams and glamour girls." Has-beens and never-weres alike had Joe on their side. He emptied his pockets daily just taking care of the poor folks who entered Hollywood glowing with ambition, the most beautiful in their high school class, and then crashed and burned once in town.

Hecht wrote, "Joe has been the Santa Claus of the Hollywood and Broadway rubbish heaps. He has supported more burned-out stars and buried more penniless alcoholics, harlots, mimes, and scribblers than any gentleman of his time." Joe had the nerve to deduct the expenses of throwing parties, get-togethers that spawned wisdom, friendship, cheer among co-workers, and a thousand other things to further the cause of filmmaking.

The American public, reading only the sensational details coming out of Joe's trial, would be made to believe that Joe's life was a dizzying and protracted orgy. The headlines ignored that Joe brought "cheer to millions and great fortune to thousands."

THE NEXT DAY, HARRY C. WILSON, A YACHT BROKER, TOOK THE WITness stand and said that Joe came to him looking to sell his yacht. He was sick and tired of his friends using the boat and then sending him all the bills.

"Did Schenck sell the yacht?"

"He did, through me."

"So, he no longer has a yacht?" Correa asked, cocking his head to one side.

"Oh no, he bought another one, also through me, called the *Caroline*."

"Is that the same yacht *Caroline* that once belonged to Marcus Loew?"

"Yes, sir."

On cross-examination, Harold Corbin asked, "Who was using the boat and not divvying up?"

Wilson said Joe named Douglas Fairbanks, Norma Shearer, Irving Thalberg, and Sam Goldwyn. He thought for a moment, and then added, "And Clara Bow and Charles Chaplin. Some of those dated back to 1929 and 1930."

"Surely, the *Invader* was used for business purposes on many of these occasions."

"I suppose."

"And there were times when the yacht was used exclusively for business purposes."

"Yes. In 1932 and 1933, Douglas Fairbanks borrowed the yacht to make a picture in the South Seas."

"In 1937, Mr. Schenck himself sailed the *Invader* from California to New York, correct?"

"Yes, sir. Wait, no, that was the *Caroline*."

"And what was the purpose of that trip?"

"It was a goodwill trip, not a pleasure cruise."

"Schenck skippered the boat through the Panama Canal, correct?"

"Yes."

"And what do you mean by goodwill?"

"Well, he made several stops, all of them for business purposes. He stopped in Jamaica, Panama City, Mexico City, which required a plane. All places where he visited Twentieth Century-Fox branch offices."

"Was he in a hurry to get to the next place during the trip?"

"Oh no, the trip was conducted at a leisurely pace."

The next witness was Captain Victor Johnson, the captain of the *Caroline*. He testified that the yacht had been used, under his watch, for "expensive and reckless" voyages, with Harpo Marx, Irving Berlin, and Douglas Fairbanks acting as seamen while the wives and girlfriends played stewardess. Joe smiled at mention of his friends' names. Fairbanks had died suddenly in 1939 of a heart attack, but Marx and Berlin remained close friends and frequent house guests.

The smile was atypical. Joe was starting to worry at the defense table. He knew he was guilty. He equated taxes with highway robbery and had been trying to get around the government since his days behind a Bowery pharmacy counter. It had been more than a week, a long week, since he'd mentioned the New York Yankees.

The next morning, the prosecution called Ruth Nolander to the stand, a tall blond woman in professional attire and a no-nonsense demeanor—not one of Joe's starlets. Nolander testified that for sixteen years she had been Joe's secretary and that, among her duties, was to be custodian of a little tin box containing cash and jewelry. Each day she delivered the box to Joe's office with the key in its lock for Joe's inspection.

"In the performance of your duties, have you met a man named Willie Bioff?" Correa asked.

"Yes, sir. He came to visit Joe on a regular basis in 1937. Sometimes it was just him coming to see Mr. Schenck, and sometimes he brought others with him."

"Do you recall a particular time when Bioff came to Mr. Schenck's office in June of that year?"

"Yes, sir. On that occasion I saw Mr. Schenck counting a stack of money. Mr. Bioff was seated in the office at Mr. Schenck's right."

"Do you know how much money was in the stack?"

"Not precisely, but Mr. Schenck was counting aloud and stopped when he got to one hundred thousand dollars."

"What happened to that money?"

"It was placed in a manila envelope, which was given to me for sealing, and then turned over by me to John B. Codd, Mr. Schenck's controller. I specifically told Mr. Codd to be careful because the envelope contained a large sum."

"When you say Mr. Schenck's controller, you mean controller for Twentieth Century-Fox, correct?"

"I believe he did some work for Mr. Schenck personally, as well. But you're right."

"Were you ever given instructions to make a note of the one hundred thousand dollars or what it was for?"

"No, sir."

"Was it like Schenck to not give you information about cash in his possession?"

"Not at all. He was usually very specific about incoming and outgoing funds. I knew for example down to the penny how much he paid for his groceries."

To illustrate this point, the prosecution offered into evidence a grocery bill for $572.50, to which Miss Nolander had attached a note with a paper clip. The note read, "Dear Boss, this is what you had to pay for groceries last month. It comes to a little more than $20 a day and includes Coca Cola, cigarettes, and caviar. And remember, sir, you changed cooks three times during the month, and each new cook when she comes has certain staples, such as condiments, which she thinks she can cook better with, and so there is some duplication on those things. And remember, you had Mr. and Mrs. Harpo Marx there living with you at the time." The note went on to say that in November of 1936 Joe ordered turkeys and caviar twice. On another occasion a high laundry bill that Joe paid was in part for the laundry of a French tutor, Mr. and Mrs. Marx, and one Sandra Rambeau." Miss Rambeau was not further identified so the jury was allowed to assume she was one of Joe's girlfriends. "The $572.50 also included food for Joe's six servants."

"During that time was there a payment for a cross-country airplane flight for a Mrs. Duffy?"

"Yes, sir."

"And who was Mrs. Duffy?"

"She was Mr. Schenck's masseuse."

"Mr. Schenck was very meticulous about items he wanted deducted from his income tax, wasn't he?"

"Objection, leading the witness," Corbin said.

"Sustained," Judge Moskowitz ruled.

"Let me rephrase. Was Mr. Schenck meticulous when it came to itemizing the expenditures he wanted to have deducted from his income tax?"

"He was." She told the jury that Joe once took tobacco heiress Doris Duke out to lunch and had Nolander list the sixty-five cents he spent on Duke as a business expenditure.

"So, one hundred thousand dollars going out with no explanation was noteworthy."

"Yes, sir."

"The envelope from which Mr. Schenck pulled the one hundred thousand dollars, did you ever see that envelope again?"

"Yes, sir. In July 1937, when Mr. Schenck was preparing to go to Europe, he took some money out of the envelope, I don't know how much, and handed me the envelope. I placed it in the safety box, turning the key in his presence. And that was the last time I ever saw that envelope."

As it was Friday afternoon, Judge Moskowitz adjourned court until Monday morning. That gave the reporter from United Press time to dig for dirt on Sandra Rambeau, whose laundry Joe once had done and claimed as a business expense.

It didn't take long for the research to become troubling. For starters, on November 19, 1940, while in Paris, Sandra Rambeau married General Franz Ritter von Epp who, according to a source just back from Europe, was the architect of the German blitz on England.

What was Joe doing *her* laundry for? Further digging was necessary.

She was born in Springfield, Missouri, and went to New York in 1933. She quickly earned a reputation as a showgirl who dated powerful men. In 1934 she'd been chummy with the Duke of Kent. She was said to have seduced Hindu Prince Vishnu of Nepal. She also liked politicians, sportsmen, and members of the "international social set." She was linked to a famous cartoonist, a Wall Street tycoon, a U.S. senator, and a South American millionaire. It wasn't much, but that was just the reporter's dispatch for Saturday. In a way, the research was a relief. She probably wasn't a spy. She liked powerful men of all sorts. She would no doubt regret marrying a Nazi one day, but politics and philosophy presumably had nothing to do with their relationship.

CORREA CALLED TO THE WITNESS STAND ENRIQUE NEIDHART, WHO managed racetrack properties for an American syndicate.

"Prior to 1935, Agua Caliente was gay and flourishing, a favorite resort of film colony residents," Neidhart said.

"What happened in 1935?"

"The Mexican government outlawed gambling at the track and three years later expropriated the holdings of the Compania Mexicana de Agua Caliente."

"Stockbroker" Paul Zuckerman took the stand and testified that Joe always paid by check when he lost a bet and insisted on cash when he won.

Joseph Rosenberg, VP of the Bank of America, testified that on June 18, 1937, his bank loaned Joe Schenck $100,000, and that Joe repaid it with cash—fifties and hundreds in a brown paper bag four days later.

That evening, columnist Jimmie Fidler wrote about the Schenck trial. He didn't know if Joe was guilty or not, but one thing was certain: The sensational testimony about a mogul throwing money around was bad for the industry. "The trial is hurting the film colony in the court of public opinion," Fidler wrote.

Back in court, Fox VP William Goetz, Louis B. Mayer's son-in-law, testified that in 1935 he gave Joe a check for $5,000 and received at the same time $5,000 in cash.

"Did you consider that money laundering?"

"Well, I considered it a year-end sale, the type the Treasury Department customarily approves of for the purpose of tax deduction," Goetz said.

Goetz's secretary, Mrs. Frances Webb, testified that Goetz gave her $5,000 in cash and instructed her to "hold it for a friend."

"So, what, if anything, did you do with the money?"

"I put it in a little green box and entered a note in my ledger."

"What did the note say?"

"It said 'Hold for V.M.'"

"Who is V.M.?"

"No one. That is just a symbol I use for an unknown person."

Huh? A few eyebrows in the jury box waxed skeptical. Several jurors were trying to figure out who V.M. could be. Victor Mature? Vincente Minelli? Virginia Mayo? Victor McLaglen?

"When was the next time you saw that cash?"

"About two weeks later, Mr. Goetz asked for the money, and I gave it to him."

At 4:30 p.m. on Thursday, March 27, after fourteen and a half days of testimony, Correa stood. "Your Honor, the government rests."

Judge Moskowitz adjourned for the weekend and ordered the defense to have its case ready to go first thing Monday morning.

Sunday's papers' headlines read: CHAPLIN TO TESTIFY FOR SCHENCK. The Little Tramp was already in town, staying at the Waldorf Towers. Chaplin had known Joe Schenck since 1912 when Joe was booking vaudeville acts for Marcus Loew and Chaplin was on the circuit. They were partners at UA for years.

And on Monday morning, in the courtroom, there he was, no mustache, gray curly hair, Charles Chaplin. Things got off to a shaky start when Chaplin lifted his left hand to take the oath.

"Other hand," Judge Moskowitz said with a frown. Was this guy trying to be fruity or what?

Chaplin smiled sheepishly, then mischievously. He very slowly lowered his left hand, then very slowly raised his right. Now the judge was convinced.

The oath taken, Chaplin climbed into the witness box with the grace of a world-class mime.

Questioned patiently by Harold Corbin, Chaplin spoke of his almost thirty-year friendship with Joe. He described the formation of UA.

"Mr. Schenck was the chairman of our company, the man who kept us together, a man we could trust, a man who settled all of our problems, a man in whom we relied, upon his judgment and his generosity," Chaplin said.

The government didn't bother to cross-examine. The facts, Correa knew, were in his favor. It was the *heart* of the jury he had to worry about. The defense was going to parade famous and powerful people to say nice things about Joe, and there wasn't much Correa could do about it. There was nothing to gain by giving Charlie Chaplin the third degree.

Irving Berlin was next. He'd known Joe since the Lower East Side, and the man was honest as the day was long. John Golden, the Broadway producer, got in his two cents. Then Chief Justice Philip Gibson of the California Supreme Court took the stand, a justice superstar.

Film czar Will Hays apparently discussed his testimony with his own lawyer before taking the stand. His comments touched only on what others thought of Joe. Hays testified: "I have known the man for twenty-two years and I know his reputation and his reputation is good. I'm very sure of his reputation."

The following Monday afternoon, Corbin tried to call four IRS agents to testify about the honest nature of Joe's tax returns, but Correa objected, and Judge Moskowitz sustained. Turned out, IRS agents were not allowed to testify without the permission of the Secretary of the Treasury, who in this case said no.

Former Postmaster General James Farley testified that Joe was "good" and "honest," without a political bone in his body. "He wouldn't be mayor of New York if you handed him the job on a silver platter," Farley said.

Outside to reporters Farley said that he'd talked to Joe recently and felt he was sincere about his interest in buying the New York Yankees baseball team.

"Would you and Joe consider going in together to run the ball club?"

"We've never had that conversation," Farley said.

Bestselling author Gene Fowler (*The Great Mouthpiece*), and Twentieth Century-Fox European executive Benjamin Miggins agreed Joe was a swell guy. Joe's banker buddy Attilio Giannini, now retired as head of the Bank of America, said Joe was honest and known for his integrity on both coasts.

The defense's case marched on. Character witnesses gave way to accountants. Corbin spent the day talking to the bottom liners. The numbers came out in Joe's favor. The government owed him money, not the other way around.

On Thursday, Joe's co-defendant, studio accountant Joseph H. Moskowitz, took the stand to defend both himself and his boss. Judge Grover Moskowitz made sure that everyone understood that he and the co-defendant were not related.

"You prepared Joseph Schenck's tax returns, Mr. Moskowitz?"

"Yes, sir."

"Do you ever falsify any figures while compiling your boss's income taxes?"

"I did not."

"How much participation did Mr. Schenck have in the process of filing a tax return?"

"None. That is, he signed the form after I was done."

"If it is determined that your tax returns were indeed faulty in some way, would that in any way be Joe Schenck's fault?"

"No, sir."

"Whose fault would that be?" Corbin asked.

"If there was a mistake on Mr. Schenck's taxes, that would be my fault, sir," Moskowitz said, willing to take the bullet.

On cross-examination, Mathias Correa asked, "During your preparation of Mr. Schenck's taxes in 1936, Mr. Moskowitz, did you ever hear of someone known as Elsie Valentine?"

"I seem to remember something about that name coming up, yes," Moskowitz replied.

"According to your recollection, was she talent discovered by Twentieth Century-Fox during the fall of 1936?"

"That sounds right."

"Isn't it true that Miss Valentine was the special friend of a Treasury agent at that time?"

"I don't know about that. My recollection is she was recommended by producer Earl Carroll."

Correa grilled Moskowitz thoroughly. Miss Poggi, was she a good deduction? How about the two women at once, was that a business deal? Special starlets get a mink, that a good deduction? What about the gambling losses? He paid with a check and collected in cash, what about that? "When you talked to Mr. Schenck about gambling did you discuss his wins and losses?"

"I went on just what the books showed," Moskowitz said.

Correa asked if all Americans are allowed to deduct all their barber shop expenses. Moskowitz argued that that was probably not the case, and further conceded that paying for a fresh haircut—especially to the tune of $475 per month—was not an expense necessary to earn a salary.

"Trips to paradise, pleasure resorts, were those good deductions?"

"I understood that business was conducted on those trips, yes."

"And those trips could not be made without the company of women, correct?"

"There was business conducted in those cases, too."

Film executive Robert T. Kane testified regarding the main contention of the defense's case, that you must spend money to make money. Joe lived in a world that partied. If the other moguls were holding parties to attract talent into the fold, Fox would have to do so also. Kane discussed parties that Joe had thrown in 1936 in Paris, parties with a 300,000-franc price tag, $20,000.

Kane testified, "Mr. Schenck was a very generous host."

"How did he pay?"

"Always with cash he pulled from his pocket."

"He paid Twentieth Century-Fox expenses out of his pocket?"

"All the time."

"Did Twentieth Century-Fox get business as a result of these parties?"

"Yes. Attending one of those parties in Paris was Gracie Fields, the English comedienne. At the time of the party, she was engaged by another company but after the Paris party we went to London and hired her."

THE DEFENSE RESTED WITHOUT JOE TAKING THE STAND TO DEFEND himself. The prosecution had put thirty-two witnesses on the stand, the defense fifteen.

Journalists portrayed the trial as one filled with figures, both feminine and mathematical—a case in which a jury would have to decide if Hollywood's "Uncle Joe" had paid Uncle Sam.

Court was adjourned for the Easter weekend. That Sunday, at Belmont Park, the daily double was a horse named "Joe Schenck" in the first race and "Witness Stand" in the second. Seriously. The racehorse "Joe Schenck" raced from 1937–44, 107 races, and won twenty-three of them, for career earnings of more than $54,000.

The judge charged the jury and sent them to the deliberation room at 4:25 p.m. on April 16. The jury worked into the night and the early morning hours. After ten hours of deliberation, at 2:33 a.m. on April 17, the jury convicted Joe of tax evasion for 1935 and 1936 but acquitted him for 1937 and on the charge of conspiracy to defraud the government.

A week later Joe was sentenced to a three-year jolt in the fed pen and fined $20,000. Co-defendant Joseph Moskowitz drew one year and was fined $10,000. Joe would not be eligible for parole for more than a year because he was also indicted for perjury regarding his statements about Willie Bioff.

And the feds were still not done with Joe. There was talk they would sue him in civil court to get back the taxes Joe hadn't paid.

Judge Moskowitz was aware that Joe's penalty was shockingly harsh. No one expected three years. The judge said, "It is in the public interest to have a salutary effect in deterring others."

Joe was unnerved by the sentence and stuttered, "I . . . I . . . I'll just have to appeal."

Correa was pleased with the sentence: "He evaded taxes for several years and has hindered government agents at every turn."

Outside the courthouse, Corbin was spitting mad. "Here is a man who never had an enemy, who lived generously, decently, and courageously. He's not a criminal. He is a great builder of a great industry. He will be more of an asset to the government out earning his salary than he would be in any jail. Fine the man if you must. Schenck would cheerfully pay any sum the government demanded."

Joe was free to go pending appeal, so—shaken but steady on his pins—Joe walked out of the courthouse, said goodbye at the curb to his friends Norma Shearer and Douglas Fairbanks's widow, Lady Ashley, got into a car, and was driven to what was then called LaGuardia Field where he boarded a plane to L.A.

Years later, Irving Berlin would tell his daughter Mary Ellin Barrett that Joe's conviction did nothing to hurt his reputation in Hollywood. In fact, he was more beloved than ever. It gave him street cred. Joe was a hero with his peers. He'd been convicted of doing something that every Hollywood executive was doing, but out of the top moguls Joe was the only one who had no wife or kids. According to Berlin, he "took the rap for everybody."

Not long after Joe's conviction, during his appeal, Joe gave an extensive interview about his life to Alan Hynd for *Liberty* magazine. The interview took place over three days, as the men sat on the veranda of Joe's cottage at Arrowhead Springs, two hours east of Hollywood. The town, now part of San Bernardino, was a weekend getaway destination for Hollywood stars. Joe's neighbors included Lucille Ball, the Marx Brothers, Judy Garland, and Humphrey Bogart.

"Sure, I'm guilty," Joe said. "This income-tax business—guilty of *carelessness*. Every man makes some sort of contribution to the jam that he is in. My contribution has been carelessness."

Joe said that, had the arrest and trial taken place twenty years earlier, he wouldn't have been bothered by it.

"You see, I've always made a point to profit from any experience, pleasant or unpleasant. For example, after I had spent the pleasantest years of my life as the husband of Norma Talmadge and, one morning at breakfast, she told me that she was in love with another man. I profited from that, even though my heart was hurt. It showed me how honest a woman could be, and it gave me a new understanding of a certain phase of life. It would be the same with this income-tax business if I were still young enough to profit. But maybe, if you tell my whole story, someone else can learn a lesson. I'm over sixty now, just how much over I don't know, and I don't know either how many years are left ahead of me. Maybe not many. So, I doubt I can benefit from this experience."

Joe explained that he "didn't give a damn" about money, that anyone in Hollywood would verify that, but he had accumulated a lot of money largely because he was restless, always urged on by something inside him, and whatever it was that he'd accomplished always brought money along with it.

He admitted that he was a gambler and had lost as much as he won.

"I would be lying if I said I wanted to be poor again. Nobody wants to be poor. But it is the truth that I have given away a good deal of what I've made, and that has been a pleasure. Maybe I've been selfish in giving big parties for people, giving them automobiles, taking a dozen friends on a long yacht cruise, because that's what I get a big kick out of—seeing that other people have a good time."

Joe confessed that he was a lonely man and enjoyed being surrounded by laughter and fun. That said, he was not a vice-ridden man. He took a drink every now and again, usually just a glass of wine.

Surprisingly, he said he didn't consider himself a ladies' man.

"I have no delusions about a pretty young girl falling in love with Joe Schenck. When I was twenty, I liked girls my own age, not women of sixty or over. It works both ways."

Hynd asked, "If you could live your life over again, would you live it the same way?"

"I'm not ashamed of anything, if that's what you mean," Joe said. "But as to marriage, I would not make the same mistake that I made when Miss Talmadge was my wife."

"How so?"

Joe said that he used to go away on long business trips and would get so caught up in work that he would forget to call Norma long distance, or to send her flowers, or a telegram. "Had I come across a script where a man as neglectful as I was succeeded in keeping the love of a beautiful wife, I would have tossed the script in the wastebasket," Joe said. "I'll admit I've done all right for an immigrant boy. In the three words of one of my dearest friends, '*God Bless America*.'"

Joe also admitted that his success story could only have happened in America.

"Still, I have no illusion that I am a great man. There are today in this country countless men with far more ability than I have. But unfortunately, it is not always ability that takes a person to the top. It is a gambling spirit. I used every bit of my ability at dangerous times while abler men slowed down at the sharp curves. If there is any philosophy of life that I have arrived at, that's it."

On May 1, Joe resigned as Fox chairman of the board. That same day, Judge Grover Moskowitz suspended Joe's tax evasion sentence, Joe pleaded guilty to perjury charges, and his prison sentence was shortened from three years to one. Joe was also placed on probation for three years. As a condition of the probation Schenck placed in escrow sixty thousand shares of Fox stock as a guarantee that his $400,000 in tax liabilities would be paid. Joe also paid the $20,000 imposed as part of his tax evasion conviction.

On May 2, 1942, Joe surrendered to the U.S. Marshal and was taken to the federal penitentiary at Danbury, Connecticut, to begin his one year, one day, sentence for perjury. The fed pen was on a hilltop two miles outside of town overlooking Candlewood Lake.

Joe, as was standard practice back then, spent his first month behind bars in quarantine, after which he was permitted considerable liberties, Danbury being one of the most "modern" prisons in the country. One of those privileges was Monday night talent shows, in which prison talent performed, often in conjunction with outside talent, top-notch some of it, stage and concert-hall performers. As Joe used to put together vaudeville shows for a living, the Monday night shows perked up with him involved.

The prison might have been modern, but it was also overcrowded, six hundred prisoners in a four-hundred-prisoner facility, the number of prisoners swollen by draft dodgers, deserters, and other wartime offenses.

On June 12, 1942, Mrs. Frank Bennett, chairman of the Citizens' Committee and owner of the Deep Well Ranch, announced that the large home on Tamarisk Road in Palm Springs belonging to Joseph M. Schenck was the newest USO hospitality center. Arrangements for the usage of the Schenck home by the USO was made by Mrs. Edward G. Robinson, wife of the great actor. The facilities of the mansion included a swimming pool, barbecue pit, sleeping quarters, guest house, recreation rooms, and tennis courts. Hearing of the transaction, experts predicted that Joe's days in stir were numbered.

And, sure enough, Joe was released on September 8, 1942. Six months later William Goetz resigned as head of Fox and was quickly replaced by Joe Schenck.

Uncle Joe, it seemed, had been completely forgiven by just about everyone for not paying his bullshit taxes.

CHAPTER EIGHTEEN

HANGOVERS AND BLACKLISTS

Throughout the war years, Loews Inc. had kept up its March of Dimes activities. Nick took over after Joe's dustup with the feds and enjoyed wooing good favor from the White House. First Lady Eleanor Roosevelt loved screen stars, and Nick saw to it that MGM stars—Nick played a hunch and sent both men and women—were regular visitors to White House balls, where the First Lady would soak up the glamour like a sponge. Their job was to stroll around arm and arm with Eleanor and point out just how hard Loew's was working for the March of Dimes.

Fund-raising continued after FDR's death. On September 5, 1945, with Harry Truman in the White House, Nick presented Basil O'Connor, president of the National Foundation for Infantile Paralysis, a check for $5,978,939.34.

In Culver City, all MGM stars were assigned to make promos, inviting theatergoers to drop a dime in the box with the picture of a kid in leg braces on it. Mickey Rooney and Judy Garland made a memorable promo. If everyone could spare one thin dime, oh, the wonders that could be done. (And they weren't lying. The March of Dimes financed the research that led to the polio vaccine.)

A report on the Loew's Inc.'s near-$6 million contribution to the March of Dimes was sent to Truman, who inherited an interest in polio from his predecessor. Interestingly, about three weeks later, Truman granted Joe Schenck, till then free only under the conditions of his parole, a full pardon.

It was good news. Joe was no longer considered a felon.

The pardon came at a time when Joe needed good news. Hollywood was going to hell. SAG planned to shut down all Hollywood studios until a seven-month-old AFL strike was settled. The aggravation wore Joe down until mid-August when he was hospitalized for a few days at Cedars of Lebanon with a fever.

When Joe felt better, he thrust himself into the life of former "poor little rich girl" (and later seller of designer jeans on TV), now twenty-one-years-old and already twice married, Mrs. Gloria Vanderbilt DiCicco Stokowski. Joe was an old friend of husband number one, Pasquale "Pat" DiCicco, a former agent who'd made many deals with Fox and UA over the years. (He was much more, too: friend of Lucky Luciano, one of the three men—with Cubby Broccoli and Wallace Beery—who beat Ted Healy to death, a murder covered up by Eddie Mannix, and a Romeo who married Thelma Todd and Gloria Vanderbilt. The man had range.) DiCicco also functioned as a bird dog for starlets, steering them to the powerful men who could make or break them, and in that capacity supplied stimulating talent for Joe's parties. Joe called him his "court jester," as his job was to keep parties lively. We'll run into DiCicco again before our tale is through.

Vanderbilt was a showbiz wannabe despite her status as society-girl gossip-column regular. Joe told her he'd keep his eyes peeled for a script that would be good for Gloria, but he never found one. She didn't make her acting debut until thirteen years later, and then only on a handful of routine TV dramas.

AS THE ALLIES MARCHED ACROSS EUROPE AND ISLAND-HOPPED IN THE Pacific, victory now an inevitability, both Joe and Nick took note of the myriad of ways WWII had drained Hollywood of its pre-war verve. Stars like James Stewart and Clark Gable went to war and were not available to make pictures. Because of rationing Hollywood was restricted in the amount of celluloid they could use—FDR's War Production Board had cut Hollywood's allotment of film by twenty million feet—plus, the theaters had trouble getting enough freon to keep their theaters air-conditioned.

During those weeks when the war in Europe was over but the war in the Pacific raged on, Nick sent Eddie Mannix to Europe, to survey areas that had only a few weeks or months before been the scenes of battles. Mannix was to scout for locations that could be used for MGM war pictures and assigned to take photos of war damages that could be used by art directors when building sets for war pictures in Culver City. When Mannix returned, Nick and Mayer debriefed Mannix about what he'd seen. No MGM war pictures went into production.

MGM came out of WWII still making happy, happy musicals. The performers' smiles remained big, but the product felt increasingly lackluster. MGM was entering post-war doldrums from which it never completely recovered. They had the stars, Judy Garland, Fred Astaire, Gene Kelly, and Frank Sinatra. But they cast Kelly and Sinatra together in an old-time baseball picture called *Take Me Out to the Ballgame* (1949), directed by a washed-up Busby Berkeley. And it was a bomb. Even baseball fans, and there were many millions of them, couldn't stand the irksome plot—something about competing ballplayers who are also in vaudeville vying for the hugs of the new team owner, who is a beautiful woman. Judy Garland was supposed to get the part but was strung out on speed and struggling. Ginger Rogers took the part, temporarily, then bailed. A bone-dry Esther Williams ended up playing the role. Berkeley started out at the helm but drank himself out of the job, so the picture had to be finished by Gene Kelly and Stanley Donen. The result was a startling unevenness, something stitched together.

To be fair, that same year MGM made *On the Town*, with much better results. The rest of Hollywood was going for dark subject matter, *noir* it would be called, with filthy murder, underworld lingo, shadowy night streets, flashing neon, dank drug dens, and sweat-stained hotel rooms. They cranked out cheap hard-boiled detective pictures with dolls and fedoras. MGM still specialized in dancing girls, just the way Louis B. liked it. In the decade-plus that Thalberg had been dead, the studio had become a wild and wonderful party, but this . . . this was the hangover.

Bottom line: MGM was slowly petering out. Costs were up. Box office was down. MGM hadn't had a hit since 1944 (*Meet Me in St. Louis*). When Nick tried to find out from Mayer what was wrong, he discovered that Mayer was spending more time overseeing his stable of thoroughbred racehorses than supervising MGM. In early 1948 Nick gave Mayer an ultimatum.

"If you want to keep your job, you'll sell those horses."

"But . . ."

"Everything has been shit since Irving died. Hire a new Thalberg right away while you're at it."

"Who?"

"I have someone in mind," Nick said.

Nick's pick for the "new Thalberg" was Dore Schary, who did have great ideas, but they were gritty and raw, nothing candy-apple about them. Nick and Schary met on a train from Washington, D.C., to New York in November 1947, and despite political differences, they were fast friends. Schary's background, a first-generation Jew from Newark, New Jersey, made him fit the template for studio executive perfectly. He'd quit school at thirteen, ran the entertainment at a Catskills resort, and dabbled in acting and writing plays. He came to Hollywood, and won an Oscar for his story for *Boys Town* in 1938. He directed for a time and worked his way up until he was hired to run RKO, the position he held when Nick decided he was the "new Thalberg."

"Streamline production, reduce costs," Nick instructed Schary.

Mayer hired Schary without complaint, but quickly learned that as a producer the man was flawed. He was a creative entity, something a producer (an MGM producer anyway) should never be, and instead of controlling the budget, he tended to be another cook in the writers' kitchen. When other execs wondered aloud how Schary had gotten into a position for which he was such an ill fit, the answer seemed obvious: Nick wanted him.

BY 1947, HOLLYWOOD WAS IN TROUBLE. BUSINESS WAS OFF BY TWENTY-FIVE percent. MGM was forced to cut their overhead by $9 million. Twelve-thousand studio workers from the seven main studios were laid off. Studios had to deal with labor unions that had grown tremendously in power during the war years. Powerful anti-Semites remained annoyed that Jewish men ran Hollywood, and were looking for ways to shrink their power.

One tack the haters used was to raise the issue of the Sherman Antitrust Act, which could be interpreted as a law against studios owning their own theaters. Men from Washington came to Hollywood and asked questions, looking to root out commies. Some studio heads thought they could kill two birds with one stone and reported troublesome union leaders as commies. During the autumn of 1947 the House Un-American Activities Committee served subpoenas and Nick got one.

Most of the witnesses said they were anti-communist and agreed that there was no place for communism in America, largely because that was what the committee wanted to hear, but others, on principle alone, refused to answer questions they thought were none of the government's business. Ten writers, in fact, refused to answer questions and became known as the Hollywood Ten. They were Alvah Bessie, Herbert Biberman, Lester Cole, Edward Dmytryk, Ring Lardner, Jr., John Howard Lawson, Albert Maltz, Samuel Ornitz, Adrian Scott, and Dalton Trumbo.

Were there communists in Hollywood in 1947? Well, sure. Of a sort.

Were there plots underway to undermine the American Way and overthrow the U.S. government by Hollywood communists? Absolutely not. The group in question was called "the parlor commies," a group consisting of liberal actors and writers, who liked to sit around someone's parlor, eat finger sandwiches, wear open-toed sandals, smoke reefers, and discuss existentialism, poetry, and radical politics.

Trouble was, it was the early days of the Red Scare. Communists, real and imagined, were being scapegoated as the source of all of America's problems, much as they had during the Great Depression. And, just as during the Depression, "communist" was a thinly veiled synonym of "Jew."

The commie conspiracy, in reality harmless meetings of mild-mannered scholarly types, was demonized by conservative politicians, until Hollywood was forced to wipe out a problem that in actuality barely existed. Nick was among the first to realize that Hollywood needed to be *publicly* anti-communist if it hoped to survive in post-WWII America.

Thus came the Waldorf Conference, Monday, November 24, 1947, in New York's Waldorf-Astoria Hotel. Many had hoped that the meeting could be put off until after Thanksgiving, but Nick was insistent that it be done immediately. Nick carried so much weight that Eric Johnston, president of the Motion Picture Association of America, cancelled his flight home for the holiday to Washington State, and flew to New York to be there. Irritated, but there.

Also there were Louis B. Mayer of MGM, Spyros Skouras of Fox, Barney Balaban of Paramount, Harry Cohn of Columbia, Dore Schary, before his move to MGM and repping RKO, and Jack Warner of Warner Brothers. For each mogul there were two or three lawyers. There were between seventy and eighty people in the room.

After Mayer and Skouras made statements saying that it was every American's duty to weed out the communists among them, Sam Goldwyn stood and said he didn't like the air of panic in the room. He was pretty much shouted down by those same panicky men, who cried out, "Are we mice or are we men? Communists need to be discharged."

Schary spoke up, like Goldwyn, warning of reacting emotionally. He pointed out that being a communist was not illegal, and there was no evidence that any of the studio personnel on the list of commie sympathizers had ever plotted to overthrow the U.S. government, or anything else subversive, for that matter. He, too, was shouted down.

The surprise of the meeting came when Eddie Mannix stood to speak. He was assumed to be on the anti-commie side, as he had been opinionated a few years earlier on V-E Day when the U.S. Army stopped at Berlin, instead of marching all the way to Moscow. Mannix, however, was very clear in his opinion. There was a law, he said, on the California books, that prohibited an employer from firing an employee because of his political affiliations.

"I wouldn't want to do anything to break the law," Mannix said, and no one even laughed.

Despite dissent, the shouters won. And so, there was a blacklist. To be fair to these men who threw the ten writers under the table, they'd only been given two choices. Denounce the Hollywood Ten or be stamped themselves as communists, enemies of the people. Preachers would call them "un-Christian filth." The WASPs would swoop in and turn pictures into Wonder Bread.

Joe Schenck tried valiantly to have it both ways, so much so that he made no sense whatsoever. Joe said, and we quote, "I don't believe there should be a blacklist, but I don't think we should hire communists either."

In the end, the "Waldorf Conference Statement" was composed. Anyone who refused to sign would be tagged a pinko. The statement read, in part, "Members of the Association of Motion Picture Producers deplore the action of the ten Hollywood men who have been cited for contempt by the House of Representatives. We do not desire to prejudge their legal rights, but their actions have been a disservice to their employers and have impaired their usefulness to the industry . . . On the issue of alleged subversive and disloyal elements in Hollywood . . . we will not knowingly employ a Communist or a member of any party which advocates the overthrow of the government of the United States . . . Nothing subversive or un-American has appeared on the screen."

Few things done in Hollywood have resulted in as much condemnation and shame as the creation of the Hollywood blacklist. According to Hollywood historian Patrick McGilligan, "It was a cultural holocaust, a tragedy from which the industry has never fully recovered. It's still a live issue because the survivors, and their children, haven't forgotten. And because it dramatically altered the climate of filmmaking. Even today, there are still risky political subjects that Hollywood won't take on."

The blacklist has been blamed for a shift in American history, from the New Deal to the Red Scare. To keep the WASPs out, Hollywood baked its own Wonder Bread. The studios, attacked on one side by TV and on the other by dogmatic conservative politicians, stopped making films that said anything.

THE MORE LIBERAL-MINDED MOGULS HATED THE BLACKLIST, EVEN IF they admitted its necessity. To soothe their consciences, Joe Schenck, Dore Schary, Paramount production head Henry Ginsberg, and producer Walter Wanger, formed the Motion Picture Industry Council, to protect members of the industry from being "falsely accused of being communists." The first meeting was held November 13, 1947, in MGM's executive dining room. It didn't help the Hollywood Ten, but maybe it would prevent future injustices.

CHAPTER NINETEEN

THE NEW NORMA

AFTER DIVORCING NORMA TALMADGE, HAVING HIS HEART BROKEN by Merle Oberon, and serving four months in prison, Joe never again considered remarrying. He'd always been a connoisseur of women. Now he indulged his passion to the fullest, and if possible, without emotional involvement. He already had a reputation as a dirty old man from the revelations of his trial. So, by the late 1940s, Joe's wants and needs were well known—exaggerated, even. Truth was, by the time World War II ended he'd lost vitality.

So it was in this diminished capacity that he became the first patron of a starlet soon to be known as Marilyn Monroe. She was young, twenty, and called Norma Jeane Mortenson (nee Baker). Young, but not naïve. She'd learned from a painfully tender age that her youth, body, and beauty had tremendous value.

IN L.A., JOE PURCHASED A DEN OF DECADENCE WORTHY OF ANY PLAYboy zillionaire. It was called Owlwood, and it stood proud and erect on Carolwood Drive just above Sunset Boulevard in Holmby Hills. The twelve-thousand-square-foot Tuscan-style mansion featured rich surfaces of limestone, marble, mahogany, oak, and wrought iron on Louis XV paneling. There were eight bedrooms and eleven baths, a grand wine cellar, and a projection room. In the den hung a larger-than-life oil painting of Norma Talmadge. The supersized portrait overlooked Joe's magnificent card games. The estate overlooked the Los Angeles Country Club, a bastion of WASP snobbery where Joe wasn't allowed to play.

One of Joe's neighbors was gangster Benjamin "Bugsy" Siegel, who built a mansion of his own nearby on Delfern Drive. Joe toured Siegel's home and picked up a few ideas. In case Siegel's home was raided, there was a secret passageway, entered through a sliding bookcase. So, Joe's den also featured a secret room behind a sliding bookcase. The passageway led to Joe's "casting room." It was a joke. Any producer could have a couch. Joe had a room.

The Schenck brothers moved with ease in the company of Jewish gangsters. They were all children of the Bowery and played by Bowery rules. Or Brownsville, or Newark rules, same thing. According to author Raymond Chandler, the Hollywood moguls, and the boys who ran the rackets, were more similar than they were different. The moguls may have had scruples the gangsters lacked, but—as Chandler wrote in a letter to a friend—the two groups shared "the same faces, same expressions, same manners, same way of dressing, and same exaggerated leisure of movement."

IN 1947, NORMA JEANE'S STANDARD STARLET CONTRACT WITH FOX EXpired, and no new contract was forthcoming.

"All they had me do was pose for stills," she complained. (Sometimes ridiculously, like that Thanksgiving shoot when they had her point a blunderbuss in the general direction of a live turkey's head while wearing a sexy Pilgrim getup.)

So, a free agent once again, she "auditioned" herself by attending all the right parties where rich men hung out looking hungrily for shapely young careers that needed a boosting. She was looking good at a party when she ran into Pat DiCicco, the agent/producer/gangster/procurer that Joe Schenck referred to as his "court jester" because his job was to "liven up" Joe's parties.

"Is it true you were married to both Thelma Todd and Gloria Vanderbilt?" Norma Jeane asked.

"All true," DiCicco said with an air of danger, and invited her to a party at Owlwood. "That's Joe Schenck's place."

With that heads-up, when the young woman first laid eyes on Joe, she approached him boldly with something to say.

"Mr. Schenck, I am named after your wife!" she said in a breathy stage whisper.

"Ex-wife. Call me Joe. How so?"

So, she told him a story. Her mom used to work for him. "At Consolidated Film Industries," she enunciated.

"What's her name?"

"Gladys Baker. She thought Norma Talmadge was the most beautiful star in the world."

"She was a film cutter."

"Yes!" The woman was delighted. "What a memory!"

"For beautiful women, yes."

The woman beamed, all eyes and teeth and lips and hair and so beautiful, like a fantasy artist had drawn her. She was again talking.

"Your Norma used to regularly visit my mom and the other ladies, the cutting ladies and the splicing ladies, bring them stuff, cookies, like that, and they loved her. So, I was called Norma."

"Norma what?"

"Well, right now I'm going by Jean Norman, but I don't like it. As a kid I was Norma Jeane Baker, to have the same name as my mom. I'm really Norma Jeane Mortenson."

"Ever read a book?"

"About one a week since I was seven. Sigmund Freud had a dirty mind; I prefer the collective unconscious. That's Jung."

Joe was impressed and asked her to stick around. He had work for her. He explained that he hosted gin rummy games—or bridge, or poker—with scary stakes, and needed attractive women to keep glasses full, cigars lit, that kind of thing.

"I would be honored to light your cigar."

"Not mine, I don't smoke. For me, there'll be other duties."

"Can't wait," Norma Jeane Mortenson said.

FADE IN. Interior. Owlwood Estate. Night.

This evening Owlwood is quiet. Joe and Norma Jeane have finished what looks like a fine meal and none of the staff are anywhere to be found. It's just the two of them. The residence is decorated for Christmas. The decorations are plush and stylish; they would give the windows at Macy's a run for their money.

NORMA JEANE

Everything was so delicious, thank you.

Joe smiles and nods.

NORMA JEANE (looking around at the decorations)

I thought you were Jewish.

JOE

In this town no one is Jewish . . . yet everyone seems to be. (pause) You enjoyed dinner?

NORMA JEANE

It's fine—really lovely—and you know how thankful I am for all your kindness.

JOE

You're my friend. I like when my friends do well.

NORMA JEANE

Well, I don't know. Mr. Zanuck looks at me as if he doesn't like me.

JOE

My dear, this is a tough business. This town mints beautiful women the way Washington mints nickels. You're meeting the right people. Be a little patient. Remember the three T's. Timing, talent, and tenacity. Of these we only control one. Tenacity. Make your career your first consideration.

NORMA JEANE

Oh, but I am. What more can I do, Joe?

JOE

I'll continue to help you. Just listen to what I say.

NORMA JEANE

Of course, Joe. You know I always will.

JOE

Come—I want to show you something.

Joe takes Norma Jeane by the hand and leads her into the den with its huge fireplace (the kind you might see in an old Universal monster picture) and painting of Norma Talmadge. Next to the mantel is a grand bookcase. Joe walks to the case and pulls out a book that is really a lever exposing a secret passage. As the case swings open toward them:

NORMA JEANE (wide-eyed)

It's so unusual, Joe. But why would you need it?

JOE

Some things we don't need but rather we want.

NORMA JEANE

But why would you want it?

JOE

It's a place to keep secrets.

After a long beat, Norma Jeane gently pushes past Joe into the passageway, into the darkness.

NORMA JEANE

I can keep a secret.

FADE.

IN THE CASTING ROOM BEGAN AN ODD LOVE AFFAIR THAT LINGERED on for them both, long after the sex part was over. There were other "girls" who worked the parties, too, of course, but from the start this new Norma was Joe's favorite—and he hers.

During the following year or so, when visitors went to Owlwood for a business meeting, it wasn't unusual to see Norma Jean—Joe advised her to drop the e—out by the Olympic-sized pool in bathing suit and sunglasses, an essential part of the scenery. She became known in the smug world of Hollywood power as "Joe's girl."

When sex was through, and it usually didn't take long, Norma Jean could talk and say things, express hopes and dreams, in a way that other starlets were unable to do. And sometimes Joe would find himself telling her all his philosophical theories as well. She was unspoiled, didn't feel the world owed her something, but was determined to work hard and get some on her own.

Joe sensed that, unlike some party girls, this new Norma didn't despise the old men with the power. It wasn't that she felt romantic toward Joe, he could have been her grandfather, but she thought he was kind of cute, and she genuinely liked him, and that made sex with him tons more tolerable. She'd grown up without a father, uncertain in fact who her father was—Gladys had two boyfriends when she got pregnant, neither worth a damn—and being with this man who had employed her mother when she was conceived might have been fascinating for her.

These were the days before Viagra and there came a time when even the most expert lover left Joe uninspired. Desperate, he received visits from a series of doctors, most of whom he kicked the hell out, until he found a Dr. Feelgood who gave him an injection. He didn't know what it was, but it worked, but only for a minute or two. So, proximity became essential. He had to have a woman nearby. For a time, that was Norma Jean's job. She and Joe synchronized schedules because, as she later put it, "this stuff can't wait for a studio limousine to drive me across town." He eventually installed her in a guesthouse behind Owlwood where she lived for six months. So she could enter Owlwood without being seen—Joe had a tunnel built with its entrance in the rear garden. She entertained men in her guesthouse, and was sometimes indiscreet, talking about Joe and his problems. (It has been said that she left Joe's guesthouse because she fell in love with her vocal coach Fred Karger. He didn't like the Owlwood arrangement so she moved out, hoping Karger would marry her. He eventually said he wasn't interested in marriage because he didn't like the idea of her being stepmother to his child from a previous marriage.)

In March 1948, Joe called Harry Cohn and arranged for Columbia Pictures to sign the actress now known as Marilyn Monroe to a six-month contract.

Soon thereafter, Joe wrote a series of letters, mostly short notes, demonstrating the honest affection the two shared. (We know because three of those letters from him to her showed up in an auction in 2018.) They were written on "Twentieth Century-Fox Film Corporation" stationery and addressed first to the Studio Club on Lodi, and then to her new home on N. Stanley Ave. in Hollywood.

Joe wrote, "I hope you will get your chance at Col and make good." Later he wrote, "Am very pleased to know you have a good part in a picture. Stick to your work and you will make good. Make your career your first consideration."

One thing that becomes clear is that spelling was not Joe's forte, and Ms. Monroe's first name was among the words he struggled with, spelling it "Maryline" on one letter, and "Marrylene" on another. On the third letter, he spelled her name correctly, although it might have been luck. Or maybe it was a subtle nod to the fact that when they met he'd known her as the new Norma, and still thought of her that way.

Marilyn screwed up the deal at Columbia by rejecting the studio head, either before or during an overnighter to Catalina on his yacht. One account has her on the boat with Cohn coming at her, member in hand. Whatever, all versions agree that Marilyn got away without giving Cohn what he wanted.

"I never saw a guy so mad," Marilyn later said.

She gave up a lot when she pushed Cohn away—maybe a starring role in the film *Born Yesterday* (1950), the role that earned Judy Holliday an Oscar.

"I only submitted to men I liked," Marilyn Monroe later said. Submitted was the key word. She been raped dozens of times, first when she was eight years old. She liked Uncle Joe. "I liked sitting by the fireplace with him," she once said in her breathless way, "and hearing him talk about love and sex. He was full of wisdom on the subjects."

As for Cohn, Marilyn was permanently on his shit list. A nanosecond after her contract at Columbia expired on September 9, 1948, she was out of work. But not for long. Uncle Joe came to the rescue. He arranged for her to have a screen test, the results of which left Zanuck chilly—Zanuck still looked at her like he didn't like her, she noticed—but she was signed anyway. Her career blossomed, and then exploded into a supernova. In 1955, Fox signed Marilyn Monroe to a huge contract, making her the highest-paid actress in Hollywood.

IRVING BERLIN'S DAUGHTER (AND JOE'S GODDAUGHTER) MARY ELLIN Barrett recalled that when she was little, Uncle Joe used to take her father and her out to lunch, sometimes at the Brown Derby, sometimes at the Twentieth Century-Fox commissary, but it was always an event. Mary Ellin noticed that Uncle Joe had many "fiancées."

Barrett later recalled, "When I was old enough to catch on, I wondered how a pretty girl could fancy such a homely, potbellied old man 'that way.' 'Power,' someone said, 'is attractive,' an odd concept to a young person."

Joe and Nick's great-nephew TV producer George W. Schenck—named after his grandfather, the first of the Schenck brothers to come over on the boat—recalled a story that lent further insight into Joe Schenck's so-called casting-couch ways. George was working on a TV show called *Pros and Cons* (ABC, 1991–92) starring the actors James Earl Jones and Richard Crenna. Playing Crenna's parents were a pair of old-time stars, Don Ameche and Maureen O'Sullivan, she being most famous as Jane to Johnny Weissmuller's Tarzan, and as Mia Farrow's mother. One early morning on the set there was a tug on George's arm.

"You and I need to lunch. I have a story about Joe Schenck I need to tell you," O'Sullivan said.

When the lunch break came, she told him that she had first come to Hollywood in the early '30s and was part of a large group of starlets under contract with MGM. She was part of a labor pool from which moguls chose their "party girls," and sure enough one day she received an invitation to a party on the *Invader*, Joe Schenck's yacht. What a moral dilemma!

At one point during the party, she was summoned to Joe's cabin.

"'Oh boy,' I said to myself, 'this is the moment of truth.' Naturally I figured I was going to be hit upon by Joe Schenck."

He told her to sit down and then explained to her what the usual rules around the town were with rich men and naïve young starlets. Then, perhaps he saw the terror in her eyes . . .

"He told me I was a pretty, young girl and that if any old goat tries to do anything with me, that I should just call on Uncle Joe and he would take care of me. He was just the sweetest man, and he never made a move on me."

And Joe didn't hinder her career in any way. On the contrary, he cast her as the female lead in a 1935 historical drama called *Cardinal Richelieu*, playing opposite George Arliss.

Everyone in Hollywood knew that the casting couch was real, and that in some form or another all the moguls used it. But, of them, Joe was considered the most generous and kindly. He liked women. Joe's old girlfriends were all on his payroll, it was said. He took care of those who took care of him—and sometimes those who didn't.

Once Joe's reputation as a sex expert got around, he became a guru, sought out for advice on all matters involving execs and starlets. One middle-aged man came to Joe seeking wisdom and Joe told him, "Just one word of advice: When you reach a certain age, and you are much younger than I am, we must not think of one thing too much. When you spread your emotions thinly you can enjoy them better and for a longer period of time."

CHAPTER TWENTY

THE MONSTER IN AMERICA'S LIVING ROOM

MGM'S DOLDRUMS WORSENED IN 1948. NICK WAS MAKING PRIvate comments to the effect that recent divorcee Louis B. Mayer, his thoroughbreds sold, had burst forth from the bachelor gates randy. He was spending more time worrying about bedding actresses than making great pictures. Mayer was a prancing erection, according to Eddie Mannix, making up for lost time—and it wasn't pretty.

Times were changing. Film noir was popular, a genre in which MGM still lagged behind. Production was way down. The studio had once cranked out a great picture once per week, and now they were struggling to crank out one mediocre film per month. "New Thalberg" Dore Schary had not improved the bottom line.

Nick still had familiar problems, one picture shooting in Rome, *another* in New York City, a lawsuit from a blacklisted scriptwriter, but Nick's real worry was TV. The threat to Hollywood presented by television had first been realized during the 1930s, but World War II set the new technology back. Now, the war over, TVs were showing up in bars across America, and even in some living rooms. In 1948 there were one million sets in the U.S., in 1949 there were four million, and six million by 1950. During the 1950s the number grew to fifty million.

MGM suffered when Nick refused to become involved in any way with television. It would have been so easy, too. RCA owner David Sarnoff offered Nick a deal whereby MGM and Sarnoff's new National Broadcasting Company (NBC) would merge. Nick would have been all set; make cheap TV shows in Culver City, lease old MGM films to a network, and count his money. But he saw TV as the enemy, an enemy he wasn't ready to join. (It would be seven more years before MGM and TV formed a limited relationship.)

As the number of TVs grew, theater stats trended in the opposite direction. Eighty million tickets sold in 1946, only sixty million in 1950. For the first time, Loew's Inc. was in the red. Theater operators made adjustments to increase revenue. Ticket prices went up. At that time many theaters still didn't have a concession stand, the picture and ambiance had long been considered enough, but by 1955 just about every theater in America sold candy, soda, and popcorn.

During one of Joe's trips east in 1949, he got together with old friend Irving Berlin, and spent the evening at the Copacabana nightclub, which was then just off Central Park. The men drank wine and watched the hysterical comedy team of Dean Martin and Jerry Lewis make their Copa debut.

"They should be in pictures," Berlin said.

"They work too blue," Joe said through the tears in his eyes. (Didn't matter. Martin and Lewis had already signed with Paramount and would make a string of hits.)

Upon leaving, Joe insisted on walking Berlin eastward to his home on Beekman Place in the Turtle Bay section of Manhattan. When they got there, Berlin insisted on walking Joe back to the Plaza Hotel, just two blocks from the Copa where they started.

It was great to have fun and feel young again—the most fun Joe'd had in years. There'd been so many worries lately. He'd about had it with work.

The business news was all distressing. Box office blues. Lawsuits. Just the previous week, Joe was sued for $2.6 million by a Mexican motion picture theater organization, accusing him of misrepresenting a stock deal.

In 1950, Joe was on the verge of retirement when events forced his hand. He fell in the bathtub, broke his hip, and was rushed to Cedars of Lebanon Hospital where he mended slowly. While still laid up, Joe dictated an ode to gratitude addressed to his Fox partners Spyros Skouras and Darryl Zanuck: "It is with great reluctance that I am compelled to inform you of my resignation as Executive Production Head of the Twentieth Century-Fox Company, to be effective immediately. I want you both to know that it is only after grave thought and consideration that I make this decision. This decision has been a doubly difficult one to make not only because of a sentimental attachment to the Company whose upbuilding I have given so many years, but because of the enriching satisfactions of my associations with you, Spyros, and you, Darryl."

Zanuck commented on Joe's resignation: "I know that Joseph Schenck's continuance with the company for several years now has entailed a sacrifice on his part, because of his many other personal interests. Ours has been a long, harmonious, and happy association, and I don't think there has been a comparable one in the history of the motion picture industry. Like everyone who had known him I have the highest affection and respect for him and am sorry he will no longer be in our official family. Everyone at Twentieth Century-Fox will share in my regret at his departure and will remember his services to the company with gratitude."

JOE MIGHT'VE APPEARED DOWN FOR THE COUNT, BUT NICK WAS STILL on his feet and swinging with both fists. Given an ultimatum by Nick, Dore Schary led MGM to a brief comeback during the early 1950s. Films such as *Battleground*, *Father of the Bride*, *The Asphalt Jungle* (noir!), *An American in Paris*, *Singin' in the Rain*, and *King Solomon's Mines* had MGM on the upswing, but momentum was against motion pictures.

If you had to pick a single moment when MGM fell apart for good it was 1951 when Dore Schary, against Mayer's wishes, poured money and talent into John Huston's film adaptation of Stephen Crane's *The Red Badge of Courage*. Mayer hated the idea.

Nick stepped in and gave Schary and Huston the green light, rendering Mayer's opinion moot. The film was a powerful, gritty First World War drama and starred real WWII hero Audie Murphy as the young protagonist. Huston later called it the best he'd ever directed—better than *The African Queen*, *The Maltese Falcon*, better than *The Asphalt Jungle*. It was a masterpiece, Huston said, but only a handful of people saw the full two-hour version. Louis B. Mayer, determined to get the last word, had the film mercilessly cut to sixty-seven minutes, and ordered the original director's cut destroyed. (After that, Huston demanded in his contracts that he be given a copy of his cut of the resulting film.) MGM lost a cool million on *Red Badge*, and the 1950s marked a steady decline. No one met at the fig tree anymore. All of Culver City needed a fresh coat of paint.

By late summer 1951, the old power structure was crumbling under the weight of television. Dore Schary was driving Mayer up the wall.

Mayer called Nick. "It's him or me," Mayer said.

Nick had no trouble making up his mind. At the time of the ultimatum, Nick and Pansy were staying at their vacation home in Miami. At the same time Schary was holidaying in Boca Raton. Nick invited him to come over for lunch and Schary came.

"How long have you been with MGM now?" Nick asked.

"Just about three years," Schary replied.

"Well, business certainly has picked up during that time. You're doing a great job."

"Thanks, Nick."

"You deserve to be rewarded," Nick said. He gave Schary a six-year extension on his contract and sweetened the deal with stock options. Mayer's "him or me" ultimatum had backfired.

Mayer was out. He left kicking and screaming, calling Nick and Schary every insult he knew, even ugly anti-Semitic remarks.

"This is the end of wholesome, decent pictures for Americans and people throughout the world," he yelled.

And he was right. Wholesome and decent moved into American living rooms via the TV set, and the cinema went slowly but surely prurient.

Mayer tried a quick but lackluster end run to regain control, failed, and soon thereafter retired. On November 19, 1952 a dinner was held for Mayer at the Biltmore Hotel where he was given the Screen Producers Guild Milestone Award. Nick didn't go because he had nothing nice to say, but Joe was there and lauded Mayer's contributions to the business.

IN 1952, GOSSIP COLUMNS WERE FULL OF STORIES ABOUT THE BUDDING romance between Marilyn Monroe and baseball legend Joe DiMaggio, who had recently retired. Columnists like Dorothy Kilgallen in New York and Louella Parsons in L.A. speculated that Monroe's studio didn't like the romance, largely because Joe Schenck, now approximately seventy-six years old, still had a thing for Marilyn.

Confidential magazine wrote that Schenck was Monroe's "Daddy," an obvious comment on their sexual relationship. The scandal sheet reported that "Joe Schenck guides the luscious blonde's career, inspires her ambitions, lauds her triumphs, and lulls her fears. He always has a paternal hug or a strong shoulder to cry on. To others, Joe Schenck might be a bald-headed old man. To Marilyn, he was and is the kind of guy that every little girl wants—the man who snaps his fingers and gets results. The stubby Galahad has been a knight in a cream-colored convertible for years for girls from six to thirty-six."

The reference to six-year-old girls sounded creepy and was meant to. To soften any potential legal problems, the rag noted that Schenck had been Shirley Temple's Daddy, and when little Shirley said she wanted a pony, Joe Schenck had an English army major bring one from the Shetland Islands aboard the *Queen Mary*. *Confidential* made it sound like there was more. Smarm was their bread and butter. The magazine brought up Joe's legal woes, four months in stir for showing a "fatherly interest in a shapely dancer or two."

(Temple herself put to rest any idea that she was abused at Joe's studio. In fact, she wrote, Joe was her protector. She didn't learn about the casting couch until she was twelve. Joe lent her to MGM for one picture called *Kathleen*. The difference was night and day. As Louis B. Mayer put awkward moves on Temple's mom, producer Arthur Freed locked the door on Shirley and stripped naked. Temple pointed, laughed at him, and escaped. Freed went on to write the lyrics to *Singin' in the Rain* and won two Best Picture Oscars as producer of *An American in Paris* in 1951 and *Gigi* in 1958. The next creep to hit on Shirley Temple was David O. Selznick, who waited until she was seventeen.)

The *Confidential* article did nothing to stifle Monroe's burgeoning career. Sexual innuendo could not harm her. Part of the MM mystique was the belief that she'd been eroticized into near nymphomania. The public was willing to believe that Marilyn had sexual relations with every man she encountered. What else was she *for*? Today, we are used to seeing photos of her dressed casually, in slacks, curled up with a book, but those pictures weren't public back then. During her life, MM in public was always a sexually needy glamour goddess.

Former roommate Shelley Winters said Marilyn was not quite the veteran of the casting couch that everyone thought she was. Norma Jeane did Joe because she liked Joe. Winters did not want to give the impression that Marilyn wasn't sexually adventurous because she was. She recalled Marilyn making a list of men she wanted to score, and then making check marks next to their names when the mission was accomplished. The men, Winters could tell, were all tops in their field. There was the world's greatest scientist, world's greatest playwright, world's greatest baseball player, world's greatest politician, etc. Albert Einstein was on the list and there was a check next to his name.

So, Marilyn was a bundle of physical love. Everyone knew it. She used sex to get ahead but enjoyed men as well. Marilyn always said in public that she and Uncle Joe were just good friends, but she didn't expect anyone to believe it. Everyone got it. Marilyn got around. Everyone except one guy, the former "world's greatest baseball player," the guy Joe Schenck usually called "that stupid dago."

Joe DiMaggio wanted to marry Marilyn; any suggestion that she had used sex to promote her career was humiliating to him. The *Confidential* article made him furious.

The article hurt Joe Schenck by (again) exposing his "immoral" lifestyle, but even more because it pissed off Hollywood power and it came up at Joe's card games.

As for Marilyn and DiMaggio, their marriage lasted less than a year, with her inability to be his and his alone. This meant more fodder for the scandal sheets. Joe D. hired a private dick to tail his wife. He and Frank Sinatra broke into an apartment, with camera in hand, expecting to find Marilyn in the arms of another man—specifically her voice coach, Hal Schaefer—and they might have had they smashed in the correct door. Instead, they burst in on a thirty-eight-year-old secretary who was sound asleep and alone. *Confidential* had a field day.

THE 1953 OSCARS (HONORING THE PICTURES OF 1952) WAS HELD ON March 19 at the RKO Pantages Theatre on Hollywood Boulevard, with a second venue in New York, the NBC International Theatre, connected via TV signal. *The Greatest Show on Earth* won Best Picture, Gary Cooper won Best Actor for *High Noon*, Shirley Booth won Best Actress for *Come Back, Little Sheba*, and Anthony Quinn and Gloria Grahame won best supporting performances. We mention this because, at those same ceremonies, Joseph M. Schenck received a special Academy Award for being a "film pioneer," and for his "long and distinguished service to the motion picture industry." Presenter Frank Capra described Joe as "all brain and iron."

Joe, who could have cared less about getting an Oscar at a ceremony he invented, was on a train headed east and Gloria Swanson accepted the statue on Joe's behalf.

Irving Berlin moved in with Joe at Owlwood and wrote five new songs for *There's No Business Like Show Business*, which would also be Marilyn Monroe's return to grace at Fox after being suspended for refusing a part.

When the film was a smash, Joe dangled a $1 million check in front of Irving Berlin, for rights to make a biopic. "I don't care how much you pay me. I don't want my life done as a motion picture," Berlin replied.

BACK EAST, NICK WAS AN HONORARY CHAIRMAN FOR A SHOW HELD AT Madison Square Garden called "Night of Stars," with proceeds going to the United Jewish Appeal. Stars included comic actress Martha Raye, funnyman Joey Adams, jazz legend Cab Calloway, cutie-pie actress Gloria DeHaven, toastmaster general George Jessel, comic pianist Victor Borge, and the high-kicking Radio City Music Hall Rockettes.

Joe and Nick were named co-recipients of the Screen Producers Guild annual Milestone Award, for their "historical contributions" to the American motion picture. The brothers were lauded as "true pioneers." Guild president Arthur Freed (the man who tried to get twelve-year-old Shirley Temple on his casting couch), said, "Both men are steeped in the history of the film industry, including distribution, exhibition, and production, and their contribution to the producer system as we know it today has been immeasurable."

In 1955, Joe suffered a heart attack and took to his bed. Business moves continued to be made in his name, and reporters still talked about him as an industry giant, but he was in decline, looking back because looking forward there was nothing to see. He'd retired from all corporate activities. Buster Keaton still visited for friendly gin rummy games.

Lights, please . . .

FADE IN. We are back in Joe's bedroom at Owlwood. KEATON is still sitting at Joe's bedside, but the cards have been pushed aside.

JOE

Buster, my old friend, I am going to leave Owlwood. It's too much for me now.

BUSTER

Are you going back east,
maybe stay with Nick and Pansy?

JOE

No, they say I shouldn't fly
and I can't do the train. Besides, I don't
want to be a burden on them.
They spend half the time in Florida anyway.

BUSTER

Where are you going to go?

JOE

I'm renting the rooftop suite at the
Beverly Hills Hilton. I'll have a staff there.
The bed'll be closer to the john. (laughs)

KEATON

Is Nurse Sunshine making the move?

JOE (smiles)

We're parting ways.

Buster looks out the window wistfully.

BUSTER

I can see Sunset Boulevard.

JOE

Fuck you, Gloria Swanson was fifty-something
in that picture, hated that picture.
I'm fucking eighty-something,
I already did it all.

BUSTER

You sure did.

FADE OUT.

As Leo the Lion's roar diminished in power until it was a barely audible purr, Nick too wound down his business career. The industry he had pioneered was aging, changing. Unlike Joe, Nick was still healthy, but his company wasn't. By December 1955, customers were demanding high-quality pictures rather than the faded glamour provided by MGM. Other studios were functioning more efficiently by taking on projects that came with a producer, director, and lead actors already attached. But Nick insisted on working the "MGM way," like an assembly line. In 1955, MGM struggled to reach the break-even point by re-releasing classic MGM pictures *Gone with the Wind* and *The Wizard of Oz* to first-run theaters.

Nick was seen by the up-and-comers as a dinosaur of show business, and by Loew's Inc.'s board of directors as one of the problems. Nick refused to cut the salaries of himself and other top execs. Almost to the end, he refused to give in to TV in any way, not allowing MGM to produce television programs, or show MGM pictures on TV. We say "almost" because two of Nick's last moves involved getting MGM into American living rooms. The first was the formation of MGM-TV, and the production of a TV show called *MGM Parade* hosted by George Murphy, which took viewers behind the scenes in Culver City and publicized upcoming pictures. The show wasn't popular. The other move was more lucrative. In 1956, Loew's Inc. sold CBS the broadcast rights to *The Wizard of Oz*, which next to *Gone with the Wind* was considered MGM's greatest picture. CBS agreed to show the picture four times and pay Loew's $225,000 for each. Neither Nick nor CBS anticipated the sustained appeal of *Oz*. When it made its TV debut on November 3, 1956, ratings were through the roof, and those numbers held for each repeated broadcast. That opened the floodgates for TV showing Hollywood pictures, and tagged an ironic kicker to Nick's career, his bringing together of one of his greatest successes (*Oz*) with his greatest foe (TV).

But that was it for Nick. His power was slipping, and he was eager to leave. Dore Schary was fired as head of production without Nick's input. Investors replaced Nick as president of Loew's Inc. with Marcus Loew's son

Arthur M. Loew, a move that Nick had promoted. In preparation for this move, Nick had assigned Arthur Loew to travel frequently to Culver City, and familiarize himself with the MGM operation.

Nick had been with the company for half a century. Thirty years after Marcus Loew's death, the company that bore his name was once again under Loew family control. Nick told the world that he fully intended to stay "active in Loew's Inc. affairs." But he didn't. After that, Nick and Pansy spent most of their time in Florida, enjoying retirement.

Arthur Loew was a nice guy with a surprisingly intriguing love life, but he had no desire to take on Nick's job as president of such a huge but aging giant. His reign was brief and in November 1956, Joseph R. Vogel was elected president of Loew's Inc.

Vogel had begun working for Loew's as a theater usher, worked his way up to president of Loew's Theaters, Inc. and now head man. Arthur Loew became chairman of the board and seventy-four-year-old Nick was given the title chairman emeritus, which meant he was history.

During Nick's last years with Loew's, Pansy easily got her name in the papers more frequently than he, usually listed as Mrs. Nicholas M. Schenck, as she would frequent charity art auctions, in which well-known artists would donate works for a cause and power wives would buy them, white-gloved hands rising daintily as the auctioneer chattered in a canine yodel. Pansy got to give a few thousand dollars to charity—e.g., the League for Emotionally Disturbed Children of Long Beach, Long Island—and she got to take home a tasteful painting or *objet* for the mansion. She also owned thoroughbred racehorses that ran in the summer at Saratoga.

IN SEPTEMBER 1957, JOE HAD A STROKE AND, STUCK IN BED, HIS DECLINE accelerated. Keaton still visited regularly. Joe always gave him a few bucks. And Keaton, aware that it made Joe feel good, always took it.

After the stroke, Keaton was urged to use Joe's infirmity to get the rights to his old comedies. But Joe wasn't himself, and Keaton refused to bring up business. Later it would be realized that Joe had not bothered to renew the copyright for Keaton's two-reelers, and they had fallen into the public domain.

According to Keaton's sister Louise, Buster never had a bad word to say about Joe. Once she became angry and said, "Look, he made a fortune off you and then he destroyed you!" Buster just got up and walked away.

ON OCTOBER 29, 1957, LOUIS B. MAYER DIED OF LEUKEMIA. ACTRESS Katharine Hepburn took charge of his funeral and bragged that she'd never had a written contract with the man. All she needed from LB was a handshake.

IN 1956, THE GEORGE EASTMAN HOUSE IN ROCHESTER, N.Y., TOOK A poll of the motion picture industry for its First Festival of Film Artists and determined Norma Talmadge to be one of the top five stars of the pre-1925 era, but she was too ill to travel to the Eastman Theater in Rochester to accept her "George" award. Long out of the limelight and chronically ill, Norma Talmadge had fallen in love with her physician, Dr. Carvel James, and married him on December 5, 1946. What Norma really needed were painkillers so, with a doctor as her husband, the supply was limitless. Her final home was on West Charleston Boulevard in Las Vegas, Nevada. On December 24, 1957, after years of crippling arthritis and addiction to painkillers (including cocaine), Norma Talmadge died of pneumonia. Her estate was still worth more than $1 million. She would have been pleased to know her death made the front pages of newspapers across the country. Her funeral was held at Pierce Brothers Mortuary in Beverly Hills. Those in attendance included both of her sisters, her husband Dr. James, old boyfriend Gilbert Roland, ex-husband George Jessel, and Marion Davies. Dr. William S. Meyer of the Emmanuel Presbyterian Church delivered the funeral sermon. She was interred with Peg in the Hollywood Forever Cemetery.

Joe, bedridden from his stroke three months earlier, was not told of her passing.

Properties that Joe had purchased for her years before were divvied up in her will. One building, at 9000 Sunset Boulevard, is noteworthy because, first, it was known as the Norma Talmadge Building, and second, when it was torn down its shutters were used in the Magic Castle on Franklin Avenue.

Norma's sad legacy unfairly includes two classic characters that she was said to have inspired: Lina Lamont in *Singin' in the Rain* (1952) and Norma Desmond in *Sunset Boulevard* (1950). Neither are accurate nor fair to her memory. Norma certainly never schemed against her co-workers in a mad attempt to save her career, and her failure as a talking actress should not take away from her greatness as a mime actress. Her demise as an addict, living out her years alone and rich, didn't mean she was delusional or psychotic, just in pain. But, like Norma Desmond, she outlived her fame, and spent her waning years a waxwork amid dusty opulence.

Two weeks after Norma passed away, Paramount founder Jesse Lasky had a heart attack and died. He too was interred at Hollywood Forever. (Lasky's partner Adolph Zukor, Marcus Loew's visionary furrier friend known for his joyless demeanor and belief in the future of cinema, lived to be 103 years old and died in 1976.)

FOR YEARS PANSY OWNED AND RACED THOROUGHBRED RACEHORSES. The highlight of her racing career came during the summer of 1958. Nick and Pansy went out to the track to see Pansy's latest thoroughbred, a two-year-old filly named Cobul, run in the Astoria Stakes at Belmont Park. As the Schencks cheered with abandon, Cobul won by a length over Hidden Talent, with the favorite Lady Be Good running third. Cobul paid an impressive $22.10. Over the next couple of years, Cobul became one of the nation's top fillies.

ON JANUARY 23, 1959, THE ACADEMY OF MOTION PICTURES AWARDED life memberships to its founding members. This included Joe Schenck. Others so honored included comic actor Harold Lloyd, superstar Mary Pickford, director Raoul Walsh, mogul Jack Warner, and the late director Cecil B. DeMille.

In the meantime, Joseph M. Schenck Enterprises (without Joe, of course) developed TV projects, and that month sold Alcoa, a sponsor, a TV series called *One Step Beyond*, which featured stories of psychic phenomena. A few weeks later, JSE announced that they were producing a show called *Around the World with Nellie Bly* about the famous nineteenth-century newspaperwoman. Nick's son-in-law Helmut Dantine—Niki's husband, best known as the actor who played the Nazi in the kitchen in the Oscar-winning film *Mrs. Miniver*—was VP and ran JSE for his ailing father-in-law.

BY 1959, LOUELLA PARSONS WAS THE ONLY WRITER STILL MENTIONING the Schencks, especially the "beloved" Joe. In a world that craved news of Fabian, Sandra Dee, Tab Hunter, and Elvis, Louella still attended Joe Schenck's weekly dinner parties and blabbed the details—never mentioning that Joe was in a wheelchair and having difficulty communicating. Louella knew how to keep a secret. By being in that center of the universe, she wanted readers to know, she was nestling against the very backbone of the entertainment world.

On March 8, while in New York, she ran an item about a recent encounter with Marilyn Monroe in which the actress spoke about how happy her marriage to world's greatest playwright Arthur Miller was, how she was glad that people enjoyed her performance in *Some Like It Hot* but regretted that she was ill during shooting and wasn't more like herself for her time with co-stars Jack Lemmon and Tony Curtis.

"Have you seen Joe?" Marilyn asked. She meant Schenck, not the long-forgotten DiMaggio. Louella understood. "I visited him the last time I was in Hollywood. I miss him," she said.

Parsons wrote, "Marilyn is that way about all her old friends—she never forgets them."

MM also mentioned that she wanted nothing more than to have a baby, and should that happen, she would take a break from her career to be a mom. Sadly, it was never to be. And the illness—depression, drug addiction—that had made her unreliable during the shooting of *Some Like It Hot* only grew worse.

Even writers who weren't Louella Parsons, such as entertainment columnist Mike Connolly, wrote about Joe when the TV show *One Step Beyond* on ABC was the most watched show on Tuesday, June 9, 1959. That this show was produced by the same "illustrious septuagenarian" who put Twentieth Century together with Fox showed that Joe, despite his age, wasn't "draggin' his wheels." Reality, which involved actual wheels, was so much crueler than that.

IN 1959, ONE OF TV'S BIGGEST STARS WAS GEORGE REEVES, STAR OF *ADventures of Superman*. The world was shocked when Reeves died at age forty-five in his Benedict Canyon home from a theoretically self-administered gunshot wound. Common belief was that Reeves, who'd had a small part in *Gone with the Wind* twenty years earlier, had grown despondent over his typecasting as the superhero. But over the years, what really happened to Reeves has remained a mystery, so it shouldn't come as any surprise that Eddie Mannix was—at the very least—tangentially involved. Reeves had recently ended a long affair with Mannix's second wife, Toni. Was Mannix's involvement more than tangential? Depends on to whom you talk.

By the mid-1950s as Toni had her affair with Reeves, Mannix had seen his day as a ladies' man, his last girlfriend being an Asian woman who was ostensibly the Mannixes' maid, and (so it is said) looked the other way when Toni took up with George Reeves. Her support of Reeves involved more than offering her body. She spent a chunk of Eddie's money on Reeves as well. She bought him a house on Benedict Canyon Drive and decorated it for him. He was a big TV star, and she did all she could to make him feel like a kept man. Things were cozy and civilized in the Mannix house. When Eddie and Toni went on vacation, they sat at the front of the plane, while George Reeves and the maid sat together in the back. Toni, it has been suggested, didn't think Eddie would survive as long as he did—he survived ten of his eleven heart attacks—and was grooming Reeves as her new husband. Instead, Eddie outlived Reeves by years.

Things took a dark turn after Reeves became bored of Toni Mannix and took up with another woman, thirty-eight-year-old Leonore Lemmon, whom he met on a business trip in 1958. Reeves broke it off with Toni and moved Leonore into the house Toni had bought. Toni called Reeves hundreds of times until he stopped answering the phone. Reeves's dog was stolen and never returned. Reeves was in a car accident, and it turned out someone had drained his brake fluid.

Then, during the early a.m. hours of June 16, 1959, Reeves was found in his bedroom nude and shot dead, a Luger on the floor. The case was treated by authorities as a simple case of suicide. Truth is, Reeves hadn't done anything to upset Eddie, but he had upset Toni, and Toni was married to a man who knew how to get things done in Hollywood. Police found two unexplained bullet holes in Reeves's bedroom, both under a rug, but the LAPD, as always in the industry's pocket, refused to investigate. Reeves's mother tried to hire people to investigate but they refused, saying that there were too many "dangerous people" involved. Some just assumed that Eddie was behind the hit, including his old co-fixer, Howard Strickling.

"Eddie did do it, of course," Strickling told writer Samuel Marx.

CHAPTER TWENTY-ONE

THE END

On October 22, 1961, Joe died at his last home on North Sierra Drive in Beverly Hills, where he lived alone except for household and medical staff. He was survived by Nick and brother George, who had run the Brooklyn Loew's theaters, as well as two sisters: Mrs. Sarah Berger and Annie Nayfack. West Coast funeral arrangements were handled by Groman Mortuary in the University Park section of L.A.

Joe's *L.A. Times* obit noted that he'd been active in the Jewish Welfare Fund, had served as the state highway commissioner during the term of Governor Culbert Olson, had control of the Federal Trust & Savings Bank in Hollywood, and held a directorship in the Bank of America.

A service was held at 1:00 p.m., October 25 at the Wilshire Boulevard Temple, Wilshire and Hobart, with Rabbi Edgar F. Magnin officiating, Y. Frank Freeman, President, Association of Motion Picture Producers, representing the industry. Four hundred mourners showed up. Buster Keaton was first to arrive.

"I have never met a finer man in show business," Keaton said.

Throughout Joe's life, Keaton had refused to say anything bad about him. Sure, Joe put the kibosh on his career as a filmmaker, but there was no way Joe could know how much the move to MGM would suffocate Keaton's soul.

Keaton was thinking of none of that. "He took care of my family when I went to war. I'll never be able to pay him back for that," was Keaton's eulogy.

Joe's pallbearers were entertainment attorney Greg Bautzer, Irving Berlin, press agent Harry Brand, son-in-law Helmut Dantine, Samuel Goldwyn, columnist John Keller, Eddie Mannix, Joseph H. Moskowitz, Joe's heart doctor Myron Prinzmetal, Spyros Skouras, Arthur Stebbins, MGM exec Benny Thau, and Jack Warner.

Honorary pallbearers included: actor Dana Andrews, Barney Balaban, song-and-dance man Dan Dailey, "court jester" Pat DiCicco, filmmaker Walt Disney, comedian Jimmy Durante, actor Henry Fonda, exec William Goetz, Senator Thomas H. Kuchel, directors Walter Lang and Mervyn LeRoy, producer Sol Lesser, actor Edmund Lowe, writer Joseph Mankiewicz, actor Victor Mature, future president Richard M. Nixon, lawyer Louis Nizer, Gregory Peck, George Raft, Randolph Scott, David O. Selznick, agent Jules Stein, Danny Thomas, Spencer Tracy, Joe Vogel, Chief Justice Earl Warren, superagent Lew Wasserman, Clifton Webb, William R. "Billy" Wilkerson (publisher of the *Hollywood Reporter*), Darryl F. Zanuck, and Darryl's son Richard Zanuck.

The rabbi called Joe "part of a dying generation, a part of an epic of Hollywood that is fading fast."

Following the West Coast ceremony, Joe's body was flown east where a second funeral was held on a seasonably cool October 27 at 11:30 a.m. at the Frank E. Campbell Funeral Chapel at Madison Avenue and East 81st St., where Nick and Pansy, and former sister-in-law Constance Talmadge paid their last respects.

The Rev. Dr. Nathan A. Perilman of Temple Emanu-El conducted the service, reading the Twenty-third Psalm. Eulogies were delivered by Spyros Skouras, and by lawyer Louis Nizer.

Skouras said, "Joe was the apostle of clean and moral films of social significance. Through his daring and enterprise, he became, together with his brother Nicholas, a guiding spirit behind the scenes of the infant industry."

Also in attendance were sister Annie Nayfack, Lillian Gish, Ricardo Cortez, and Adolph Zukor. Joe was entombed in Maimonides Cemetery in Cypress Hills, Brooklyn, about forty yards from Marcus Loew's final resting spot. Nick and Pansy, and sister Annie were at the tomb, tossing flowers atop Joe's casket.

The United California Bank was appointed as special administrator of Joe's $3.5 million estate. When Joe's will was read, he left numerous bequests, almost everything went to his brother Nick, but nothing to Buster Keaton. Apparently, after years of handing his friend cash, Joe felt he and Keaton were finally square.

Because Joe had no family in California, his friends sent condolences—cards, letters, and telegrams—to Nick and Pansy. And Pansy returned printed thank-you cards that read, "The family of Joseph M. Schenck acknowledges with sincere appreciation your kind expression of sympathy." Inside, she wrote personal notes to each mourner. To Lillian Gish, Pansy penned, "Dear Lillian, Nick and I appreciate your lovely note so much. We shall miss our dear Joe deeply, for he filled a large space in our lives, as well as that of his friends. Somewhere his light is shining, and it always will, in our hearts. With love, Pansy and Nick."

In 1962, brother George died. The following year, Eddie Mannix had his twelfth and final heart attack, this one fatal, and in 1964 Pansy's brother Fred Wilcox died at age fifty-nine.

ON MONDAY NIGHT, MARCH 4, 1969, NICK SUFFERED A STROKE AND died in Miami Beach, Florida, at age eighty-seven. He had divided his later years between his estates at Sands Point and Miami Beach. In his dotage he suffered from a delusion that he'd lost his money, and often refused to go places and do things because he "couldn't afford it." His family would explain that he was still a very rich man and could do whatever he wanted. But that wasn't true. Nick sought to buy off the tide of time, and for that he lacked the funds.

Services were held on March 8 at Frank E. Campbell's funeral home in Manhattan, a veiled Pansy in front, with her three daughters and their families. The same rabbi as for Joe conducted services. Eulogies were delivered by Louis Nizer and by Spyros Skouras.

Nizer said, "Nicholas Schenck was a great man. The architect of and the civil genius behind this country's motion picture industry. He was a quiet, humble, but noble man. He truly was The General."

Skouras added, "Nick was a compassionate human being."

It was freezing with an icy wind in Cypress Hills and no one dillydallied as Nick was interred in Maimonides in the same tomb as brother Joe, still the same pitching wedge from Marcus Loew's final resting place.

Across the Hudson, at Palisades Amusement Park where a new monorail was being installed, Irving Rosenthal—the same man who purchased the park from Nick more than thirty years earlier—renamed its main drag, Nick's all-time favorite place, his Rosebud, "The Schenck Midway."

Fade out.

That's a wrap.

APPENDIX

FILMS BILLED AS "JOSEPH M. SCHENCK PRESENTS"

(Includes only films for which Joe gets a Producer or "Presented by" credit, and does not include films like *Redemption*, the Evelyn Nesbit picture, and Roland West's *Lost Souls* [1916], for which Joe invested money, made tremendous profits, but took no credit.)

Panthea (1917). 1hr 18m. Director and Writer: Allan Dwan. Cast: Norma Talmadge, L. Rogers Lytton, George Fawcett, Erich von Stroheim. The expertly lit Norma was cute, unpretentious, warm, and funny—instantly America's sweetheart, master of the gestural soliloquy. Distributed by Lewis Selznick. Based on a hit play by Monckton Hoffe—and considerably cleaned up for the screen. Unlike the play, the picture has a happy ending. Joe and Norma were married during production. The picture opened in Times Square in two theaters simultaneously. *Variety* (January 19, 1917) wrote, "If future Talmadge special releases are of equal caliber as *Panthea*, Miss Talmadge is certain to remain in the front rank of sensational drawing cards." Film's last known screening was in 1958 and is now considered lost. The picture received much glowing press. The fact that it took four months to shoot was impressive. The story told of a Russian girl, a musician, whose brother is a socialist and enemy of the government. A big impresario who stands well politically, and is a friend of the prefect of police, falls in love with her. He arranges for her brother to be arrested so that he can come to her aid, but the brother kills a Russian soldier and escapes. She is accused of the crime, is arrested, and escapes with the assistance of a Russian soldier, her school days sweetheart. She leaves on a steamer for England, pursued by a Russian agent, shipwrecked on the English Coast, falls in love again, is discovered by the Russian agents, flees to Paris, and . . . You get the idea—enough plot for ten pictures! Norma was great in it. Director Dwan had a long career, directing more than four hundred pictures between 1911 and 1960.

The Butcher Boy (1917). 30m. Director and Writer: Roscoe Arbuckle. Cast: Arbuckle, Buster Keaton, Alice Lake, Al St. John, Josephine Stevens, Arthur Earle, Luke the Dog (as himself). The portly butcher boy is in love with the boss's daughter Alice Lake, in conflict with his romantic rival (Al St. John), all as an innocent bystander customer (Buster Keaton) tries to purchase meat. When Lake is sent away to boarding school, Arbuckle follows her pretending to be her cousin. Luke was a Staffordshire terrier, and Arbuckle's real-life pet.

The Law of Compensation (1917). 1hr 12m. Director: Joseph A. Golden, Julius Steger. Cast: Norma Talmadge, Fred Esmelton, John Charles, and Chester Barnett. *Motion Picture* magazine in July 1917 wrote, "I cannot honestly say that I consider this play worthy of Norma Talmadge. It hinges on the old plot of a woman who forsakes her home and child for another man." Critics were impressed by Norma's versatility as she begins the picture playing a child and ends it playing a mature woman. Joe was lauded as well. As producer, he "lavishly mounted" the new Norma feature. The only extant copy of the film, incomplete, is in the Library of Congress.

Poppy (1917). 1hr 32m. Director: Edward José. Cast: Norma Talmadge, Eugene O'Brien, Frederick Perry, Jack Meredith, Dorothy Rogers, Edna Whistler. The photoplay was filled with soap opera elements that made Norma a hero for women. Here she unwittingly marries an abusive man, falls for and is impregnated by an amnesiac, hits the road, and becomes a famous writer. Whew! At the Library of Congress only two reels of the second half are extant. *Moving Picture World* (June 9, 1917) commended the photoplay for holding the audience's attention despite the long running time. *Photoplay* said this picture established Edward José as a "big-time director."

The Moth (1917). 1hr 12m. Director: Edward José. Cast: Norma Talmadge, Eugene O'Brien, Hassard Short, Virginia Dare, Adolphe Menjou, Donald

Hall. Adventure. When our heroine's father dies, he leaves her in the care of his best friend's son, who turns out to be no good. Library of Congress has only a partial print.

The Secret of the Storm Country (1917). 1hr 12m. Director: Charles Miller. Cast: Norma Talmadge, Edwin Denison, J. Herbert Frank, Niles Welch. Drama. Norma plays a desperately poor girl who marries a rich man. He is embarrassed by her class and keeps her a secret from his parents. Film considered lost.

Reckless Romeo (a.k.a. *A Creampuff Romance*) (1917) 23m. Director: Roscoe Arbuckle. Writer: Joseph Anthony Roach. Cast: Arbuckle, Agnes Neilson, Al St. John, Corinne Parquet, Alice Lake. Filmed in part at Palisades Park. Arbuckle is a married man who flirts with a girl in a park. Later he takes his wife to the photoplays and, in a surreal twist, sees himself on the screen flirting with the girl in the park. Long thought lost. In 1999 a copy was made available to the public by the Norwegian Film Institute and can be seen in its entirety online.

The Rough House (1917). 19m. Directors: Roscoe Arbuckle, Buster Keaton. Writers: Arbuckle, Keaton, and Joseph Anthony Roach. Cast: Arbuckle, Keaton, Al St. John, Alice Lake, Agnes Neilson, Glen Cavender. Keaton's directorial debut. Arbuckle plays a rich man who falls asleep smoking, sets his bed on fire, and then takes his time putting the fire out. Keaton plays a delivery boy who comes to the house and competes with the cook for the affections of the maid. While all of this is going on, two thieves show up at the house and try to steal a necklace.

His Wedding Night (1917). 19m. Director: Roscoe Arbuckle. Writers: Arbuckle, Joseph Anthony Roach. Cast: Arbuckle, Buster Keaton, Al St. John, Alice Mann, Arthur Earle. Comedy includes a brief appearance, as the pretty lady in the car, by Natalie Talmadge. Set in a pharmacy, Arbuckle is about to marry the pharmacist's daughter (Mann) but still must worry about his rival (St. John). Comedy ensues when a deliveryman (Keaton) delivers to Mann her wedding dress, models the dress for her, and then is mistakenly kidnapped by St. John.

Oh Doctor! (1917). 23m. Director: Roscoe Arbuckle. Writers: Jean C. Havez, Joseph Anthony Roach. Cast: Arbuckle, Buster Keaton, Al St. John, Alice Mann, Alice Lake. Gags at the racetrack. Arbuckle plays the married Dr. Holepoke who is at the track with his son (Keaton), flirts with a pretty girl (Mann), and bets his money on a thoroughbred named Lightning that runs the wrong way.

Coney Island (1917). 25m. Director, writer: Roscoe Arbuckle. Cast: Arbuckle, Buster Keaton, Al St. John, Agnes Neilson, Alice Mann, Jimmy Bryant, Alice Lake, and Luke the Dog. After his wife drags him to the beach, Fatty sneaks away and enjoys the rides at the Coney Island amusement parks.

A Country Hero (1917). 20m. Director and Writer: Roscoe Arbuckle. Cast: Arbuckle, Buster Keaton, Al St. John, Alice Lake, Joe Keaton (as Cy Klone, the garage owner), Scott Pembroke, Natalie Talmadge. First Arbuckle picture to be shot in California and distinguished itself from previous vehicles with its large outdoor sets. Keaton again appeared in drag, in this case to do the "Fatima snake dance." Arbuckle, too, ended up in women's clothes, dressed as a "Spanish dancer." Film concluded with a crash-filled car chase sequence. Film is considered lost, the only one of Keaton's films for which no print exists.

The Ghosts of Yesterday (1918). 1hr 12m. Director: Charles Miller. Writer: Mildred Considine. Cast: Norma Talmadge, Eugene O'Brien, Stuart Holmes. Based on the play *Two Women* by Rupert Hughes. Norma plays a dual role. A poor artist doesn't get to finish a portrait of his wife when she dies of starvation. Things get weird when he soon thereafter runs into a woman who greatly resembles his wife.

De Luxe Annie (1918). 1hr 12m. Director: Roland West. Writer: Paul West. Cast: Norma Talmadge, Eugene O'Brien. Norma plays a Jekyll/Hyde-type character. She is a woman who, while suffering from amnesia, becomes a criminal. When her memory returns, she must face the consequences for her actions.

Out West (1918). 25m. Director, writer: Roscoe Arbuckle. Based on a story by Natalie Talmadge. Cast: Arbuckle, Buster Keaton, Al St. John, Alice Lake,

Joe Keaton (as man on train). A wandering bartender out west survives an attack by Indians, teams up with a saloon keeper (Keaton), and tries to protect a Salvation Army girl (Lake) from an evil villain named Wild Bill Hiccup. Film makes excellent use of its California locations shots. That sunlight, desert, and mountains helped turn the "Western" into a solid Hollywood genre. Modern audiences are appalled by one scene in which cowboys shoot at the feet of a Black man to "make him dance."

The Bell Boy (1918). 33m. Director, writer: Roscoe Arbuckle. Cast: Arbuckle, Buster Keaton, Al St. John, Alice Lake, Joe Keaton, Charles Dudley. Fatty and Buster as incompetent bellhops. Alice Lake's character, a manicurist, is named Cutie Cuticle. Our bumbling heroes make good when they inadvertently stop a bank robbery.

Moonshine (1918). 23m. Director, writer: Roscoe Arbuckle. Cast: Arbuckle, Buster Keaton, Al St. John, Alice Lake, Charles Dudley. Fatty and Buster are revenuers hunting bootleggers in hillbilly land where a family feud is raging. Film contains the first known example of a screen performer "breaking the fourth wall"—later widely used by Oliver Hardy. Arbuckle appears to have been blown to smithereens by a bomb, but is saved when the film is run backward, putting his pieces back together again.

Her Only Way (1918). 1hr 12m. Director: Sidney Franklin. Writers: George Scarborough, Mary Murillo. Cast: Norma Talmadge, Eugene O'Brien, Ramsey Wallace, E. Alyn Warren. Norma marries for wealth rather than love. She soon becomes a neglected wife and appears to commit suicide but wakes up to find that the whole thing was a nightmare, teaching her to follow her heart not her pocketbook.

The Forbidden City (1918). 1hr 2m. Director: Sidney Franklin. Writer: Mary Murillo. Cast: Norma Talmadge, Thomas Meighan, E. Alyn Warren, Michael Rayle. Norma plays a Chinese princess in a tale of interracial romance. Today, the pigeon-English intertitles gather unintentional laughter: "Oh, Budda [sic], please send love-man here to give me million sweet kisses." When palace officials learn that she has been impregnated by a white man, she is sentenced to death—but not until the baby girl is born.

In act two Norma plays the now-grown daughter, who is in the Philippines searching for her father.

Good Night, Nurse! (1918). 26m. Director, writer: Roscoe Arbuckle. Cast: Arbuckle, Buster Keaton, Al St. John, Alice Lake, Joe Bordeaux, Kate Price, Joe Keaton (as man in bandages). Fatty's wife takes him to the sanitarium to have his alcoholism surgically removed (by surgeon Buster Keaton). Three scenes were cut in some markets by censorship boards, twice when Fatty kicks a woman in the butt and a third in which he pulls the dress off a woman revealing her in undergarments.

The Cook (1918). 22m. Director, writer: Roscoe Arbuckle. Cast: Arbuckle, Buster Keaton, Al St. John, Alice Lake, Luke the Dog. Arbuckle is the cook, and Keaton the waiter at a fancy restaurant. Considered lost for seventy years, only a partial version is extant. The scene for which the film is most famous involves the cook (Arbuckle), in the interest of efficiency, tossing food at the waiter (Keaton), who performs great dexterity in always catching it on a plate.

The Sheriff (1918). 18m. Director, writer: Roscoe Arbuckle. Cast: Arbuckle, Betty Compson, Monty Banks, Luke the Dog. A schoolteacher (Compson) has been kidnapped and it is up to rootin' tootin' sheriff Arbuckle to save her. Film is considered lost.

The Heart of Wetona (1919). 1hr 12m. Director: Sidney Franklin. Writer: Mary Murillo. Cast: Norma Talmadge, Fred Huntley, Thomas Meighan, Gladden James. Set against a backdrop of Native Americans preparing for their "Corn Dance," Norma plays a mixed-blood daughter of a Comanche chief who falls in love with a fickle young engineer.

The New Moon (1919). 1hr. Director: Chester Withey. Writer: H. H. Van Loan. Cast: Norma Talmadge, Pedro de Cordoba, Charles K. Gerrard, Stuart Holmes, Marc McDermott. At the grand opening, the Rivoli Theatre was so packed that Norma and sister Constance couldn't get in. At one point, police warned the Rivoli's box office to stop selling tickets as the crowd represented a fire hazard. Today, one reel of this film is lost.

The Probation Wife (1919). 1hr. Director: Sidney Franklin. Writer: Angie Ousley Rooser, Kathryn Stuart. Cast: Norma Talmadge, Thomas Meighan, Florence Billings, Alec B. Francis. Comedy/drama. Norma plays a woman who grew up as a B-girl in a saloon, cheats the patrons, but gets a chance at redemption when a famous writer and his wife enter the saloon and offer to buy her way out.

Back Stage (1919). 26m. Director: Roscoe Arbuckle. Writer: Jean C. Havez. Cast: Arbuckle, Buster Keaton, Al St. John, Charles A. Post, Molly Malone. Arbuckle and Keaton are stagehands in a theater where the entire cast has just quit, so they are forced to do the show themselves. To put it mildly, things go wrong.

The Isle of Conquest (1919). 1hr. Director: Edward José. Writers: John Emerson, Anita Loos. Cast: Norma Talmadge, Wyndham Standing, Charles K. Gerrard, Hedda Hopper, Natalie Talmadge. When a woman who hates men is shipwrecked on a deserted island with a man who hates women, how will they ever get along? Norma's final picture before she and Joe headed west. Considered lost.

The Hayseed (1919). 27m. Director: Roscoe Arbuckle. Writer: Jean C. Havez. Cast: Arbuckle, Buster Keaton, Molly Malone, John Henry Coogan, Jr., Luke the Dog. Not a tremendous amount of plot here. Arbuckle delivers mail, Keaton manages a store, a constable played by Jack Coogan Sr. (Uncle Fester's dad) turns out to be a thief, and everyone likes Molly Malone.

The Garage, a.k.a. *Fire Chief* (1920). 25m. Director: Roscoe Arbuckle. Writer: Jean C. Havez. Cast: Arbuckle, Buster Keaton, Molly Malone, Harry McCoy, Dan Crimmins, Luke the Dog. The garage where Arbuckle and Keaton work is also a fire station, so the hijinks focus on fixing cars and putting out fires. This is the last film starring both Arbuckle and Keaton.

A Daughter of Two Worlds (1920). 1hr 12m. Director: James Young. Writer: Edmund Goulding. Cast: Norma Talmadge, Jack Crosby, Virginia Lee, William Shea, Frank Sheridan. A girl who grew up in a speakeasy gets in trouble for writing a bad check. Her criminal dad wants her in a classier environment and with the help of his brother sends her to boarding school. She falls in love with her roomie's brother, but will he love her back when he learns where she came from? Adventure/drama.

She Loves and Lies (1920). 1hr 12m. Director: Chester Withey. Writer: Grant Cooper. Cast: Norma Talmadge, Conway Tearle, Octavia Broske, Philips Tead, Ida Darling, John T. Dillon. When a young woman is left a large inheritance by an elderly admirer, with the caveat that she must marry her true love, she wears disguises (an old woman, a romantic rival) to make sure her prospective husband loves her back and isn't out for her money.

The Woman Gives (1920). 1hr 12m. Director: Roy William Neill. Writers: Grant Carpenter, Waldo Walker. Cast: Norma Talmadge, John Halliday, Edmund Lowe, Lucille Lee Stewart, John Smiley. Norma plays a model whose boyfriend is a sculptor. When he catches her in the arms of another man, he falls apart and moves into an opium den. The model spends the rest of the picture putting the pieces back together again. Adventure/drama.

The Perfect Woman (1920). 1hr. Director: David Kirkland. Writers: John Emerson, Anita Loos. Cast: Constance Talmadge, Charles Meredith, Elizabeth Garrison, Joseph Burke. A Constance Talmadge comedy—and the first "Joseph M. Schenck Presents" feature film not to star Norma. Constance wears an ugly-girl disguise to work for a man who believes beautiful women have no place in the workforce. When the office is invaded by Bolsheviks (hate when that happens) Constance removes her disguise and uses her appeal to save her boss and his business.

One Week (1920). 25m. Directors, writers: Buster Keaton, Edward F. Cline. Cast: Keaton, Sybil Seely, Joe Roberts. Contains a scene of a side of a building falling on Keaton—almost. First Keaton picture without Arbuckle. Keaton attempts to build his prefabricated home unaware that the villain has changed the numbers on the pieces.

The Branded Woman (1920). 1hr 24m. Director: Albert Parker. Writers: Anita Loos, Burns Mantle. Cast: Norma Talmadge, Percy Marmont, Vincent Serrano, George Fawcett, Grace Studdiford. A woman's mother once worked in a house of ill repute. Will her boyfriend still love her if he learns the truth about Mom? The question is forced to a head by a blackmailer.

Convict 13 (1920) 19m. Directors, writers: Edward F. Cline, Buster Keaton. Cast: Keaton, Sybil Seely, Joe Roberts, Joe Keaton, Louise Keaton. Premises in Keaton films did not need to be feasible, only funny. Here a golfer is bugged by an escaped convict and, in a case of mistaken identity, ends up in prison. How will he get out? Should he go along with the escape plans or foil the plot and hope the authorities realize he should be on the links and not in chains?

Neighbors, a.k.a. *Backyard*, a.k.a. *Mailbox* (1920) 18m. Directors, writers: Edward F. Cline, Buster Keaton. Cast: Keaton, Virginia Fox, Joe Roberts, Joe Keaton, Jack Duffy. Keaton and Fox are a young couple who live next door to each other, which would be convenient if their families were not feuding.

The Scarecrow (1920). 19m. Directors, writers: Edward F. Kline, Buster Keaton. Cast: Keaton, Sybil Seely, Joe Keaton, Joe Roberts, Luke the Dog. Buster and Joe Roberts are farmhands competing for the affections of a farmer's daughter (Seely) and come up with increasingly ridiculous plans to catch her eye.

Mama's Affair (1921). 1hr. Director: Victor Fleming. Writers: John Emerson, Anita Loos. Cast: Constance Talmadge, Effie Shannon, Kenneth Harlan, George LeGuere, Katharine Kaelred. Romantic fluff in which a wealthy woman tries in vain to control her selfish daughter. Eighteen years later, director Victor Fleming would direct *The Wizard of Oz* and *Gone with the Wind*.

The Haunted House (1921). 21m. Directors, writers: Edward F. Cline, Buster Keaton. Cast: Keaton, Virginia Fox, Joe Keaton, Joe Roberts, Edward F. Cline, Mark Hamilton, Natalie Talmadge (as fainting girl in bank). One of the first haunted house pictures. Keaton is a bank clerk who finds himself in a spooky house. In a resolution that would become cliché when repeated by the Three Stooges, the Bowery Boys, Kay Kyser and others, the haunted house turns out to be a gangster hideout.

The Goat (1921). 23m. Directors, writers: Buster Keaton, Malcolm St. Clair. Cast: Keaton, Virginia Fox, Joe Roberts, Malcolm St. Clair, Edward F. Cline. Through ridiculous happenstance mild-mannered Keaton is mistaken for outlaw "Dead Shot Dan." Famous scene: Keaton sits on the front of a freight train.

Hard Luck (1921). 22m. Directors, writers: Edward F. Cline, Buster Keaton. Cast: Keaton, Virginia Fox, Joe Roberts, Bull Montana. Suicidal Keaton can't even kill himself correctly.

The "High Sign" (1921). 20m. Directors, writers: Edward F. Kline, Buster Keaton. Cast: Keaton, Bartine Burkett, Charles Dorety, Al St. John. Drifter Keaton is hired to work at a carnival shooting gallery and is such a marksman that he's hired by that most murderous of gangs, the Blinking Buzzards.

Wedding Bells (1921). 1hr. Director: Chester Withey. Writer: Zelda Crosby. Cast: Constance Talmadge, Harrison Ford, Emily Chichester, Ida Darling, James Harrison. Comedy. Boy meets girl, boy marries girl, boy divorces girl, boy gets back with girl, boy marries girl again. The End. Or so they say. Film is considered lost.

The Play House (1921). 23m. Directors, writers: Buster Keaton, Edward F. Cline. Cast: Keaton, Virginia Fox, Joe Roberts, Edward F. Cline, Monte Collins. This film is most famous for the first reel in which Keaton plays every part, sometimes appearing on screen multiple times simultaneously. The trick helped mask the fact that Keaton was shooting with a broken ankle.

The Boat (1921). 23m. Directors, writers: Buster Keaton, Edward F. Cline. Cast: Keaton, Sybil Seely. Man vs. machine. Keaton and his family go for a voyage in a boat he built himself. Oh-oh. The boat's name is *Damfino.*

The Paleface (1922). 20m. Directors, writers: Buster Keaton, Edward F. Cline. Cast: Keaton, Virginia Fox, Joe Roberts. It is an ugly fact of American history that, when oil was found on land owned by Native Americans, that land was stolen by white men, often by killing the rightful owners. Here, Keaton darkens his skin, calls himself Little Chief Paleface, and teams up with the Native Americans to foil the murderous oil barons.

Smilin' Through (1922). 1hr 36m. Director: Sidney Franklin. Writer: James Ashmore Creelman. Cast: Norma Talmadge, Harrison Ford, Wyndham Standing, Alec B. Francis, Glenn Hunter, Grace Griswold. An orphaned Irish woman can't marry the man she loves because her guardian forbids it. Mary Pickford called this examination of a woman's spirituality one of her favorite films.

Cops (1922). 18m. Directors, writers: Edward F. Cline, Buster Keaton. Cast: Keaton, Virginia Fox, Joe Roberts, Edward F. Cline, Steve Murphy. One relentless chase scene, the entire Los Angeles Police Department versus our hero.

The Primitive Lover (1922). 1hr 8m. Director: Sidney Franklin. Writer: Frances Marion. Cast: Constance Talmadge, Harrison Ford, Kenneth Harlan, Joe Roberts, Chief John Big Tree. A married woman faces temptation when a handsome adventurer comes into her life.

My Wife's Relations (1922). 25m. Directors, writers: Buster Keaton, Edward F. Cline. Cast: Keaton, Monte Collins, Wheezer Dell, Harry Madison, Kate Price, Joe Roberts, Wallace Beery. Our hero "accidentally" marries a plump and domineering woman (Price).

The Blacksmith (1922). 21m. Directors, writers: Buster Keaton, Malcolm St. Clair. Cast: Keaton, Joe Roberts, Virginia Fox. Gags revolve around a blacksmith trying to show a horse and repair an automobile.

The Frozen North (1922). 17m. Directors, writers: Buster Keaton, Edward F. Cline. Cast: Keaton, Joe Roberts, Sybil Seely, Bonnie Hill, Freeman Wood. First Joseph M. Schenck film after Roscoe Arbuckle's arrest. In a satire of melodramas, Keaton is a dastardly yet blundering villain.

The Eternal Flame (1922). 1hr 36m. Director: Frank Lloyd. Writer: Frances Marion. Cast: Norma Talmadge, Adolphe Menjou, Wedgwood Nowell, Conway Tearl, Rosemary Theby. Based on the Balzac novel. Norma plays a duchess who has an affair. Two of the eight reels are considered lost.

The Electric House (1922). 23m. Directors, writers: Buster Keaton, Edward F. Cline. Cast: Keaton, Virginia Fox, Joe Keaton, Louise Keaton, Myra Keaton, Joe Roberts. Our hero is accidentally given a degree in electrical engineering and tries to rewire a house.

Day Dreams (1922). 28m. Directors, writers: Buster Keaton, Edward F. Cline. Cast: Buster Keaton, Renée Adorée, Edward F. Cline, Joe Keaton, Joe Roberts. Our hero wants to marry the girl of his dreams but lacks the means, so he sets off into the world to find his fame and fortune in hopes that one day he'll return home to domestic bliss. Filmed on location in L.A., San Francisco, and Oakland.

The Balloonatic (1923). 22m. Directors, writers: Buster Keaton, Edward F. Cline. Cast: Keaton, Phyllis Haver, Babe London. Our hero works at a (West Coast) amusement park. Keaton rides in a hot-air balloon. One reviewer wrote, "It is in searching for adventure that Buster meets with a certain blonde Diana, who wears sport clothes, especially the breeches, with no little charm." A-oo-ga!

The Voice from the Minaret (1923). 1hr 10m. Director: Frank Lloyd. Writer: Frances Marion. Cast: Norma Talmadge, Eugene O'Brien, Winter Hall, Carl Gerard, Claire Du Brey, Lillian Lawrence, Albert Prisco. A British lord in India marries our heroine but she doesn't love him. Her attempt to escape her predicament takes her to several continents.

The Love Nest (1923). 20m. Directors, writers: Buster Keaton, Edward F. Cline. Cast: Keaton, Joe Roberts, Virginia Fox. A loser in life and love sets off to sea in a boat called the *Cupid*, and eventually finds himself on a whaling ship with an Ahab-like captain. Famous scene: Keaton yanked into the water by a whale.

3 Ages (1923). 1hr 3m. Directors: Buster Keaton, Edward F. Cline. Writers: Clyde Bruckman, Jean C. Havez, Joseph Mitchell. Cast: Keaton, Margaret Leahy, Wallace Beery, Lillian Lawrence, Joe Roberts. Keaton's first feature-length film. The picture is divided into three distinct parts, same characters at a different time: caveman, ancient Rome, modern times. One benefit of this format was that, should the project not have worked as a feature, it could have been divided into three short subjects. As it turned out, audiences had no trouble sitting through a full hour of Keaton.

Ashes of Vengeance (1923). 1hr 51m. Director, writer: Frank Lloyd. Cast: Norma Talmadge, Wallace Beery, Conway Tearle, Josephine Crowell. A dashing romance of Old France, based on an H. B. Somerville play. About this production Joe said, "I have spared nothing in the way of costumes, settings, excellent cast, or authenticity and elaborateness as in details of the period." The sets were replicas of the Renaissance period of architecture in France. The Louvre ballroom set was 328 feet long, three hundred dancers learned the steps of the day, one thousand extras were used, four hundred horses. In the street scenes for the Huguenot massacre on St. Bartholomew's Eve, the streets were four hundred feet long, streets lined with French houses, inns, and public buildings of the Charles IX period. Architect Stephen Goosson was brought in to make sure the sets were one-hundred-percent authentic. Weapons were as authentic as possible as well—matchlock rifles, swords, pikes, armor, and cannon are duplications of the real thing. The fencing scenes were choreographed and performed by graduates of the National Fencing School of Brussels.

The Dangerous Maid (1923). 1hr 20m. Director: Victor Heerman. Writer: C. Gardner Sullivan. Cast: Constance Talmadge, Conway Tearle, Morgan Wallace, Charles K. Gerrard. According to the ad, "Miss Talmadge in an entirely new role in a romance of the seventeenth century. Dramatic and yet filled with the impish pranks and delightful fun of this winsome, madcap rebel, who defied King James and his whole army and captured the heart of his handsomest officer."

Our Hospitality (1923). 1hr 5m. Directors: Buster Keaton, John G. Blystone. Writers: Clyde Bruckman, Jean C. Havez, Joseph A. Mitchell. Cast: Buster Keaton, Joe Roberts, Natalie Talmadge, Joe Keaton as the locomotive engineer. Family feud picture, a hayseed *Romeo and Juliet*.

The Goldfish (1924). 1hr 10m. Director: Jerome Storm. Writer: C. Gardner Sullivan. Cast: Constance Talmadge, Jack Mulhall, Frank Elliott, Jean Hersholt, Zasu Pitts, Nellie Bly Baker. Tagline: "A Tale of Four Matrimonial Knots with Laughs in Every Twist." Only a partial print of this picture exists.

Director Storm told a reporter, "Constance Talmadge has the most expressive hands in filmdom. Hands have always been my directorial hobby. Things can be said with the hands that even the eyes cannot express. Without changing the expression of her eyes, or the pose of her head and body, Constance can get over her thoughts in a manner which instantly stamps her as a great artist. I delight in sitting back and watching Constance work."

Sherlock Jr. (1924). 45m. Director: Buster Keaton, Clyde Brackman, Roscoe Arbuckle. Writers: Clyde Bruckman, Jean C. Havez, Joseph A. Mitchell. Cast: Keaton, Kathryn McGuire, Joe Keaton, Erwin Connelly, Ward Crane, Ford West. Distributed by Metro Pictures. A poor young projectionist falls asleep and dreams he is the famous detective. Who directed what in this picture is up to conjecture. Roscoe Arbuckle began production at the helm but was relieved of duty part way for being "unproductive." Keaton finished up. Selected for restoration by the National Film Registry.

The Navigator (1924). 59m. Directors: Buster Keaton, Donald Crisp. Writers: Clyde Bruckman, Jean C. Havez, Joseph A. Mitchell. Cast: Keaton, Kathryn McGuire, Clarence Burton, H. N. Clugston, Noble Johnson. A spoiled upper-class couple find themselves alone on a passenger ship. Famous scene: Keaton deep-sea dives to repair a hole in the ship's hull. Selected for preservation by the National Film Registry.

Her Sister From Paris (1925). 1hr 10m. Director: Sidney Franklin. Writer: Hänns Kraly. Cast: Constance Talmadge, Ronald Colman, George K. Arthur, Gertrude Claire, Mario Carillo. Constance plays twin sisters, one a housewife, one a scandalous dancer. Will the housewife pretend to be her twin to teach her husband a lesson? Yes. Yes, she will. Art director: William Cameron Menzies.

Go West (1925). 1hr 9m. Director: Buster Keaton. Writer: Lex Neal. Cast: Keaton, Kathleen Myers, Howard Truesdale, Ray Thompson. Fish out of water story: New York city slicker Buster goes west and finds himself being chased by a thousand steer through the streets of L.A.

The Eagle (1925). 1hr 13m. Director: Clarence Brown. Writer: Hanns Kräly, George Marion, Jr. Cast: Rudolph Valentino, Vilma Bánky, Louise Dresser,

Albert Conti, James A. Marcus. Drama. Here's a rare example of Joe Schenck producing a picture that didn't star Keaton or a Talmadge. Joe co-produced with John W. Considine, Jr. Here Valentino plays a Russian Zorro type, a masked vigilante seeking vengeance on the man who stole his family's land. He is conflicted when he falls in love with the villain's lovely daughter.

Seven Chances (1925). 56m. Director: Buster Keaton. Writer: Clyde Bruckman, Jean C. Havez, Joseph A. Mitchell. Cast: Keaton, T. Roy Barnes, Snitz Edwards, Ruth Dwyer. Film's opening sequences shot in Technicolor. Famous scene: Keaton runs downhill pursued by hundreds of aggressive boulders.

Kiki (1926). 1hr 48m. Director: Clarence Brown. Writer: Hanns Kräly. Cast: Norma Talmadge, Ronald Colman, Gertrude Astor. Rare Norma comedy. Not a bad picture, but it wasn't what the public wanted from Norma and lost money. Norma plays a female newsie who goes into showbiz.

The Bat (1926). 1hr 26m. Director: Roland West. Production design: William Cameron Menzies. Cast: André de Béranger, Charles W. Herzinger, Robert McKim, Jack Pickford, Jewel Carmen. A mystery writer rents a house to entertain guests but finds the place haunted by a masked criminal dressed like a bat. Based on a play that made $10 million on the "legitimate stage."

Battling Butler (1926). 1hr 17m. Director: Buster Keaton. Writers: Al Boasberg, Lex Neal, Charles Smith, Paul Gerard Smith. Cast: Keaton, Sally O'Neil, Walter James, Budd Fine. One of Keaton's best. A butler's girlfriend comes from a family that finds him weak and mild, so he proves his toughness through pugilism. Realistic boxing scenes.

The Duchess of Buffalo (1926). 1hr 15m. Director: Sidney Franklin. Writers: Hanns Kräly, George Marion, Jr. Cast: Constance Talmadge, Tullio Carminati, Edward Martindel, Rose Dione. A Buffalo, N.Y., candymaker's opera-singing daughter marries a Russian duke. Romantic comedy.

Camille (1926). 1hr 48m. Director: Fred Niblo. Writers: Fred de Grésac, Olga Printzlau, Chandler Sprague, George Marion, Jr. Cast: Norma Talmadge, Gilbert Roland, Lilyan Tashman. No complete print known to exist. A Parisian courtesan has her romance forbidden by her father. After many trials and tribulations, she wants her boyfriend back, but does he still love her?

Breakfast at Sunrise (1927). 1hr 2m. Director: Malcolm St. Clair. Writers: Gladys Unger, Fred de Grésac. Cast: Constance Talmadge, Don Alvarado, Marie Dressler, Bryant Washburn, Alice White, Paulette Duval. A boy and girl, both dumped by their significant others, fall for each other.

The General (1927). 1hr 7m. Director: Clyde Bruckman, Buster Keaton. Writers: Al Boasberg, Charles Henry Smith, Paul Gerard Smith. Cast: Keaton, Marion Mack, Glen Cavender, Jim Farley, Frederick Vroom. Keaton's last film as an independent filmmaker and considered one of the greatest pictures ever made. Keaton plays a locomotive engineer who is refused by the military during the Civil War because of the importance of his civilian job. His sweetheart, however, believes he is not in the army due to cowardice. He gets a chance to prove his spine when Union spies abduct his train, and he must go behind enemy lines to rescue his train and bring it back home.

College (1927). 1hr 6m. Director: James W. Horne, Buster Keaton. Writer: Bryan Foy, Carl Harbaugh. Cast: Keaton, Anne Cornwall, Harold Goodwin, Flora Bramley. When a bookworm is rejected by his girlfriend for not being athletic enough, he goes to college and tries sports. Most famous scene, shot in an empty L.A. Coliseum: Keaton tries track and field and attempts to throw the hammer. But he forgets to let go and scatters a crowd with his spinning weapon. First Keaton film to be distributed by United Artists.

Venus of Venice (1927). 1hr 10m. Director: Marshall Neilan. Writer: Wallace Smith, George Marion, Jr. Starring: Constance Talmadge, Antonio Moreno. Filmed in France. One reel lost. *The New York Times* complained of "unconscious humor." Constance's last picture with Joe.

Steamboat Bill, Jr. (1928). 1hr 10m. Director: Charles Reisner. Writer: Carl Harbaugh. Cast: Buster Keaton, Ernest Torrence, Marion Byron, Joe Keaton as the barber. Another Keaton classic filled with inventive sight gags. Strong wind blows Keaton and his bed down a street. A house almost falls on Keaton—again. It goes on and on. Selected for preservation by the National Film Registry.

Tempest (1928). 1hr 42m. Director: Sam Taylor. Writers: Vladimir Nemirovich-Danchenko, C. Gardner Sullivan. Cast: John Barrymore, Camilla Horn, George Fawcett, Louis Wolheim. Set in Czarist Russia, a peasant falls in love with a princess. Winner of the first Academy Award for Art Direction.

The Woman Disputed (1928). 1hr 48m. Directors: Henry King, Sam Taylor. Writer: C. Gardner Sullivan. Cast: Norma Talmadge, Gilbert Roland, Arnold Kent, Boris de Fast, Michael Vavitch. Norma's last silent film. An "adventuress" falls in love on the eve of the First World War, but happiness is elusive when she offers her charms to a Russian officer for the release of Austrian hostages.

Lady of the Pavements (1929). 1hr 25m. Director: D. W. Griffith. Writer: Sam Taylor, Karl Vollmöller. Cast: Lupe Velez, William Boyd, Jetta Goudal. In England, this film was known as *Lady of the Night*. When a woman is caught cheating on her boyfriend, he tells her he'd rather be with a "girl of the streets" than her. She decides to give him his wish and secretly sets him up with a "dancer" from a disreputable "nightclub," who turns out to be Lupe Velez.

Eternal Love (1929). 1hr 11m. Director: Ernst Lubitsch. Writers: Katherine Hilliker, Harry H. Caldwell, Hanns Kräly. Cast: John Barrymore, Camilla Horn. Romantic drama set in the Swiss Alps, with Barrymore as lead mountain man.

New York Nights (1929). 1hr 22m. Director: Lewis Milestone. Writer: Jules Furthman. Cast: Norma Talmadge, Gilbert Roland, John Wray, Lilyan Tashman, Roscoe Karns. Norma's first talking picture, not well received. Thirty-something Norma plays a chorus girl stuck in an unhappy marriage who is tempted toward infidelity by a gangster.

Glorious Vamps (1930). 10m. Director: Orville O. Dull. Writer: Sidney Lazarus. Cast: Bobby Watson, Joyzelle Joyner. Weird really-short subject, in which our hero casts himself and his girl as famous lovers from the past—Adam and Eve, Samson and Delilah, and things always go wrong. Film comes off as an excuse to show off scantily clad women and huge sets by William Cameron Menzies.

Be Yourself! (1930). 1hr 5m. Director: Thornton Freeland. Writer: Max Marcin. Cast: Fannie Brice, Robert Armstrong, Harry Green, G. Pat Collins, Gertrude Astor, Budd Fine. Musical comedy. Ethnic comedy in which a chorus girl manages a boxer. How ethnic? The tagline read: "*Peecture wot ever wassit. Sungs und smotcracks make you roar witt leefing.*"

The Bad One (1930). 1hr 10m. Director: George Fitzmaurice. Writers: John Farrow, Howard Emmett Rogers, Carey Wilson. Cast: Dolores del Rio, Edmund Lowe, Boris Karloff. An American sailor has a complex romance with a Marseilles dancing girl.

Abraham Lincoln (1930). 1hr 36m. Director: D. W. Griffith. Writers: Stephen Vincent Benet, John W. Considine, Jr., Gerrit Lloyd. Cast: Walter Huston, Una Merkel. Episodic bio. D. W. Griffith's first talkie. He only made two.

The Lottery Bride (1930). 1hr 20m. Director: Paul L. Stein. Writers: Howard Emmett Rogers, Horace Jackson, Herbert Stothart. Cast: Jeannette MacDonald, John Garrick, Zasu Pitts, Joe E. Brown. Dramatic romance set in a mining camp in northern Norway. The final reel shot in Technicolor.

Du Barry, Woman of Passion (1930). 1hr 30m. Director and Screenplay Adaptation: Sam Taylor. Writer: David Belasco (play). Cast: Norma Talmadge, William Farnum, Conrad Nagel, Hobart Bosworth, Ullrich Haupt. Norma's second and last talkie. She plays a French milliner who becomes a casino hostess, a courtesan, and eventually King Louis XV's mistress.

The Bat Whispers (1930). 1hr 23m. Director: Roland West. Writers: Mary Roberts Rinehart, Avery Hopwood. Cast: Chester Morris, Una Merkel. Directed by Joe Schenck's good friend West, this is one of the first films to be shot in widescreen format. Return of the archvillain "The Bat," who steals a rich woman's necklace, taunts police, robs a bank, and terrorizes the occupants of a desolate mansion. Tagline: "You'll laugh and gasp, throb and thrill." The picture ends with an actor making the audience promise that they won't spoil the surprise and tell anyone The Bat's secret identity. Story goes that Bob Kane saw this picture, and invented Batman.

Reaching for the Moon (1930). 1hr 31m. Director and Writer: Edmund Goulding. Songs: Irving Berlin. Cast: Douglas Fairbanks, Bebe Daniels, Edward Everett Horton, Bing Crosby, the Paul Whiteman Rhythm Boys. Musical in which a prince of Wall Street (Fairbanks) loses everything in the stock market crash. Will his girl (Daniels), whom he met after drinking a love potion, still want him even though he's on the skids?

One Romantic Night (1930). 1hr 13m. Director: Paul L. Stein. Writers: Maxwell Anderson, Melville Baker. Cast: Lillian Gish, Rod La Rocque, Conrad Nagel, Marie Dressler, O. P. Heggie. After six pictures at MGM, Gish came to Joe and UA for her first talkie, playing a princess facing an arranged marriage with a prince.

Indiscreet, a.k.a. *Careless Heart* (1931). 1hr 32m. Director: Leo McCarey. Writers: Buddy G. DeSylva, Lew Brown, Ray Henderson. Cast: Gloria Swanson, Ben Lyon. Originally planned as a full-fledged musical comedy, but after drastic editing, only two song numbers remained in the finished picture. Swanson is radiant as a young woman whose romance is threatened by a bum from her past. Five years earlier this part would have gone to Norma.

Rain (1932). 1hr 34m. Director: Lewis Milestone. Writer: Maxwell Anderson. Cast: Joan Crawford, Walter Huston, Fred Howard. Drama. Sex worker's soul is saved by a missionary. Filmed on location on Catalina Island. The first time Nick's MGM lent out Joan Crawford, she went to Joe's UA. Joan, it is said, didn't get along with the UA crowd and spent evenings on the island in her cottage playing Bing Crosby records. To be fair, Joan was going through a divorce and had a lot of her mind. There are also stories that she told her ex that she was pregnant while making *Rain* but lost the baby when she slipped and fell on a ship's deck.

Hallelujah I'm a Bum (1933). 1hr 22m. Director: Lewis Milestone. Writers: S. N. Behrman, Ben Hecht. Cast: Al Jolson, Madge Evans, Frank Morgan,

Harry Langdon, Tammany Young. Musical comedy, songs by Richard Rodgers and Lorenz Hart. Jolson plays an NYC tramp who rescues the mayor's amnesiac girlfriend from a suicide attempt and falls in love.

Blood Money (1933). 1hr 5m. Director: Rowland Brown. Writers: Hal Long, Speed Kendall. Cast: George Bancroft, Judith Anderson, Frances Dee, Chick Chandler, Blossom Seeley, Etienne Giradot. A corrupt L.A. bondsman (Bancroft) falls for a slumming socialite (Dee). At one point the heroine says, "If I could find a man who would be my master and give me a good thrashing, I'd follow him around like a dog on a leash."

The Last Gentleman (1934). 1hr 12m. Director: Sidney Lanfield. Writers: Maude T. Howell, Leonard Praskins, Paul Schofield. Cast: George Arliss, Edna May Oliver, Janet Beecher, Charlotte Henry, Ralph Morgan. Dark comedy in which a rich New Englander calls his family to his estate to see who is worthy of his inheritance.

Born to Be Bad (1934). 1hr 2m. Director: Lowell Sherman. Writer: Ralph Graves. Cast: Loretta Young, Cary Grant, Jackie Kelk, Marion Burns. Trials and tribs of an unwed mother. The public found it distasteful. A mother whose son is the victim of a hit-and-run (though not seriously injured) learns the driver's identity and blackmails him. Picture was twice rejected by the Hays Office because of the horrible things Loretta Young said, sometimes while not wearing much.

Cardinal Richelieu (1935). 1hr 22m. Director: Rowland V. Lee. Writer: Cameron Rogers. Cast: George Arliss, Maureen O'Sullivan, Edward Arnold, Cesar Romero, Russell Hicks, John Carradine. Historical drama. The cardinal saves King Louis XIII from treachery.

Folies-Bergère de Paris (1935). 1hr 22m. Director: Roy Del Ruth. Writers: Jessie Ernst, Bess Meredyth, Hal Long, Darryl F. Zanuck. Cast: Maurice Chevalier, Ann Sothern, Merle Oberon. Picture in which Joe became Merle Oberon's producer. But the picture is all Chevalier, playing a dual role as an entertainer and a lookalike banker.

Under Two Flags (1936). 1hr 52m. Director: Frank Lloyd. Writers: Bess Meredyth, Allen Rivkin, Walter Ferris, W. P. Lipscomb. Cast: Ronald Colman, Claudette Colbert, Victor McLaglen, Rosalind Russell. Adventure/romance. After taking the blame for a crime his brother committed, our hero joins the French Foreign Legion and falls in love with a sophisticated lady.

As You Like It (1936). 1hr 36m. Director: Paul Czinner. Writers: J. M. Barrie, R. J. Cullen. Based on the Shakespeare play. Cast: Laurence Olivier, Elisabeth Bergner, Felix Aylmer, Henry Ainley, Sophie Stewart. Bergner, who played the role of Rosalind in Germany, tries to reprise the role here in English—the actress had fled to escape Hitler—but her accent remained thick and American audiences were put off. Joe's last film as producer. After this, he is exclusively a studio head.

BIBLIOGRAPHY

BOOKS

Anger, Kenneth. *Hollywood Babylon*. New York: Dell Publishing, 1981.

Barbas, Samantha. *Confidential Confidential: The Inside Story of Hollywood's Notorious Scandal Magazine*. Chicago: Chicago Review Press, 2018.

Barrett, Mary Ellin. *Irving Berlin: A Daughter's Memoir*. New York: Simon and Schuster, 1994.

Basinger, Jeanine. *Silent Stars*. Middletown, Connecticut: Wesleyan University Press, 2000.

Baxter, John. *Hollywood in the Thirties*. New York: A.S. Barnes, 1968.

Belletti, Valeria. *Adventures of a Hollywood Secretary: Her Private Letters from Inside the Studios of the 1920s*. Oakland, California: University of California Press, 2006. Author was personal and social secretary to Samuel Goldwyn.

Bergan, Ronald. *The United Artists Story*. New York: Crown Publishers, 1986.

Black, Shirley Temple. *Child Star*. New York: McGraw-Hill, 1988.

Bohn, Thomas W., and Richard L. Stromgren. *Lights and Shadows*. Mountain View, California: Alfred, 1987.

Brownlow, Kevin. *Hollywood: The Pioneers*. New York: Knopf, 1980.

Carey, Gary. *All the Stars in Heaven: The Story of Louis B. Mayer and MGM*. New York: E.P. Dutton, 1981.

Caso, Frank. "Marcus Loew." *Immigrant Entrepreneurship*. Washington, D.C.: German Historical Institute, 2014.

Curtis, James. *Buster Keaton: A Filmmaker's Life*. New York: Alfred A. Knopf, 2022.

Custen, George F., *Twentieth Century's Fox*. New York: Basic Books, 1991.

D'Agostino, Annette M. *Filmmakers in the Moving Picture World*. Jefferson, North Carolina: McFarland & Company, Inc, 1997.

Eyman, Scott. *20th Century-Fox: Darryl F. Zanuck and the Creation of the Modern Film Studio*. New York: Running Press, 2021.

Fleming, E. J. *The Fixers: Eddie Mannix, Howard Strickling and the MGM Publicity Machine*. Jefferson, North Carolina: McFarland & Co., 2005.

Friedrich, Otto. *City of Nets: A Portrait of Hollywood in the 1940s*. New York: Harper Perennial, 2014.

Gabler, Neal. *An Empire of Their Own: How the Jews Invented Hollywood*. New York: Crown Publishers, 1988.

Gargiulo, Vince. *Palisades Amusement Park*. New Brunswick, New Jersey: Rutgers University Press, 1995.

Golden, Eve. *Golden Images: 41 Essays on Silent Film Stars*. Jefferson, North Carolina: McFarland & Co., 2000.

Gussow, Mel. *Don't Say Yes Until I Finish Talking: A Biography of Darryl F. Zanuck*. New York: Pocket Books, 1983.

Hay, Peter. *MGM: When the Lion Roars*. Atlanta, Georgia: Turner Publications, 1991.

Headley, Robert K. *Motion Picture Exhibition in Washington, D.C.* Jefferson, North Carolina: McFarland & Co., 1999.

Higham, Charles. *Merchant of Dreams: Louis B. Mayer and the Secret Hollywood*. New York: Dell, 1993.

Huston, John. *An Open Book*. Cambridge, Massachusetts: Da Capo Press, 1994.

Koszarski, Richard. *Hollywood on the Hudson*. New Brunswick, New Jersey: Rutgers University Press, 2008.

Landingham, Andrea Van. *Hollywood Horrors: Murders, Scandals, and Cover-Ups from Tinseltown*. Guilford, Connecticut: Lyons Press, 2022.

Leaming, Barbara. *Marilyn Monroe*. New York: Crown Publishers, 1998.

Loos, Anita. *The Talmadge Girls: A Memoir*. New York: Viking Press, 1978.

Lowe, Denise. *An Encyclopedic Dictionary of Women in Early American Films: 1895–1930*. Philadelphia, Pennsylvania: Haworth Press, 2004

McCaffrey, Donald W., and Christopher P. Jacobs. *Guide to the Silent Years of American Cinema*. Westport, Connecticut: Greenwood Publishing, 1999.

Marx, Samuel. *Mayer and Thalberg: The Make-Believe Saints*. New York: Random House, 1975.

Meade, Marion. *Buster Keaton: Cut to the Chase*. New York: HarperCollins, 1995.

Mordden, Ethan. *The Hollywood Studios*. New York: Simon and Schuster, 1988.

Perelman, Dale Richard. *Death at the Cecil Hotel in Los Angeles*. Charleston, South Carolina: History Press, 2022.

Schatz, Thomas. *The Genius of the System: Hollywood Filmmaking in the Studio Era*. New York: Pantheon, 1988.

Slide, Anthony. *Silent Players: A Biographical and Autobiographical Study of 100 Silent Film Actors and Actresses*. Lexington, Kentucky: University Press of Kentucky, 2002.

Sobel, Robert. *The Entrepreneurs*. New York: Weybright & Talley, 1974.

Spears, Jack. *Hollywood: The Golden Era*. New York: A. S. Barnes, 1971.

Summers, Anthony. *Goddess: The Secret Lives of Marilyn Monroe*. New York: Macmillan, 1985.

Talmadge, Margaret L. *The Talmadge Sisters*. Philadelphia, PA: J. B. Lippincott Co., 1924.

Thomson, David. *Showman: The Life of David O. Selznick*. New York: Knopf, 1992.

Williams, Gregory Paul. *The Story of Hollywood: An Illustrated History*. Los Angeles, California: BL Press, 2011.

PERIODICALS

Action
Americus Times-Recorder
Anaconda Standard
Bennington Banner
B'nai B'rith Messenger
Boston Globe
Brooklyn Chat
Brooklyn Times Union
Buffalo Times
The Butte Miner
Cherry Hill Courier-Post
Confidential
Exhibitors Trade Review
Fall River Daily Evening News
Film TV Daily
Films in Review
Fortune
Hackensack Record
Harrisburg Evening News
Hollywood Reporter
Hollywood Spectator
Indianapolis Star
Liberty
Lima Gazette and Republican
Los Angeles Daily News
Los Angeles Evening Citizen News
Los Angeles Evening Post-Record
Los Angeles Magazine
Los Angeles Times
Monrovia News-Post
Motion Picture
The Moving Picture World
Muncie Star Press
Nashville Banner
New York Daily News
New York Evening World
New York Times
New York Tribune
Oregon Daily Journal
Pasadena Post
Paterson Morning Call
Paterson Evening News

Philadelphia Inquirer
Photoplay
Pittsburgh Press
Pomona Progress-Bulletin
Rochester Democrat and Chronicle
San Bernardino County Sun
San Francisco Examiner
San Luis Obispo Tribune
Saturday Evening Post
Shamokin News-Dispatch
Shepherdstown Register (Shepherdstown, West Virginia)
Spokane Chronicle
Tacoma Ledger
Time
Variety
Venice Evening Vanguard
Virginia Chronicle
Visalia Times-Delta
Wilmington News Journal
Winona Republican-Herald

WEBSITES

dailymail.co.uk
denofgeek.com
filmreference.com
filmsite.org
imdb.com
mediahistoryproject.org
usc.edu

ACKNOWLEDGMENTS

The Schencks' story began in Russia, but the story of this book, and how it came to be, starts in Brockton, Massachusetts, with a kid named Alvin Marill during motion pictures' Golden Age, the 1940s and '50s. Marill was a kid who's spent way too much time at the cinema, sometimes going from one double feature to another, sometimes with his sister, sometimes alone. Those hours in the dark paid off as Marill grew up to become a well-respected film historian and writer, covering subjects during his career as diverse as the Three Stooges, Edward G. Robinson, and Tommy Lee Jones. During his later years it was Marill's dream to write the definitive biography of Joe and Nick Schenck.

In the meantime, a friend of Al's, New Jersey filmmaker Craig Singer, was directing a picture called *A Good Night to Die* (2003). Singer was a childhood friend of Al's son Steve. The gritty streets-of-New-York action thriller debuted at the Cannes Film Festival, produced by Jeff Schenck, a great-great-nephew of the moguls. Through Jeff, Singer met others in the Schenck family, the pronunciation now softened to *Shenk.*

George W. Schenck (Jeff's dad) agreed to be principal liaison between the family and the "project," which was initially to be a feature or a miniseries. George was producer of TV's number-one drama, *NCIS*. Knowing his friend Al Marill's intense interest in the subject, Singer brought Marill in to help develop the idea. Of course, for Marill, this was a dream come true.

Like Singer before him, Marill was practically offended by how little the world knew of the Schencks. He once wrote in a letter to Richard Zanuck, "Joe and Nick Schenck turn up in virtually every book about the moguls of the time, but they have never been front and center—outrageous considering that they were among the founders of the motion picture industry. My goal is to introduce them to a whole new generation of film enthusiasts and historians."

Marill spent long hours in the Motion Picture Academy Library, and the USC Library, putting together the largest collection of Schenck info anywhere. Marill repeatedly interviewed George Schenck. He spoke with Joe Schenck's secretary Juanita Portillo.

Marill was full swing into the Schenck project when, on Christmas Day 2010, he had a stroke and died in Glen Rock, New Jersey.

Now that might have been the end of the Schenck project except Marill's son Steve knew how much his dad's research meant to him and didn't want it to go to waste. Steve Marill asked Singer to oversee the big bundle of Schenck material. The project was now to produce a book that could be later adapted into a film or miniseries.

The authors wish to thank the following persons and organizations for their help: Lisa Grasso Benson; Matthew Benson; Tekla Benson; Keith Brenner; Logan Brunkhurst; Arthur Bryant; Cassandra Bryant; James Bryant; Miriam Coon; Max Dobson; Wyatt Dobson; Ed Edelson; Melinda Elliott; our editor extraordinaire Gary Goldstein; our intrepid agent Doug Grad of the Doug Grad Literary Agency; Miranda Hambro and Tomoko Kawamoto at the Museum of the Moving Image; Richard and Diane Koszarski at the Fort Lee Historical Society; Brandon Levanduski; Christian Wayne Levanduski; Isabella Nicole Levanduski; Torri Levanduski; Rick McKay; Leonard Maltin; Valerie and Steph at Maimonides Cemetery, Brooklyn; John Calhoun and Jeremy Megraw, Billy Rose Theatre Division, the New York Public Library for the Performing Arts; Nelson Page, Executive Director, and Jen Livesey at the Barrymore Film Center, Fort Lee, N.J.; Marvin Paige; Jim Parish; Juanita Portillo, Joe's secretary; Ann Pryor; George W. Schenck; C. J. Singer; Jamie Singer; Judy Singer; Laurie Erlenmeyer Singer; Susan Singer; Hollywood historian Lisa Slopek; Eve Smith; Stephen Smith; Sylvia Wang at the Shubert Foundation; Sherry Wasserman; Tom Weaver; and Roslyn Yarborough at the office of Samuel Goldwyn, Jr.

INDEX